ALLIANCE

BRAND

'It is not enough to bring big names together simply because it seems to make sense. An alliance must create a value proposition that could not have existed within either enterprise. Mark Darby's practitioner expertise and extensive research have brought him unique insights. Using accurate and dynamic models, he provides us with powerful tools to address the tough questions that the daily business of alliance management obscures.'

Jonathan Cohen, Practice Principal, HP

'Alliances provide the opportunity for both commercial and not-for-profit organisations to build competitive advantage, increase sustainability and brand value. However building the necessary relationships can be a high risk undertaking for all sides. Mark Darby brings insight tempered by his extensive experience to guide directors and managers when considering the strategic and operational implications of this option for their business.'

David Yates, President, Chartered Institute of Marketing, Sussex

'SEEDA is dependent on alliances for success. Mark Darby helped our Enterprise Team make positive strides forward. We have enthusiastically embraced his advice, and his book can help you to also get great results from alliances and a positive reputation for partnering.'

Jeff Alexander, Executive Director, Business and International, SEEDA

'FDM has relationships with companies that have resource constraints at the point of software product implementation. We built our unique IT staffing "Mountie" model on the principal of alliances embedding it into our company's culture and philosophy. We have worked extensively with ALLIANTIST to shape and refine this approach. Alliance Brand shows you how to build that partnering capability too.'

Rod Flavell, CEO, FDM Group Limited

'Alliance Brand achieves three things. First, it helps optimise ROI from alliances at an operational level. Second, it provides for good corporate governance. Third, and probably most important, alliances are now part of the business planning strategic agenda. Get this right and the other two fall into place. Mark shows you how to do it all in this book.'

Antonio Betes, CEO, Vetlab Services Limited

'As an SME we work closely with a number of partners but don't have the budgets that many large corporates might have for alliance management. However, our reputation as the dispensing solution partner of choice for our customers, suppliers and stockists relies on us continuing to develop our capability and invest in those relationships. By working with Mark and following his philosophy we have got smarter about where we invest and how we work internally as well as with our partners, to great effect. His philosophy is not just for the large corporates; everyone who partners, especially SMES, will need a positive reputation for alliance management just to compete in the future, let alone prosper. Buying this book and applying his simple yet effective methods could be the best return on investment you ever make.'

Stephen Woolmer, Managing Director, Brightwell Dispensers Limited

ALLIANCE
BRAND

Fulfilling the Promise of Partnering

Mark Darby

John Wiley & Sons, Ltd

Published by   John Wiley & Sons Ltd, The Atrium, Southern Gate, Chichester,
West Sussex PO19 8SQ, England
Telephone (+44) 1243 779777

Email (for orders and customer service enquiries): cs-books@wiley.co.uk
Visit our Home Page on www.wiley.com

Other Wiley Editorial Offices

John Wiley & Sons Inc., 111 River Street, Hoboken, NJ 07030, USA

Jossey-Bass, 989 Market Street, San Francisco, CA 94103-1741, USA

Wiley-VCH Verlag GmbH, Boschstr. 12, D-69469 Weinheim, Germany

John Wiley & Sons Australia Ltd, 42 McDougall Street, Milton, Queensland 4064,
Australia

John Wiley & Sons (Asia) Pte Ltd, 2 Clementi Loop #02-01, Jin Xing Distripark,
Singapore 129809

John Wiley & Sons Canada Ltd, 6045 Freemont Blvd, Mississauga, Ontario, L5R 4J3, Canada

Wiley also publishes its books in a variety of electronic formats. Some content that appears
in print may not be available in electronic books.

Library of Congress Cataloging-in-Publication Data

Darby, Mark
   Alliance brand : fulfilling the promise of partnering / Mark Darby.
     p.   cm.
   Includes bibliographical references and index.
   ISBN-13: 978-0-470-03218-3 (cloth: alk. paper)
   ISBN-10: 0-470-03218-9 (cloth: alk. paper)
   1. Strategic alliances (Business)   I. Title.
   HD69.S8D387 2006
   658'.044—dc22   2006016561

British Library Cataloguing in Publication Data
A catalogue record for this book is available from the British Library

ISBN 13 978-0-470-03218-3 (HB)
ISBN 10 0-470-03218-9 (HB)

Typeset in 11.5/15pt Bembo and Univers by SNP Best-set Typesetter Ltd, Hong Kong
Printed and bound in Great Britain by TJ International Ltd, Padstow, Cornwall, UK

For:
Marshall and Tegan

In memory of:
Sandra Darby; only after Mum had been taken did I realise that what she gave me was so valuable.

Timothy Foster; founder of Adslogans.com. A truly gifted and charming man who helped establish ALLIANTIST.

CONTENTS

FOREWORD

Productivity. Innovation. Reputation. All of these buzzwords seem to have an ubiquitous presence in company mission statements and long term strategic plans. Yet I believe that the new keyword, the golden thread permeating company visions, must be 'partnership'.

Organisations can no longer work in isolation. To compete effectively in a fiercely contested global marketplace, we all have to build robust, resilient and vibrant alliances to succeed. We must collaborate on ideas, pool skills, share creativity, exchange information, combine resources and work together to secure new opportunities. The call to business is to champion new partnerships because it makes compelling commercial sense.

However, we have to recognise that alliances can be difficult to manage. Adding new groups to networks, for example, can often generate increased issues. In this book, Mark Darby not only powerfully illustrates the importance of cementing alliances, but also considers how to manage and exploit them effectively. Most importantly, he then shows in detail how to do it yourself and build a sustainable alliance capability. His maps and methods are comprehensive and easy to use, offering fast and effective results whether you are a multinational or a sole trader.

The South East England Development Agency (www.seeda. co.uk) is the Regional Development Agency (RDA) responsible for the sustainable economic development and regeneration of the South East of England. Our aim is to accelerate business competitiveness and drive enterprise, in order to build a thriving environment where people want to live and work. In such an intense and prosperous business environment we must work imaginatively and collaboratively to succeed. We therefore understand the pivotal importance of alliances and joint ventures both in formulating strategies and executing the delivery of ambitious transformational plans. Partnering not only enhances best practice working, but can also assist with wider business issues such as research and development.

Partnering is critical to the success and delivery of many of our initiatives. Sector consortia are driven by business leaders to focus on new opportunities and market failures to deliver sustained business growth. Without strong partnering, dissemination of knowledge and close engagement with a range of key players these would never work – especially when attempting to increase access to global markets. Partnership working is therefore aligned to business success, and the forming of imaginative relationships vital to achieving our vision of a region synonymous with business enterprise and success. SEEDA itself in its relationship with central government and regional partners is dependant on alliances for success. As you will see in chapter 6, we are doing well but looking to extract more value from this field in future. ALLIANTIST helped our Enterprise Team make positive strides forward, and we have enthusiastically embraced Mark's advice. We intend to strive towards being a strong, trusting and confident alliance brand, intrinsically linked to working collaboratively with others and fulfilling our partnering promises. With this book, you too can get great results from alliances and a positive reputation for partnering.

Jeff Alexander
Executive Director, Business and International, SEEDA

ACKNOWLEDGEMENTS

This book reflects learning and experiences from nearly 20 years of working around alliances. During that time I have collaborated with many colleagues, customers, suppliers, business partners, academics and others. So in a way, this book must combine some element of their contribution and therefore I say thanks to everyone I have touched and been fortunate enough to meet.

Many people have helped me on my journey and a few really stand out. David Johnson is a special person who gave me both the encouragement and environment to spread my wings and I will be forever indebted to him. Rosemary Martin was also another inspiration at Reuters and enabled me, with some success, to challenge a few deeply held beliefs and assumptions in the 152-year-old organisation, some of which are reflected in the book. Without the early support of Graham Norton, Martin Yates, Christine Twells and Nigel Ewens many of the things you read about in this book may not have happened. Paul Davies, Tim Phillips, Grant Murray, Aidan McGuinness and the late Ron Gamblin have all been influential and I am grateful to them for their mentoring and guidance while at Rank. More recently, other colleagues at Deloitte and its clients have also played a part. In particular my thanks go to Tim Mumford who helped in many ways. Keith Wright was a demanding yet terrific client at the NHS who helped me see there was another way forward and our little chats reinforced my desire to focus on alliance solutions through ALLIANTIST. Richard Baker has been another tremendous influence and his coaching for both business and life has been a tower of strength for me in the past few years. Steven Shove and Graham Constantine have put up with my passionate and sometimes intense desire to improve this emerging discipline of alliance management and I thank them for both their friendship and time, not least in critiquing early drafts of the book. Francis Booth from Ernst & Young, Steven Sharpe and Bala from Reuters, Phil Mehrtens from Thus, Robert Hayward from BT, along with Hugh Barton of HP have all been terrific with their input. As leaders in their respective fields I really appreciate their contributions and constructive feedback as the book has taken shape. Joe Palmer brought the ALLIANTIST VIP Map to life with his innovative graphics. Nick Horslen, Graeme Hodges, Richard Wolfströme, Danny Roberts, Goetz Boue, Clive Bonny, Roy Purtill, Simon Farncombe, Luke Johnson, Michael Myers, Andy Brimacombe, Mark Whitmore, Chris Exeter, Emma Baylis, Giovanni Tepedino, Gemma Tuxford, Gail Warrander, Ole Siig, Matthew Gadd, Mindy Cockeram, Karl Pick, Mark Aplin, Alan Logan and the late, amazing, Val Elliott have all played a part in my journey, so thank you.

A great degree of thanks must also go to others such as Stephen Woolmer, for so long my trusted advisor and close friend who took his support to a new level by allowing Brightwell to become an SME case study for the book. Greg Ward, Julie Kapsalis, and the whole Enterprise Team at SEEDA have been great as has Rod, Julian, Jon, Andy, Jacs, Sheila, Alistair, Stuart and everyone else at FDM Group, the leading AIM listed IT services organisation. I am pleased that my work, based on the maps and models you will find in the book, have made such a difference for them all in such a short space of time. They and many others have made sure that this stuff works in practice!

From an academic perspective Chris Pendleton and others like Louisa, Carita, Darren, Richard, Julian and Ken from my time at the University of Reading were a source of great strength in the early days doing primary and secondary research. Martin Aylward, now at Henley Management College, has been a tremendous inspiration and constantly challenged my thinking. He like others also urged me to publish my work more widely, so Martin, this is it, I hope you approve! Mark Moore and in particular Mark Bickerton, now a leading light at London Metropolitan University, were tremendous influences in the beginning, and I have to thank them for pointing me in the right direction early on. Claire, Jo, Sam and Darren at Wiley have been super and I am grateful for the time and support they invested in this project and the help they gave me as a first time author.

Finally, I owe a huge debt to my wife Paula, mother to our wonderful children, Marshall and Tegan. She has supported me unconditionally since I left the relative comfort of Deloitte and started up ALLIANTIST. Paula, not being a business person, has also proved tremendously helpful in ensuring that my work is easy to digest and void of consulting jargon; if Paula 'got it' then my hope is others can too! She is also partly responsible for many of the simple mnemonics and frameworks you will encounter in the book. Our wider families and friends have also shown great support and for every one of them, thanks very much.

Mark Darby
May 2006

PREFACE

NEW RULES

The world of business has changed significantly in recent years. Business is no longer just a zero-sum game and pressures continue to grow on organisations to achieve more success with less resource. Resulting from forces of globalisation, emerging technologies, heightened competition, customer demand, growing risks and an increasing pace of change, there is a movement to alliances and extended enterprises, where organisations collaborate to compete and operate more effectively.

Mergers and acquisitions also continually fail to deliver value so organisations are increasingly turning to alliances as a primary strategic solution. Whether it is for reducing costs, growing sales, improving operations or aiding innovation it is a fact that many organisations, regardless of size or sector, now depend on other parties for much of their business success.

But this is not new information. Surveys and reports in the late 1990s and early this millennium made it clear that alliances are big news. Fifty-seven per cent of CEOs in companies surveyed rated their alliances as either critical or very important for their company's present and future growth[1]. A Partnership Sourcing survey highlighted that more than 80% of UK companies believe that partnership sourcing will have a crucial impact on competitiveness[2]. The Economist Intelligence Unit and Accenture (Anderson Consulting at the time) produced a report in 1997 called Vision 2010. The report suggested that by the end of this decade, 40% of organisations would be loose-knit 'virtual' organisations that buy in skills and collaborate for services as needed rather than be monolithic corporates[3]. Research presented while with Deloitte in 2004 reinforced these findings and announced others, and brought out the concept of the extended enterprise to a wider audience.

These forces, backed up by the survey results, do indicate there is a need to work more closely with other parties who will undoubtedly have an impact on the organisation's future prosperity, and its competitive advantage, more so than ever before. Regardless of whether the other party is a customer, competitor, supplier, complementor or another department in the same company, a new set of 'rules' has emerged but few understand the changes or how to play the game. There are some good examples of winning alliances that generate significant business value; however, research indicates that over 50% and up to 70% of alliances fail to meet their objectives. In addition, there is a growing body of compliance and controls legislation that heightens the financial and reputational risks from failure.

Many organisations find it difficult to change and adapt to these rules but being capable of partnering is now just the price of entry to the beauty parade, it won't guarantee success in itself. The choice of who the organisation works with in the future, why, what for, and crucially how, will be the difference between success and failure. This book shows you how to succeed. It introduces, quite simply, the rules of how to play the game the smart way with the three critical success factors that create value through alliances. The three critical success factors are:

1. Having a capability to partner
2. Having the right partners
3. Having effective relationship architectures

By following the maps, and using the tools and techniques in this book, you will be in the minority that wins with alliances and gains attractive rewards, standing out as the partner to work with in your chosen field, gaining a positive reputation and great results as shown in Figure i.

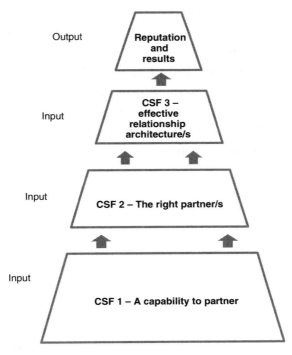

Figure i Steps to success with alliances.

THE IMPORTANCE OF ALLIANCE BRAND FOR FUTURE SUCCESS

Why do organisations need to stand out? Regardless of industry or competence it is clear that firms are increasing the use of alliances to execute their business goals. This means that the available pool of potential partners is growing and there is greater choice. However, given the alarming failure rates and growing consequences and risks from poor partnering, organisations need to get smarter about who they partner with and how they go about it. So the importance of a positive reputation and results for alliances starts to make sense if organisations want to identify the best partners, as well as differentiate themselves as an attractive partner and organisation that can be trusted to deliver on its promises.

Organisations who achieve the three critical success factors will not only get great results from alliances, over time they will get an alliance brand, characterised as having **'a positive reputation and results from its alliance activity'.** Going further it is considered that organisations that have a 'leading' alliance brand will be seen as **'the partner to work with, delivering on its promises and creating superior value for their customers, partners, shareholders and other key stakeholders from its alliance activity'.**

The tangible results that organisations can enjoy from becoming a leading alliance brand include:

- Faster time to positive value creation
- Lower costs of partnering and higher returns from investments
- Lower risks of partner or alliance failure
- Improved relationships internally and externally
- Governance friendly, transparent and auditable processes
- Improved staff skills, satisfaction and knowledge retention

■ Being seen as the partner of choice in their chosen field and first option for new alliances
■ Increased alliance brand attractiveness

Leading alliance brands will clearly stand out in the future and a league of attractive alliance brands to work with will emerge. This 'alliance brand index' will reinforce them as an attractive partner, and further enhance their asset attractiveness to give even greater returns.

Those firms that develop an alliance brand will go from success to success whereas the businesses that fail to execute the three critical success factors may struggle to survive, let alone prosper.

Alliance brand and the three critical success factors is not just a good idea. There is a significant body of research from various sources which has informed the approach and relevant parts are touched on in the book. It demonstrates that those organisations that get it right enjoy very attractive returns on their investments and much higher long-term success rates. This secondary research coupled with primary research and extensive practical experience forms the basis of how the maps and tools you will find in the book have been built and developed. The term 'map' is used for the frameworks specifically because the 'map' is not the territory. By that it means that things you will encounter in the real world (the territory) may have some slight differences to the map. However, with a map to guide you there is a much greater chance of success and a likelihood of getting to that holy grail of winning alliances and alliance brand status more quickly and cost effectively than without it.

Over the years of working with third parties there has been exposure to some of the best and worst practice in the public and not so public domain. Some of the not so public experiences or worst practice examples drawn from will remain anonymous for obvious reasons! At Rank and Reuters, then leading Deloitte's extended enterprise practice in the UK, and now with ALLIANTIST, there have been opportunities to work with some smart people. Working together the teams designed, built and managed many alliances and other business relationships as well as coached large numbers of customers, partners and suppliers. There have been local, national and global programmes for R&D, sourcing, operations and sales as well as marketing-based alliances, and low value alliances as well as alliances with billions of pounds at risk. Some of what was created did not lead where the team first envisaged, for better or worse. Part of that was the team's fault, and part was due to factors way beyond its control or influence. As a result of all those experiences, both good and bad, this book represents a comprehensive yet pragmatic approach to building business value using alliances.

Much of what you will read in this book may strike you as common sense. It is. The sad part is that it is not common execution. The purpose of the book is both to inform and offer the maps, tools and techniques that enable you to make it more commonly executed and with it, create the value that you and your organisation desire from your alliance activity.

HOW THIS BOOK DIFFERS FROM OTHER MATERIAL

There is a growing body of information about alliances; some of it is helpful while much of it adds little value. Paradoxically, as the amount of new alliances continues to steadily increase and the wealth of information grows bigger, the reported alliance success rate remains pathetically low suggesting that much of the learning and available good practice is not filtering through to the workplace. There are five challenges for interested parties that this book aims to address:

1. Need for a swift and focused return on investment: there are significant pressures to move quickly nowadays and an increasing pace of change. As such there may not be the time to distil and then execute the few key things that can make a difference to your alliance activity and positively affect business success. This book introduces the three critical success factors that make a real difference and is presented in a manner that you will find easy to digest and work with on a day-to-day basis.

2. Aligning with the wider business: alliances are just a means to an end. Alliance success is also affected by so much more than just the alliance itself. Much of the material in existence today fails to address this key point and looks at alliances in too narrow a capacity without considering how it all fits back into the wider organisation context. This book introduces the elements that create or destroy value at both an organisational and an alliance infrastructure level. Addressing these elements forms an integral part of critical success factor one (CSF 1) which is having a capability to partner. Part II shows you how to achieve it by following ALLIANTIST VIP Map.

3. Balancing academia with real life business need: reviewing academic material can be useful. As Kurt Lewin apparently once said, there is nothing so practical as a good theory[4]. However, there are few good practical theories so not much of the academic material available has application in the workplace where practitioners needed it most. This book is mainly a 'how to' fieldbook with maps, tools and guidance to aid your journey to success and includes underpinning theory and context to reinforce the pragmatic approach. The hope is it will become a trusted advisor for your day-to-day operation and have a place on your desktop and not just the book shelf.

4. Extracting learning from different arenas and working as a team: there are some fundamental differences between joint go-to-market alliances and buyer/supplier outsourcing alliances, not least the measures of success. There are also differences between doing an R&D alliance in the pharmaceutical industry and a marketing alliance in the information technology industry, for example the pace of change and risks involved. Despite these differences, there are many similarities, not least the need to collaborate, to allocate resources effectively, to construct workable and effective governance architectures and so on. Personal experience suggests the groups that manage the various external relationships in an organisation, for example sales and sourcing professionals, rarely work closely together and share learning. Yet they have many common issues and can leverage each other's talents. This book is therefore focused on translating the learning from various different competency areas and different industries into a practical alliance advisor aid regardless of the type of alliance or industry. The book shows a bias towards building alliances such as joint go-to-market alliances and outsourcing alliances given their added complexity over (say) R&D and marketing alliances. The information, communication and technology (ICT) industry features more than other industries given the complex nature of some alliances and pertinent case studies to draw from.

In real life now with ALLIANTIST, and in previous lives, the aim has been to work closely with the client who brings its depth of specific industry expertise, or (say) its deeper legal and financial know-how into a powerful team. Working together the maps and processes are tailored according to the actual business environment and organisation needs in order to deliver the project or alliance objectives. So to gain the best from this book you should add in your key skills and experience, and share it with colleagues in your team who may have different skills. Then use the maps and tools for your 'territory' while bearing in mind ALLIANTIST copyright at all times. This book is not focused on giving deep insight into a particular industry, nor is it a substitute for legal and financial advice so make sure those resources are in your team, and to enable them to contribute and buy into your alliance aims, engage them early in the process!

5. A UK and broader Europe centric perspective: many of the books available in the market today have a US centric context. This book, while it covers global alliance activity as well as international business and is relevant to all geographic audiences, is taken from a UK and Europe centric perspective. It includes examples of alliances and organisations originating from the UK and Europe, and touches on issues such as the Combined Code and Operating and Financial Review from an alliance governance standpoint.

STRUCTURE OF THE BOOK

Part I

Part I is organised into six chapters and acts as an overview of alliances with insight and background on the relevant theory and research in the field. There are exercises throughout this part to help challenge your thinking and raise probing questions about alliance excellence within your firm.

Chapter 1 is about understanding competitive advantage and value creation as this should be the overarching goal for any alliance activity. Chapter 2 introduces alliances. Starting with a definition it then demystifies the complexity by understanding what gets accessed in alliances as well as breaking down the types of alliances that exist, and how they pervade the value chain. It explains how alliances have differing values and importance and addresses the various sources for potential partners. Chapter 3 assesses why alliances are growing in popularity and seeks to uncover the forces behind their increasing use. Chapter 4 takes a look at what a good alliance looks and feels like as well as what leading alliance organisations do with their alliance infrastructure to generate great returns. Research that explains leading alliance performers is discussed and put into perspective. Alliances are not all plain sailing, despite many folk considering they are, so in Chapter 5 the forces challenging alliance success are revealed. Chapter 6 brings out the importance of reputation and results as a key differentiator and research around brand in its traditional sense is explored. Alliance brand is introduced along with the three critical success factors that underpin it, with some examples of organisations with alliance brands.

Part II

Part II gets into much deeper territory and is where the rubber really starts hitting the road on how critical success factor one (CSF 1), having a capability to partner is achieved. ALLIANTIST Value Inflection Point (VIP) Map, as shown in Figure ii, is introduced to help you address the factors that create and destroy value at both an organisational and alliance infrastructure level. A chapter is devoted to each underpinning element. During each chapter there are a number of exercises and tools to help you build the capability and use it effectively back in the real world.

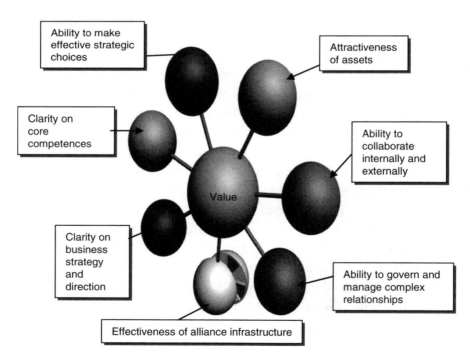

Figure ii   ALLIANTIST VIP Map.

Part III

Having a capability to partner is critical but not enough for success on its own. Building winning alliances can't happen without the right partners (CSF 2), nor will those alliances flourish unless they have effective relationship architectures underpinning them (CSF 3). These two CSF are addressed in Part III. ALLIANTIST ICE Map addresses CSF 2, and this map aids the Investigation, Creation and Execution of alliances. A six phase process is shown in Figure iii. It covers the lifecycle of alliance activity from alliance idea through to partner selection using ALLIANTIST TOPSCORER Map, then into alliance launch, delivery and renewal or termination.

Many organisations operate a one size fits all approach to how they work with their partners, and fail to give this aspect due care and attention so Part III also offers solutions on achieving CSF 3. As shown in Figure iv ALLIANTIST ERA Map is used in With-Partner Planning, Phase 3 of the ICE Map. This map looks closely at how to craft an Effective Relationship Architecture with partner/s to facilitate alliance success and mitigate the risk of failure or surprise. Each chapter within Part III is also underpinned by supporting tools and techniques to aid practical activity whether in the classroom or the workplace.

A final chapter in Part III brings it all together as you embark on your journey to an alliance brand. This chapter introduces

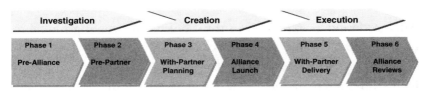

Figure iii ALLIANTIST ICE Map.

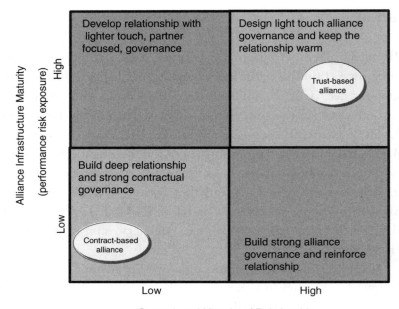

Figure iv ALLIANTIST ERA Map.

guidance around how to get started and where to go for help. In order to really stand out from the crowd final commentary introduces an emerging model called alliance brand index, an embryonic league table of alliance brands.

Concluding thoughts before reading the book

Alliance brand as expressed in this book is an evolving model so there are few explicit examples of leading alliance brands today. Not one organisation scored 100% during interviews and assessments although many organisations do exhibit some alliance brand characteristics. Those organisations that are used as examples in the text may not stay relevant over the lifetime of this book. As is so often the case in business as with football, things change. Just as Manchester United were the team of the 1990s, the baton appears to have been handed on to Chelsea early in the new millennium. Who knows if those firms listed in the book will maintain their positions. The signs are good given their current commitment and leadership.

This book is a deliberate attempt to raise the bar on alliance performance and there are no apologies for some of the tough exercises within it and the standards set for alliance brands. The goal is to help organisations beat the growing challenges that successful partnering brings at both an organisational and alliance infrastructure level, now and in the future. If you aim for the stars you might reach the moon. Put another way, you will at least improve upon the current 30% alliance success rate!

Before going any further you can test your capability for partnering and assess your alliance brand status now on line at www. ALLIANTIST.com or do the quicktest diagnostic in Appendix 1 at the back of the book. This will help you identify where best to start in Part II if you want to jump right into that section. Keep connected to the website www.ALLIANTIST.com for the latest tools and ideas in this field and email mark.darby@ALLIANTIST. com if you have any comments, questions or wish to share your own ideas for developing a positive reputation and results with alliances.

Andrew Ewing is a successful alliance director who has a favourite saying about idle chat, 'that's all very well but what are we going to do at 9 am on a Monday morning?' Well, this statement goes to the heart of the book's ethos. During each chapter there are practical exercises and initiatives that you can use to keep adding value at any time of the day! So let's kick off right now. . . . Good luck.

NOTES

1. PricewaterhouseCoopers barometer surveys 30 November 2000 – http://www.barometersurveys.com/pr/tb001130.html
2. Partnership Sourcing Limited March 2000 – http://www.pslcbi. com/findings.html
3. Vision 2010 – Economist Intelligence Unit 1997.
4. Kurt Lewin was a German psychologist studying groups, organisation development and one of the pioneers of social psychology.

USING ALLIANCES TO CREATE VALUE

T he book starts with a basic introduction to the world of value, advantage and alliances, and then moves up a pace to consider leading edge activity that affects alliance and business success. By the end of this part you will understand the components of value and competitive advantage, and have a high-level perspective on the types of analysis required to take decisions on whether to make, buy or ally. In addition you will have a clear understanding of what alliances are, what they are not, what good looks like in a successful alliance and what it takes to achieve great returns from alliance activity. You will get to understand why alliances go wrong and why. In addition you will gain a view of why alliances are increasing and what the major challenges are which will continue to force firms towards smarter alliance execution. Finally, this part introduces why a positive reputation and results from partnering are becoming growing standards for doing business, and what it means to have an alliance brand. Before you get started in Part I, consider the following questions in Table 1.0 and note your thoughts alongside.

Table 1.0 Introductory questions.

Question	Answer/Comments
How does your organisation measure success?	
What does value mean and where is it created in your organisation?	
Does your organisation have a competitive advantage and if so do you know how is it achieved?	
Does your organisation have consistency in recognising the type, value and importance of its third party relationships?	
How many alliances and other third party relationships does your organisation have today?	
How dependent is your organisation on alliances and other third party relationships for its success now?	
Is that dependency likely to change in the future? If yes, why and how?	
Is the alliance activity creating or destroying value for your organisation?	
Can your organisation place a monetary value on the benefits, cost and return on investment from its alliance activity?	
Does your organisation have a positive identity and reputation for alliances and partnering internally and externally?	
What would your organisation's best and worst partners say about doing business with it?	

## CHAPTER 1

HOW VALUE AND ADVANTAGE AFFECT FIRM ACTIVITIES

WHAT IS VALUE

Organisations exist for a reason. They must have a purpose that drives their strategy. Regardless of whether it is public, private, for profit or nonprofit, the business will have some underlying reason for being in existence. If that purpose and strategy is not clear or well understood it can affect alliance activity, and more importantly impact whether the business creates or destroys value. The purpose should have something to do with creating value for stakeholders such as itself, its shareholders, customers, suppliers and other interested parties. So what is value?

At an individual stakeholder or customer level, value means different things to different people and at different times it can be valued in vastly different ways. Treacy and Wiersema[1] suggested that 'value' is made up of components including: price, time, premium service and quality, and see 'value' as being the combination of the costs customers pay and the benefits they receive. This applies to both the products sold and services offered. Product costs include 'price and less than perfect reliability including the whole life cost of ownership. Service costs include mistakes, delays and inconvenience because customers are said to pay with both their time and money.' Outlining the benefit side, value comes out of the features and needs fulfilled by the product and from the kinds of service benefits provided, and these are only seen as benefits if they 'substantially exceed competitors' offerings'.

Many people value low price, others high quality, some fast service, while others are concerned about environmentally friendly goods and are prepared to pay more for that benefit because they value it. So in simple terms value is 'the overall price paid or investment made for the benefits gained in return'.

As suggested, the 'overall price' can be made up of both explicit and implicit factors. For example, the 'price' you pay for access to a daily newspaper might include the face price of the newspaper, the time it takes you to get that paper, and the effort in researching which paper to buy. It also includes the hidden implications of not buying another paper or a substitute (e.g. reading a website) which could provide you with the same or better benefits at a lower overall price, such as reduced cost of disposal afterwards. There are also psychological prices paid as well, perhaps less for buying a news-paper but imagine the stress and risks involved in some investments such as buying a house, changing job, or perhaps selecting and managing alliance partners . . . although much of that stress disap-pears when purchasing from a trusted brand or someone who has a positive identity and reputation in that field.

Businesses talk about their 'value proposition' for customers. What they aim to communicate is the benefits achieved by investing in a product, service or solution from their organisation instead of others. Failure to articulate this message succinctly and clearly may mean the customer can't see the value in the proposition and the sale is lost. Sometimes an organisation's product or service by itself is not enough to solve a problem so customer prospects go elsewhere. Take the simple example of buying a car. Without servicing, financing support, car insurance and breakdown protection the car may not be attractive for some people. This is where an example of a joint value proposition using alliances would make sense for some customers and is why many car dealerships have just those relationships in place, either with sister companies or external partners.

Organisations measure and define value for their shareholders and key stakeholders in different ways. For profit businesses emphasise the value they achieve in the form of financial revenue and profitability statements. When taken together with the future prospects for the firm these translate into higher value share prices if it is a listed organisation. Not for profit and public sector organisations may emphasise the creation of other value, for example people treated and lives saved by the National Heath Service (NHS) as well as value for money indicators and stakeholder satisfaction metrics. Many organisations now also generate more holistic scorecards that address not just financial value creation but also other metrics, for example customer and employee satisfaction, innovation, process improvement and others such as those termed 'the triple bottom line', which includes social and environmental measures as well as financial. All of these metrics should relate back to the purpose of the organisation and align with the value proposition for customers as well, because clearly the source of a company's long-term prosperity is in its satisfied customers. However, consideration also needs to be given to suppliers and other partners, and from an alliance perspective, any alliance activity should also relate to one or more of those goals.

Exercise 1: Value proposition

Select one of your products or services. Can you articulate in one sentence a compelling value proposition for your customer? How does it compare against competitors and other alternatives?

In this age of increasing competition and choice, customers, suppliers and others usually have many avenues to realise their benefits and goals. So in order to attract and retain its target audience an organisation must deliver greater value than other options available. For example, Tesco, the leading supermarket and growing retailer, seeks to offer equal or better products at the same or lower cost and in a more convenient location than its competitors either online at Tesco.com, or via its Express and large edge of town outlets. The benefit for the shopper is that they can trust Tesco to offer them a similar or better basket of goods when and where they want it at a cost that is at least as good as the other suppliers. Sainsburys by comparison suffered in the late 1990s with poor stock and inventory management so they lost out for many years, as have many of the specialist retailers and food operators that cannot compete with Tesco on price even though many may offer better service. Supply chain management is a key factor in successful retailing. As organisations rely more on external sources, and suppliers move to become alliance partners, it will be interesting to see whether the alleged adversarial practices by some dominant leading players can be sustained in the future.

In order to continually beat its rivals or maintain its position as the favoured supplier of its customers, organisations need to deliver better value and do it more consistently for their customers and other stakeholders than other options. At its most fundamental, this is the basis of competitive advantage.

UNDERSTANDING COMPETITIVE ADVANTAGE

For a prosperous future an organisation needs to ensure that its strategy will produce both value and competitive advantage. Alliances done well will enhance value, but done badly could result in serious value destruction, increased risk and erosion of competitive advantage. While luck and indeed hope are not unknown strategies for winning, and are important for success, they are not enough. There is usually something more powerful underpinning any firm advantage. It is also one of the reasons why prospective partners might see the organisation as attractive to work with in the future.

So value is now understood but what is competitive advantage and how do you get it? A brief step into the academic world with a skim of the literature will help clarify but remember, this book is not an academic critique or deep review of all the related concepts. These factors are introduced here to help the learning and reinforce the practical approach addressed in Part II.

Rappaport stated that productivity, the value of output produced by a unit of labour or capital, was the foundation for creating competitive advantage. He then went on to say 'a business creates competitive advantage when the long term value of its output or sales is greater than its total costs, including its costs of capital. This advantage can be achieved by providing superior value or lower prices.'[2] Tate & Lyle is a world leading manufacturer of renewable food and industrial ingredients. They have a competitive advantage in the manufacturing of speciality syrups (e.g. Lyle's) and treacles through the nature of the manufacturing process and sheer scale of the business. Focus and ongoing development, both in manufacturing capabilities and the increasing variety of products available to its customers, as well as development of market share are used as measures to ensure continued competitive advantage.

Michael Porter, the leading strategy guru, has written extensively about competitive advantage[3]. He said that competitive advantage 'grows fundamentally out of the value a firm is able to create for its buyers that exceeds the firm's cost of creating it. Value is what buyers are willing to pay and superior value stems from offering lower prices than competitors for equivalent benefits or providing unique benefits that more than offset a higher price.'[4]

In his early work Porter[5] presented his three 'generic strategies': cost leadership, differentiation and focus as the basis for competitive advantage. Porter argued that you should only focus on one generic strategy or there is a risk of getting 'stuck in the middle'. The concept of only being able to adopt one of the generic strategies has, however, been dismissed by many authors[6], most notably citing the Japanese car industry and its approach to the US, and Walmart, both offering differentiation and lower costs.

Depending on how you define focus, in the UK, Tesco and BT are examples of firms following all the generic competitive strategies. The BT website[7] states eight strategic priorities which include each of the strategies above:

- Keep a relentless focus on improving customer satisfaction
- Put broadband at the heart of BT
- Create mobility services and solutions
- Transform our network for the 21st century
- Achieve competitive advantage through cost leadership
- Lead the world in network centric ICT solutions
- Reinvent our traditional business
- Motivate our people and live the BT values

In their book *The Discipline of Market Leaders*, Treacy and Wiersema[8] argued that new rules meant that a different strategic approach was needed for competitive advantage. They suggested that four new premises underpinned the 'New World of Competition' where the buyer was now king:

- Companies can no longer raise prices in lockstep with higher costs; they have to try to lower costs to accommodate rising customer expectations.
- Companies can no longer aim for less than hassle-free service. Their customers enjoy effortless, flawless and instant performance from one industry and want it from every other.

- Companies can no longer assume that good basic service is enough; customers demand premium service – and raise their standards continuously.
- Companies can no longer compromise on quality and product capabilities. They must build products to deliver nothing less than superiority and eye-popping innovation.

The disciplines proposed by Treacy and Wiersema were built on the overarching value proposition the companies pursued and these disciplines shaped the entire organisation, from its culture to its public perception. The disciplines all needed to be in existence but with a clear focus on one. They are best total cost, best product or best total solution. Calling them their Value Disciplines the authors presented each as:

Operational Excellence (best total cost) – providing the customer with reliable products or services at competitive prices, delivered with minimal difficulty or inconvenience. Current well-known examples include Tesco, Vodafone and Dell.

Product Leadership (best product) – providing products that continually redefine the state of the art. Current examples include Starbucks, Intel, Cisco, HP and Disney.

Customer Intimacy (best total solution) – selling the customer a total solution, not just a product or service. Current examples here include Reuters, BT, IBM and the top professional services firms like Ernst & Young and Deloitte.

Exercise 2: Value disciplines

Which of the three value disciplines does your company adopt as its primary focus? Would your customers, suppliers and other stakeholders agree?

Each of the 'generic' strategies presented above is fundamentally a 'competitive' strategy. These strategies may have underlying tactics and objective where third parties and alliance partners are used. Indeed Porter[9] presented seven different ways for firms to consider differentiation, and one of the ways was to link with other firms in alliances (the others being: product features, links between functions, timing, location, product mix and reputation).

In more recent times, Porter has discussed the basis of competitive advantage as being drawn from the activities that an organisation undertakes. He stated 'ultimately all differences between companies in cost or price derive from the hundreds of activities required to create, produce, sell and deliver their products and services. Overall advantage or disadvantage results from all a company's activities not only a few.'[10] He later went on to highlight the risks of outsourcing and partnering without due care as it might deliver operational effectiveness but compromise future competitive advantage. Therefore before thinking about alliances or any other form of external relationship, the organisation must first know what it wants to focus on and where value is really created for customers, as it needs to be sure that it is going to deliver value and competitive advantage, and not erode or destroy future benefits.

There are various methods of analysis to support strategic decision-making and this is a well-trodden path for academics and practitioners alike. Kenneth Andrews is one of the earliest individuals to be associated with work about how strategy should be designed or formulated in order to achieve competitive advantage. He wrote, 'The interdependence of purpose, policies, and organised action is crucial to the particularity of an individual strategy and its opportunity to identify competitive advantage. It is the unity, coherence, and internal consistency of a company's strategic decisions that position the company in its environment and give the firm its identity, its power to mobilise its strengths, and its likelihood of success in the marketplace.'[11]

Andrews held the view that the principal 'subactivities' of strategy formulation were identifying opportunities and threats in the environment, including undertaking some form of risk assessment to the alternatives available. He also outlined the need to undertake a review of the internal situation to assess the resources 'on hand and available'. Rumelt[12] argued that competitive advantage could normally be traced to one of three roots; superior skills, superior resources or superior position, again reflecting that advantage can come either internally or externally. Position in this context could be associated with either size or scale and brand, and once in a good position it is usually defensible.

In their influential article 'Competing on Capabilities: The New Rules of Corporate Strategy' Stalk, Evans and Shulman[13] explain that the key to competitive advantage now is '*how*' the company chooses to compete and not just '*where*' it competes. As also proposed by Andrews, the '*how*' is determined by two separate but complementary forms of analysis, the external, industry-based analysis, and the internal, resource or core competence based perspective.

We shall focus in much more depth in Part II on the need for effective internal and external analysis. There is, however, a view that even with all the internal and external analysis available, uncontrollable factors and in-situ events may impact the chosen strategy and affect competitive advantage potential, both positively and negatively[14]. Good old luck also plays a part, although you will probably not come across too many examples where luck has resulted in any lengthy form of value creation or advantage!

To summarise, value and competitive advantage mean different things to different people. You are on the right track if you are delivering more value to your customers, more consistently than your competitors or other substitutes. Enhanced brand and reputation as well as increasingly positive results are an output from successful execution and past performance. To attempt to define value and advantage it could be considered that 'competitive advantage is determined by the sum of the activities undertaken by an organisation and value is created from the effective deployment of a firm's core competences and broader assets into attractive well qualified external opportunities'.

The capabilities to deliver the activities can be built organically within the organisation, purchased at arm's length, acquired from merger or acquisition, or borrowed from alliances with other organisations. As will be seen in Part II, knowing which option to use and when, then executing well, is important as it affects value creation and advantage, yet is a competence lacking in many organisations.

Having now got a perspective on value creation and competitive advantage, Chapter 2 introduces one of the major options for achieving it, alliances, which is increasingly becoming a primary strategic choice for delivery of organisation strategy.

UNDERSTANDING ALLIANCES

ALLIANCE AMBIGUITY

Language ambiguity in life, let alone business, is one of the major problems that cause communication and relationship breakdown. Anthony Robbins, the leading motivator and NLP guru, said that 'the quality of your life is dependent on the quality of your communication.'[15] To offer a simple example, there have been many situations where someone's implicit definition and terminology around alliances has been markedly different from not only the organisation they were negotiating with, but also other members of their team! To demonstrate some of the complexity and potential for ambiguity surrounding alliances, observe the mind map in Figure 2.1.

The terms partnering, PPP, PFI, outsourcing, consortia, franchising, corporate venturing and so on are all well used. Their meaning is less clear to some stakeholders because the devil is in

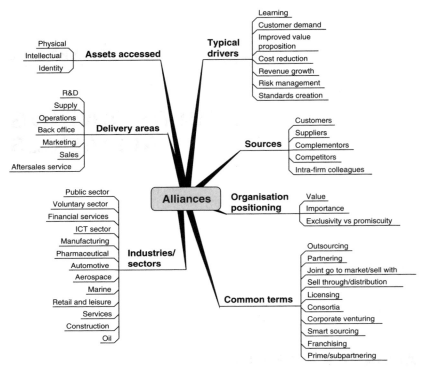

Figure 2.1   Alliance complexity map.

the detail. Each of these terms needs to be defined very clearly for each specific initiative. While indirect channel sales distribution is effectively outsourcing, it is rarely considered as such. Outsourcing at its most basic is about taking a hitherto internal practice and passing it over to a third party. In a start-up organisation with no previous practice, outsourcing that process or piece of work would more likely be considered an alliance.

DEFINING ALLIANCES

Given the potential for confusion here is a definition of alliances to ensure alignment for the remainder of the book. An alliance is 'two or more partners working closely together to achieve some-thing one cannot easily do or chooses not to do alone'. Exploring this definition it is useful to understand:

'**partners**' in this instance can mean internal colleagues in other departments or sister companies in the same organisation as well as external individuals and other organisations. There is no limit to how many partners may participate in an alliance. Partner is used to describe an entity participating in an alliance and is used consistently throughout the book although in practice the term needs careful consideration before use. Partner is a 'one size fits all' phrase and not appropriate when alliances have differing values and importance to the organisation as will be seen shortly. Partner also has legal implications with most organisations that use the term having a clause in their alliance agreements to reflect the term is only used in a marketing context.

'**working closely together**' means a need for collaboration and some form of interdependence where one partner is reliant on the other partner to some degree for achievement of its goals. Given this interdependence it is usual to see some form of shared risk and reward between the partners.

'**to achieve something**' indicates that alliances are about creating value and have some underlying goal, as with a project. This might be a short-term goal (e.g. drive cost and inefficiency out of a process) or a longer-term goal (e.g. research and develop then market a new drug) but either way it needs to relate back to the organisation goals and purpose.

'**one cannot easily do or chooses not to do alone**' not only reinforces the interdependence, but recognises that while an organisation might be capable of executing alone, there are good reasons not to. There are many examples expressed later but in simple terms this means that they either want to focus on something they are better at and find a partner to help (e.g. by outsourcing a noncore but important process), or work with someone who has something of value to them they can't immediately or easily access (e.g. in entering a new industry or different geography).

In addition to these factors there are other characteristics that alliances exhibit as well. These include an ability to influence but not control the other party, and an evolving or incomplete contract where decisions affecting the alliance need to be made on an ongoing basis and cannot be determined at the time the contract is first written. Trust is also exhibited, but built within appropriate safeguards. Both or all partners will normally have some 'visibility' to the end user, whether it is in actual delivery of the alliance tasks, or through some other means, for example by use of a brand asset, such as Intel Inside, the logo demonstrating Intel products is contained within its partner's hardware.

WHAT ALLIANCES ARE NOT

Alliances are definitely *not* fully specified contracts involving arm's length transactions with other parties that don't make a significant difference to an organisation's performance. So unless the organisation is hugely dependent on stationery it is highly unlikely they will be engaged in a strategic alliance with the staples and envelope supplier, despite that supplier's best effort to tell its client otherwise!

Mergers and acquisitions (M&A) in the general sense are not alliances because they exhibit full control characteristics for the parent; however, at an operational level there could be alliances between different product groups or departments as suggested above.

Less clearly categorised are joint ventures. If a relationship with another party involves equity exchange, whether minor or major, it is normally viewed as a joint venture. Three additional points need to be considered that may affect its categorisation of alliance or joint venture:

- Equity injection may result in an increasing form of control or influence, for example through a voting seat on the board of the partner.
- A full joint venture would normally include the creation of a separate entity and standalone board made up of both partners.
- Equity exchange activity in large companies usually involves the corporate finance or M&A team being engaged rather than an alliance team and a greater range of tax and accounting issues to consider (although clearly tax and accounting issues exist in many alliances, especially cross-border activities).

ASSETS ARE WHAT YOU ACCESS

It can be dressed up many ways but basically, alliances provide organisations with access to assets they don't have internally or don't want to own directly, for whatever reason. These include:

- **Physical:** for example, products, people, capital, equipment and property
- **Identity:** for example, brand, reputation and association, including alliance brand itself
- **Intellectual:** for example, specialist knowledge, processes and confidential information

One of the key questions addressed during Part II in the chapter on strategic choice is whether alliances are the most appropriate means to access these assets. Investing in an alliance to access assets when an arm's length purchasing agreement would be more appropriate is likely to waste internal resources time, cash and may concede future rewards unnecessarily. Conducting an alliance when it may be more appropriate to acquire the assets, e.g. through merger or acquisition (M&A), may subsequently destroy value by allying away a competence or asset that could yield a future competitive advantage. Conversely, undertaking either option when an alliance is more appropriate will also destroy value. Chapter 10 in Part II also looks at the range of assets an organisation has and addresses their attractiveness and use in practice.

Exercise 3: Assets

What assets are there in your organisation that might be attractive to other parties?

ALLIANCES PERVADE THE VALUE CHAIN

There is almost no area of business or industry where firms have not sought to construct alliances. The typical value chain as shown in Figure 2.2 indicates some examples where alliances have taken place.

ST Microelectronics, Motorola and Philips set up an R&D alliance in 2003 as part of a five-year partnership to jointly develop processes from the 90 nm to 32 nm nodes on a 300 mm manufacturing line at ST's French R&D facility. The alliance demonstrates cooperation for standards setting, lowering of production costs and management of risks.

GlaxoSmithKline and Human Genome Sciences have an alliance that spans R&D, production, sales and marketing for an anticancer drug. Brightwell Dispensers works closely with Anglia, a leading electrical component supplier on various R&D initiatives and in return for its support on R&D, Anglia enjoys an almost

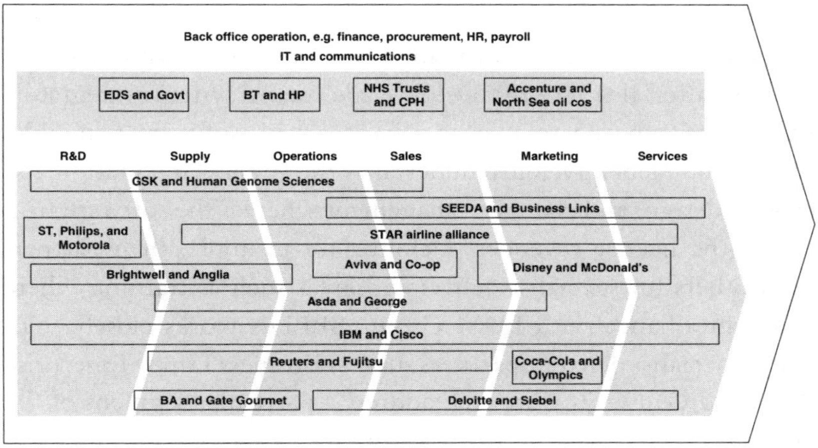

Figure 2.2 Cross-value chain examples of alliance activity.

exclusive supply contract with Brightwell for electronic components.

Disney and McDonald's have had a 10-year marketing and merchandising alliance that has brought great rewards for both parties. McDonald's has accessed Disney assets to appeal to the family audience and Disney got access to the powerful promotion and distribution of McDonald's 30 000 restaurants that serve 50 million people across 119 countries every day. Reckitt Benckiser like Procter & Gamble is an example of FMCG (fast moving consumer goods) organisations that licenses their assets to others in relatively simple but nonetheless attractive alliances in order to innovate and build brand equity as well as derive income streams from the licence revenue. Tate & Lyle is increasingly turning to marketing and sales-based alliances which leverage its strong brand name and ingredients for mutual benefit with partners. Its long standing alliance with McVities in a co-branded alliance for McVities Lyles cakes is one example where it helps differentiate against supermarket 'own label' offerings.

IBM and Cisco have a large cross-value chain alliance that encompasses joint R&D through to ongoing service and maintenance on aftersales activity. Deloitte like many systems integrators has vendor type go-to-market alliances with software firms like Oracle and Siebel. Deloitte undertakes the systems integration and process design, and change management whereas the software firm enjoys the licence revenues. Deloitte, for example, then partners with others for specialist delivery in areas such as training where it has an alliance with FDM Group. SEEDA works closely with many specialist delivery partners such as Business Links, Enterprise Hubs and Gateways who each address a particular segment of the business market, helping firms at different stages of their lifecycle or with different types of challenges.

Given in-country regulations and the structure of the airline industry, participants work together in alliances such as STAR and Oneworld. STAR Alliance was the first global alliance to take off in 1997, and now has 16 member airlines including Air Canada, Air New Zealand, ANA, Asian Airlines, Austrian, BMI, LOT Polish Airlines, Lufthansa, Scandinavian Airlines, Singapore Airlines, Spanair, United, US Airways, VARIG and TAP Portugal. South African Airways is scheduled to join in 2006. Benefits for the partners include the ability to offer customers seamless travel and loyalty rewards as well as increased scale and cost reduction from acting together in sourcing fuel, infrastructure, marketing and other goods and services.

Back office activities are increasingly being seen as noncore with a proliferation in outsourcing shared services and offshoring services now available. Common areas to ally for include ICT such as the government and its many IT services partners like EDS; financial services, procurement, and HR where organisations like Accenture and IBM excel. In late 2004 the NHS started building collaborative procurement hubs (CPH). The purpose was to allow the primary and secondary Trusts to focus on what they do best (saving lives) as well as increase the quality of purchasing activity and improve scale from aggregating volumes in areas not addressed by PASA (Purchasing and Supplies Agency).

Organisations from different industries and sectors are also joining forces to create more value for themselves and their customers. An example of this is with the Information, Communication and Technology (ICT) sectors where convergence is happening at great speed where mobile phone providers, network operators and content providers are working more closely together. BT Fusion works just like a mobile phone when you are out and about, but switches automatically and seamlessly onto a BT Broadband line when you get home. That means users get all the convenience and all the features of a mobile phone but with fixed lines prices and quality.

ALLIANCES HAVE DIFFERING VALUES AND IMPORTANCE

Alliances have differing values and importance yet few organisations are able to demonstrate an effective categorisation for how they position their alliances and external relationships in the context of an alliance portfolio. As a result it can adversely affect the allocation of resources in alliances and destroy the value of assets if used in an ad hoc manner.

Organisations that categorise their alliance portfolios tend to use terminology such as strategic partner, premier partner, or gold, silver and bronze alliances, or tier 1, 2, 3, 4 alliances and so on where strategic alliances or strategic partners have similar attributes to other alliances but in addition they will have a 'material' effect on the organisation. The segmentation is usually underpinned by clear definitions and sensible criteria such as business or financial impact, return on investment, risk and partner profile. It should be noted that one organisation's strategic alliance may not have the same value or importance for the other party. This is an important

facet to remember when seeking alliance partners as is explored in
more detail during Part III.

Exercise 4: Value and importance of alliances

**Consider how your organisation determines the value
and importance of its alliances. Is there a clear and
consistent method to support allocation of assets and
resources to the alliances?**

Other aspects that need consideration in alliance activity are
the optimum amount of partners for a particular type of initiative.
In some cases it may just be one, for example when outsourcing a
back office process. However, when looking at routes to market
and sales distribution it could be thousands of partners are needed.
IBM has tens of thousands of 'partners' in the loosest sense of the
word but it categorises its partners in a similar vein to that expressed
above where higher value alliances get access to more attractive
IBM assets. Partners are important to IBM as they contribute some
30% of its $90 bn revenues! A key consideration is therefore around
exclusivity and whether to grant it to partners. Used well, exclusivity is a significant asset to offer; however, used badly value may
be destroyed, for example if the exclusive partner fails to execute
on its commitments or does not have the capacity to deliver what
more partners could do overall. Conversely, channel conflict is
another significant issue for organisations with large portfolios of
'partners' with overlapping assets and if poorly managed can cause
value destruction for all parties.

Other factors in terms of value and importance come about
when partners consider whether to win together and lose together
in alliances. Imagine your organisation has agreed a joint go-to-
market 'sell-with' alliance with a partner, committed to investments for a long-term partnership and started out on the sales
cycle. An early customer prospect is a big corporate with potentially large revenues and a great case study. They suggest that the

alliance value proposition is interesting, they like your organisation, but have had a bad past experience with your partner so under no circumstances will engage them. What do you do? Let's assume that the partner has been well qualified and has a good name generally but there is no way the customer will have them on site. This issue is one at the heart of alliance commitment. Do you win together and lose together, so walk away, or do you drop the partner in favour of an impromptu move with another firm to win that account? This happens in real life and it is one reason why some organisations do not engage in exclusive alliances. Unless exclusivity and degrees of commitment are addressed at the early stage of alliance planning, it can prove very destructive.

Failure to execute on commitments and/or act opportunistically can be caused by many things. For example, consider the anonymous case of Services Plc (primarily a services organisation but with access to some technology) and Technology Plc (primarily a technology organisation but with a strong services capability). They had senior meetings and after some time agreed to collaborate rather than compete and target a particular audience. During the very first sales engagement a joint team came together and customer account managers from both partners connected, although not very well, and a joint proposal was submitted to the customer prospect. During negotiations the customer was sent signals that actually one of the two partners might be better placed to execute the contract alone and the customer would also benefit more. As a result the customer chose to negotiate with one of the partners alone and it won the business. In order to win one order worth circa £2m and a hefty bonus for the customer account manager, the joint go-to-market alliance crumbled before it had really started. The overall market opportunity was actually worth hundreds of millions if they had structured the alliance well to start with and given it the importance it needed across the firm. Both organisations really needed to invest for success and treat that alliance as different to the multitude of other ad hoc opportunistic relationships being engaged in by both parties to win business. In addition they needed to encourage a change in behaviour from the sales floor up, for example through metrics, incentives, consequences and relationship building well before tenders were received or customer engagement was made. Despite the value proposition being attractive for the partners to neutralise a threat from their competitors it was not compelling enough for the customer. The alliance never did recover and both parties went their separate ways. The market remained dominated by others.

Exercise 5: Alliance behaviour

Is your organisation known more for opportunistic alliance behaviour or investing in longer-term relationships? What messages does your organisation's alliance behaviour send to partners and is it appropriate for the future?

PARTNERS COME FROM VARIOUS SOURCES

Partners can come from various sources depending on the nature of the alliance, value chain area affected and the underlying drivers or forces pushing for the alliance. Alliance partners are drawn from five generic sources:

1. Internal colleagues and other departments or subsidiaries
2. Customers
3. Suppliers
4. Competitors which also takes on broader meaning when thinking about co-opetition[16]:
   (a) Customer side – if customers value your product less when they have the other firm's product then that firm is a com-

petitor. This implicitly includes substitutes as well as direct competitors.

(b) Supplier side – if it's less attractive for a supplier to provide resources to you when it's also supplying another firm then that firm is a competitor too, for example in the case of scarce resources or limited edition work.

Alliance activity with competitors may be for collusion although the interest in this book is legal value creation activity that benefits stakeholders such as shareholders and customers as well as the alliance partners. Any risks of collusive or anticompetitive behaviour should be addressed by lawyers early on. Competitors become complementors and form alliances for various reasons including the creation of industry standards, sharing risk and improving buying power as evidenced with the airline alliances and the microcontroller examples stated earlier. They also work together to add more value for their customers and compete against common enemies. A good example is the 2004 alliance announced between HP the global IT organisation, and BT the leading telecoms provider. Both organisations have some overlapping capability and compete against each other in the desktop services space. However, they have successfully united to provide a compelling integrated ICT outsourcing solution for customers and neutralise threats from common foe such as IBM. The joint alliance helps their clients become more agile and turns ageing inflexible systems into adaptable responsive competitive environments. They achieve this at lower cost and with much lower risk, for example, by guaranteeing end-to-end service delivery underpinned by what they call Integrated Services Architecture which offers a single governance model, single delivery architecture and a single delivery model. The alliance has recorded several big wins including First Group and Hertz, the global car rental company where the alliance has unified Hertz workplace enabling it to reduce time to market, open branches faster and ultimately improve its competitive position.

5. **Complementors** – Brandenburger and Nalebuff coined the term complementor in their breakthrough book about co-opetition which means combining competition and cooperation. Any of the four sources above can also be a complementor. For example:

   (a) Customer side – a firm is your complementor if customers value your product more when they have that firm's product than when they have your product alone. Examples include software and hardware suppliers bundling solutions in a complementary alliance and then having a complementary alliance partner offer installation and maintenance services.

   (b) Supplier side – a firm is also your complementor if it's more attractive for a supplier to provide resources to you when it's also supplying the other firm than when it's supplying you alone. Examples here include the design and build of high investment products with standards, such as planes, cars, ships and microchips which can be sold to many clients to help amortise the investment over a wider group and make the unit price more palatable.

COMPLEX RELATIONSHIPS

Relationships with other parties can also become even more complicated when an organisation has multiple alliances or relationships with one party. For example, the BT HP relationship has multiple alliances where BT has outsourced its desktop services to HP, and HP has outsourced much of its call centre support to BT. This sign of commitment towards each other also enables both organisations to demonstrate what is commonly known as a 'dog food', or 'drink your own champagne' story to customers in a multibillion pound joint go-to-market sell-with alliance. This is where the partners use the products of the alliance internally with each other to reinforce the attractiveness of the go-to-market alliance to customers. In addition, the two partners engage in other activities together which make the overall relationship very complex yet both organisations have worked hard to create a model that facilitates success as will be seen in Chapter 12 in Part II, which explores complex governance solutions in more detail.

Exercise 6: Learning from success

Where in your organisation are the most successful and unsuccessful alliances found? Are they with your internal colleagues, customers, suppliers, complementors or competitors? What lessons can be learnt from alliances in other parts of your organisation?

This chapter has explored the role of alliances and understood that they mean different things to different people, and can have different values and importance for their participants. The next chapter explores more about the forces pushing for alliances and seeks to understand why they are becoming an increasingly attractive vehicle.

## CHAPTER 3

FORCES DRIVING
FOR ALLIANCES

*O*rganisations are increasingly turning to alliances. Results from a Deloitte and Economist Intelligence Unit survey published in 2004[17] suggested that two thirds of companies surveyed had significantly increased their dependency on alliances during the previous three years. A similar percentage (66%) felt that their dependence on alliances would significantly increase over the next three years as well. So what are the drivers behind this increase? Many of the forces behind alliances growth are highlighted in Figure 3.1.

These forces are consistent with CEO and firm-wide issues around how best to create value. The Conference Board publication of CEO-level challenges in 2004[18] listed the following in their Top 10 challenges: sustained and steady top line growth (no. 1), speed, flexibility and adaptability to change (no. 2), stimulating innovation/creativity/enabling entrepreneurship (no. 4), cost/ability to innovate (no. 5), seizing opportunities for expansion (no. 9).

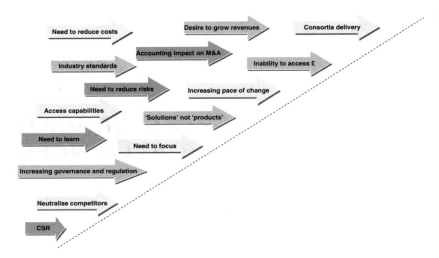

Figure 3.1 Forces pushing for alliances.

CUSTOMER DEMANDS AND INDUSTRY STANDARDS

There is more pressure on providing solutions not products. At an enterprise level global corporates are seeking better efficiencies in the way their facilities are managed yet few firms can deliver this alone, which is why alliances like that between HP and BT have emerged. In the public sector there is a drive for alliances following public and government demands, for example, with greater choice in education and health service provision. Customers are also getting far smarter nowadays and at a business-to-business level, the days of 'logo sharing' alliances are gone. Prospective suppliers are asked to list all their partner logos in their proposals and some naïve customers look no further. Smart customers, however, will get inside this detail and look to see if the alliance goes beyond smiling sales forces into the execution stage with effective governance and positive past experience underpinning the alliance. Customers are also demanding firms improve their corporate social responsibility (CSR) and increasing measures are being seen around the so-called triple bottom line to include environmental and social factors as well as financial. This means firms need to take greater care on who they work with as Nike and others will testify following a series of bad press around their supply chain relationships in recent years.

INCREASING PACE OF CHANGE WITH GROWTH AND COST PRESSURES

Many organisations cannot keep up with the pace of change and their own operations cannot meet the growing customer demands or competitive threats. Increasing globalisation and lowering barriers to change may mean that firms are too costly or too slow in responding, especially if the competence to be accessed is not core. Firms cannot invest and build new channels or access new markets, especially overseas, as quickly as necessary or with the degree of knowledge needed for success. By undertaking alliances they can achieve these goals and also mitigate many of the business risks.

Cost pressures have seen many firms now start to focus on what they do well and seek to outsource or stop what does not add value. Reuters entered into a high risk alliance in 2000 when it chose Fujitsu to deliver its IT field services, distribution and logistics for its UK customers. The primary reason for this alliance was to allow Reuters to focus on what it did well and to bring in an added value partner who could deliver better service and value for clients on IT hardware, software and related services. Offshoring alliances have also grown quickly in recent years, and this is likely to continue. However, the haste or short-term outlook within which many of these alliances are constructed and the focus on cost savings may lead to a destruction of value in the future for some. Porter[19] back in 1996 suggested that short-term improvements to operational effectiveness by outsourcing to generic service providers may result in longer-term problems for competing effectively, as evidenced in 2005 by an airline clashing with its catering provider, which subsequently affected more than its direct profits.

FDM Group, the AIM listed IT organisation, has built its unique IT staffing model on the principle of alliances at both an individual and organisation level. FDM seeks to cultivate alliances with software technology companies and end user organisations that wish to outsource or have resource constraints at the point of product implementation. It provides these partners with a flexible IT worker 'the Mountie', who works as part of the customer or partner implementation team. This model brings about lower cost as well as lower risk than other alternatives with onshore delivery to maintain the closeness of client relationship and ability to respond to change quickly.

Brightwell Dispensers is another example of an SME (small/medium size enterprise) that opted for an extended enterprise business model and also bucked the offshoring trend. Brightwell has sought collaborative alliances with UK and European suppliers and international sales and marketing partners. The company designs and manufactures chemical dispensing equipment in the UK and offers a unique service to its customers, who are mainly large corporates and chemical consumables supplies organisations. By taking much of its plastics and electronics manufacture to China (for example) it may marginally reduce production prices but the opportunity cost could be significant. The downside may be in longer lead times, higher inventory and shipping charges, inferior quality and an inability to respond to customer needs for flexibility and own branding. Brightwell is customer solution oriented, has effective domestic upstream supplier alliances and is able to flex its production, adapting quickly for key customers needs and has far greater control over development, quality and price as a result. As its business continues to expand internationally it is also building tighter downstream sales and marketing alliances with in-country partners who have great local knowledge and value added capability attractive to end user customers.

In the public sector there are huge cost pressures following the Gershon Review in 2003 and as a result it is anticipated that more close knit risk and reward-based alliances will be brought about to transform business practices as opposed to the more traditional supplier price focus of the past which have caused significant problems, not least in the delivery of IT services in areas such as benefit processing and child support services.

In the financial services arena, Aviva, the UK insurance giant, agreed an alliance with Co-operative Insurance Services (CIS) in August 2005 securing distribution of a range of its products through CIS's 2,200-strong sales force. Aviva, which owns the Norwich Union brand in the UK, is the sole provider of personal pensions, unit-linked bonds and inheritance tax planning services through CIS's direct sales force, which is the largest in the country. The Co-op markets a Norwich Union life insurance product to its existing customer base. At the end of 2004 Bradford & Bingley linked up with Legal & General in a similar alliance.

REGULATION AND GOVERNANCE

Changes in regulation and governance may help push firms into closer more collaborative alliances and away from more traditional arm's length noncollaborative buyer/supplier contracts. This should be seen as an opportunity to transcend old style relations and craft more mutually rewarding, innovative and yet transparent contracts, controls and governance mechanisms. In the UK the move to a more tightly regulated business environment started in the 1990s, principally in financial services, but has now extended across all listed organisations. The Combined Code issued by the Financial Reporting Council in July 2003 placed greater demands on risk management of material relationships, in particular the aspects around the Turnbull requirement to report on the quality of internal controls. It is applicable to listed organisations but also impacts those parties on whom the listed organisations have some dependency, even if those parties are themselves not listed.

The most radical change to regulation and compliance, however, emerged in 2002 in the US as a result of financial improprieties in WorldCom, Enron and others. Organisations that also have a Securities and Exchange Commission (SEC) registration in the US need to comply with the Sarbanes Oxley Act legislation that came about as a result of these scandals. The board must make statements to its shareholders on internal control that include disclosing any material uncontrolled risks arising from joint ventures, associates and outsourced activities[20]. Failure to manage these relationships by not putting in place effective controls may have a significant impact on share price and on directors' futures although the Combined Code is less draconian than Sarbanes Oxley in this regard.

A more recent piece of important legislation in the UK is encapsulated within Reporting Standard 1 (RS1), on the Operating and Financial Review, issued in May 2005 by the Accounting Standards Board (ASB). While the implementation of this standard has been delayed as the result of statements made by the Chancellor of the Exchequer, most listed UK groups are expected to comply with its requirements. The standard requires a forward-looking orientation and directors must report their analysis of market conditions of the businesses in the group and the strategies that are being adopted to increase shareholder value. This information will be of interest not just to shareholders but also other stakeholders including current and potential alliance partners. Sections 55, 59 and 60 of RS1 have particular relevance to how the firm might use alliances to execute strategy and the overall relationships that are likely to impact business performance. Even if the OFR does not find its way back in the front door, the International Accounting Standards Board (IASB) is understood to be planning global guidance that looks similar to the OFR in practice, and the Transparency Directive will push in that direction as well. It has often been said that alliances have been conceived over dinner or on the golf course between friends with little regard to any due diligence. These regulations don't necessarily challenge who you partner with but they do bring more transparency to the questions of why and especially how, which will then raise questions of whom!

One of the other positive effects of the growing compliance agenda and external alliances is where it raises standards and helps reduce business risks that might not be effectively addressed internally at present. For example, the creation of internal shared service centres is becoming more popular but one of the potential problems is the risk of poor process management and ineffective internal control. This arises from a poorly documented understanding of the roles and responsibilities of the various internal parties and this can result in a high risk of relationship problems and service failure. Internal intra-company service level agreements are often rather casually worded and rarely have the rigour or discipline that are necessary to support a strong control environment. However, the creation of an external alliance for a similar service is usually the subject of detailed governance and contract negotiations and it is more likely that there will initially be less trust between the parties and a greater perception of risk at the alliance formation stage. As a result the external partner will probably be required to sign a contract and build a governance model with its partner which has incentives and penalties (risk and reward) to ensure its preventive (front end) and detective (back end) controls management processes demonstrate that activities are executed to the quality standards set out in the contract.

INCREASING M&A CHALLENGES

Alliances fail pretty regularly, as will be seen shortly; however, some reports suggest that there are more significant risks and issues from M&A activity. One report suggested 83% of acquirers failed to create shareholder value from their acquisitions[21] and a study by Mckinsey found only the cost of capital was returned or better in just 23% of acquisitions[22]. M&A also have greater integration challenges than alliances and may bring about unwanted baggage in terms of unwanted assets. Distractions may be likely as well. People are normally productive for about 5.7 hours in an 8 hour working day; however, when confronted with a change of control their productivity falls to less than an hour[23].

The International Financial Reporting Standards (IFRS) may also have a small influence on some firms whereby it could affect their behaviour if the treatment of goodwill means some potential acquisitions become less attractive and an alliance may be more suitable. The treatment of tax liabilities may also affect M&A activity as well as that of alliances.

CAPITAL, SIZE, LEARNING AND COMPETITIVE THREAT

Many firms, in particular SMEs, struggle to access capital to fund organic or acquisitive growth. As a result they seek financial help from partners in exchange for some of the future rewards. Others seek learning alliances where they can work together for mutual benefit and transfer knowledge or other assets over time. These alliances are very popular but need careful consideration to manage any future threats, e.g. by creating a new competitor! Many SMEs encounter significant challenges from large corporates who prefer to work with larger organisations, perhaps for risk management purposes, better capacity, greater economies of scale and so on. Consortia alliances spring up from trade associations to counter some of these issues although there can be challenges around governance, decision-making and leadership in less well-constructed consortia. Government funded bodies such as the South East

England Development Agency (SEEDA) act as enablers and facilitators of consortia to aid firms to collaborate and compete more effectively for new business as well as neutralise competitive threats. This is evidenced through SEEDA's successful Sector Consortia programme led by SEEDA's Enterprise team[24].

Exercise 7: Forces pushing for alliances

1. **Identify the forces driving for alliances in your industry and in your organisation**
2. **Rank the forces in terms of priority and assess whether an opportunity or threat**
3. **Consider the possible future scenarios and implications of action or inaction to meet the opportunities or threats**

This chapter has addressed the forces pushing for alliances and outlined why they are becoming more attractive for organisations. This means that the available pool of partners is also growing, although it does not mean that all partners are attractive! The next chapter demonstrates what good looks like and how the organisation's achieved it.

## CHAPTER 4

WHAT WINNING ALLIANCES LOOK LIKE

ALLIANCE SPIRIT

Alliance Competence is an excellent book by Spekman, Isabella and MacAvoy[25], who introduce the terminology of 'alliance spirit' and suggest it is present in successful alliances. Adapted from their work Figure 4.1 summarises the essence of what they wrote, with alliance spirit having four key 'talking points', represented as pillars, underpinned by descriptors of common views.

Exercise 8: Alliance spirit

Pick one of your organisation's key alliances and reflect whether it has an alliance spirit. How many of the pillars and descriptors above do you recognise being present in the alliance? What is missing and why?

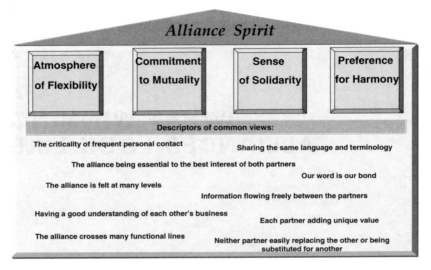

Figure 4.1   Alliance spirit.

Alliance spirit is a great concept and a useful one to have a picture of when assessing alliance capability. However, two important traits jump out when thinking about successful alliances that are implicit but not present in Figure 4.1. They are trust and effective communication.

BUILDING TRUST

Neither trust nor effective communication or the broader alliance spirit materialises overnight so how do alliance partners obtain them? Jordan Lewis is a guru in this field and he goes some way to answering the question about trust. His Trusted Partners work[26] demonstrates the key characteristics of trust from an alliance perspective. He suggested that trust in an alliance can be defined as 'each firm can depend on the other to get results that exceed what a transaction can do'[27]. Lewis then presented eight conditions for trust[28] which are adapted in Figure 4.2 and presented as a trust framework.

Figure 4.2   Trust framework (adapted from J.D. Lewis). Adapted with permission of The Free Press, a division of Simon & Schuster Adult Publishing Group, from TRUSTED PARTNERS: How Companies Build Mutual Trust and Win Together by Jordan D. Lewis. Copyright © 1999 by Jordan D. Lewis. All rights reserved.

This framework is helpful when considering a 'textbook' alliance success using a well-publicised alliance between IBM and Siebel for Customer Relationship Management (CRM) solutions. This alliance has been discussed many times[29] since its inception in 1999, although not in this context.

Compelling mutual need: Lewis talked of a priority mutual need where firms regard each other as being the right choice for meeting important objectives. Neither IBM nor Siebel had the best of breed capability alone to win, but by working together they could pool resources to lead the CRM market. It was a very attractive value proposition as well. For every dollar of revenue earned by Siebel, IBM could win between two and seven dollars. In 2001 IBM reported $5bn revenue from Siebel related sales. For the 2000 plus clients served by IBM and Siebel together since the alliance began it was also a very compelling story as they benefited from a joined-up integrated solution from two market leaders. (Whether the alliance will remain in force is open to question following Oracle's acquisition of Siebel late in 2005.)

Complementary objectives: Lewis suggested mutual objectives were essential to building trust. Objectives do need to be aligned and although they don't need to be the same, they do need to be complementary. IBM and Siebel had complementary goals to grow revenues quickly and penetrate then dominate the growing CRM sector.

Complementary is used (for example) because sometimes the detailed objectives behind buyer and supplier alliances are less clear than joint sales goals like IBM and Siebel above. One partner (buyer) might want to reduce its costs and the other (supplier) might want to grow its revenues in the buyer account. First impressions might suggest this is a conflict but it is not in itself a problem if the available market (spend) exists and the share desired by the supplier is feasible. Without an explicit discussion and agreement around these objectives it could end in tears. This happens when buyers and suppliers have been a little resistant about sharing their information and kept some goals hidden. Imagine a simple case when the buyer has costs of £10m in a supply category and its goal (ceteris paribus) is to re-engineer, consolidate suppliers and drive out cost by 40% to lower spend to £6m for the category. It does not share the actual target. The partner currently has a revenue share of 50% of that spend, i.e. £5m, and would like to grow its revenues to £8m by offering improved prices, better service, joint innovation resources and so on, still offering the client a significant saving and performance improvement. It too does not share its sales target and bonus threshold for the sales manager. The conflict arises when spend is not as high as the supplier forecast or savings not as great as budgeted by the buyer. In simple terms organisations have to make sure that the objectives are explicit, bought into by both parties (if not contracted) and the available market share will exist to achieve the goals for both parties.

Interpersonal relationships: fundamentally alliances are about people and without trust pervading the key touchpoints, success of the alliance may be compromised or inhibited. Sometimes one has to deal with the devil on basic sales or sourcing initiatives in arm's length transactions and lack of trust or interpersonal relationships are not a barrier to performance. However, there are few examples where an alliance succeeded without trust and good relationships with the key people on either side. The IBM and Siebel alliance had a number of mechanisms in place to encourage the building of trust including joint targets and incentives, joint planning, shared information repositories, and the opportunity for relevant touchpoints to work closely together and build their relationships on an ongoing basis.

Joint leaders: Lewis raised the importance of senior leaders being seen to collaborate and set examples for staff below. The IBM Siebel alliance had sponsorship at the highest level with the (then) founder and CEO Tom Siebel and (then) IBM CEO Lou Gerstner actively involved in the early days.

Safeguards: alliances involve collaboration and movement beyond arm's length agreements. They normally include sharing sensitive information or practices that affect competitive advantage. Agreements are therefore essential, but the depth and breadth of those agreements, and whether verbal or written, is dependent on factors such as what the alliance seeks to achieve, the risks, rewards, strength of relationships and each party's ability to execute as will be demonstrated in Part III. IBM and Siebel did not have an exclusive alliance and therefore needed a number of safeguards. These included documented agreements on things such as IPR and investments but also a number of mechanisms to help manage the growth and performance of the alliance. These included CEO-level governance bodies having quarterly reviews and monthly governance reviews of senior executives in regions with weekly pipeline reviews at operational touchpoints. Alliance methods and operating models were aligned, and policies around rewards, targets and channel conflict were agreed. In addition rules of engagement were put in place to manage the competitive threat (co-opetition policy) from each other's technology and service arms.

In his book called *Partner Risk*[30], Warnock Davies reinforces the need for safeguards and suggests that 'opportunistic behaviour' is the principal reason why alliances fail. He suggested there were three pre-conditions to such risk. The partners need to have access to privileged information; they need to have the opportunity to behave opportunistically and the motive to do so as well.

In a clear lesson about the importance of safeguards such as clearly written agreements that transcend personal relationships consider Marks and Spencer (M&S) and William Baird. For 30 years Baird supplied M&S without a formal contract. Sadly the relationship ended in despair for Baird when it lost a £50 m court case against M&S after M&S terminated the agreement in 1999. Baird closed 16 factories, made 4500 staff redundant and made provisions for losses of £113 m in its accounts before being sold off to a venture capital firm[31]. This is also an example of where the alliance affected one party far more than the other and reinforced the need for safeguards protecting the smaller player.

Commitment: both IBM and Siebel made significant commitments to each other. Commonly termed 'skin in the game', IBM, as part of a major strategic shift in its application business, exited its own CRM technology. It had roughly 300 staff on the alliance team as well as thousands of consultants trained to integrate Siebel for clients. IBM also has the largest Siebel CRM deployment globally with over 60 000 seats. Siebel adopted IBM technology and some 5% of the Siebel sales force joined IBM.

Collaborative internal organisations: Lewis suggested organisations need to be 'adaptable' and those that have the ability to collaborate well internally have the skills to do so externally. Ability to collaborate internally and externally is a crucial element that is addressed in some detail during Part II, as that perhaps more than any other element is a frequent underlying cause of alliance failure. IBM and Siebel had made the commitments and put in place the safeguards noted above. In addition to encourage collaboration they had joint targets and rewards, joint training, sales hotlines and radio, newsletters and webinars as well as shared databases.

Continuity: many alliances rely heavily on one or two key passionate staff and when they move on, the alliance stumbles and some never recover. IBM and Siebel (although much larger anyway) sought to embed processes to transcend individuals. They worked hard on sharing of knowledge and information widely including recruiting, through to pre- and post-sales such as demonstration and technical centres and had broad senior management buy-in.

Exercise 9: Trust comparison

Pick two alliances from your organisation's portfolio, one of your best performing and one of your worst performing alliances. Drawing on the trust framework above can you determine whether any of the conditions differ from the best to worst performing alliance? If yes, what can you do to help build the conditions into the other alliance for future benefit?

SMEs don't have the resources that IBM and Siebel had, yet the principles for success are the same. Brightwell Dispensers has a strategic alliance with Anglia, a provider of electronics components and associated services. Anglia worked closely with

Brightwell on design and development of Brightwell's leading Brightstar® laundry dispensing equipment. Anglia provided assistance on the design and selection of key components and has enjoyed an almost exclusive supply relationship for the electronic components. The relationship has been in place for many years and trust is in place from the managing director down although both firms work hard on maintaining and developing the relationship. There are lightweight but effective contracts and governing bodies in place. The governing relationship architecture has recently been expanded to include improved reporting and metrics as well as allow greater engagement with other team members to ensure continuity as the firms both continue to grow.

In 2000 Reuters decided it wanted to focus on the provision of its core information services to financial markets clients in the UK and Ireland as well as develop new and innovative services. It sought an alliance partner for the provision of complementary hardware, software and network services which until then had always been provided in-house but was in danger of being left behind key competitors such as Bloomberg. This was a business critical alliance for Reuters with much of its £500m plus UKI revenues potentially at risk if the alliance did not deliver. After a lengthy beauty parade process to help select the best partner and build relationships, Fujitsu were chosen as the sole partner. Their commitment and intent to develop the business together saw them beat established Reuters suppliers like Compaq and IBM. There was a compelling value proposition for both parties, in particular for Fujitsu who saw the alliance as a springboard into penetrating the UK financial markets and were prepared to make that very attractive for Reuters and its clients. The client benefited by getting access to the latest hardware, software and networking solutions with better service and prices than Reuters or they could achieve alone, and with a completely joined-up customer service interface. There was a significant risk for both Reuters and Fujitsu and neither had worked together before. As such very clear safeguards in the form of service-level ground rules and contract terms were spelt out, many specifying formulas and policies to help anticipate unknown future decisions. Governance policies such as dispute resolution, audit and joint investment decisions were specified early on and senior management held regular reviews with the operational teams. Some resources transferred to Fujitsu from Reuters yet both teams were co-located where possible to help accelerate learning and relationship building. Joint rewards and incentives were agreed at both an organisational level and to encourage the teams to work together. For example, if Fujitsu helped Reuters improve its service and increase efficiency, it could enjoy a sizeable share of the subsequent cost saving or performance improvement benefits. There were significant challenges in the early months, and at times both parties became very frustrated, not least because of the deep cultural challenges in each organisation and a range of issues over collaboration. However, because of the overall opportunities for working together which were clearly spelt out in an alliance roadmap, strength in senior management support and continuity with the operational team leaders, the alliance has flourished and extended beyond the initial roadmap.

One great alliance does not, however, mean the organisation achieves ongoing business success. What do organisations do that have a much greater dependency on alliances and need to manage many relationships? How do they achieve ongoing success from their alliances?

WHAT AN ORGANISATION THAT WINS WITH ALLIANCES DOES FOR SUCCESS

Type alliances into Google and there are over 50 million results! Despite that and much published material on alliances, there is little of value around the broader concepts of alliance programmes or how alliance capability dovetails back into the wider organisation goals. From the primary and secondary research, along with significant past experience, the following things stand out in organisations that win with alliances:

- There are very attractive rewards for those that invest in success and build an alliance capability.
- Investment in alliance infrastructure is growing in terms of people, processes, tools and systems to help execute more effectively and efficiently. This means the standards for alliance performance are getting higher and those who don't ally well or fail to invest will get left behind.
- Alliance activity must be aligned with organisation strategy and metrics relate to strategic goals. Each alliance needs to stand alone as a commercial proposition as well as complement the broader portfolio.
- Alliance activity must be optimised. Less is more in this instance and more partners does not necessarily mean better results. The days of 'spray and pray' partnering and logo sharing are gone.

The most influential secondary research includes:

How to make strategic alliances work. Dyer, Kale and Singh (2001)[32]: in a breakthrough piece of work, the authors suggested that developing an alliance function was imperative for competitive advantage. Their research studied 200 organisations and over 1500 alliances. Companies with such a capability achieved approximately four times more wealth than those without a dedicated function with stock prices jumping on average 1% ($54m) on the announcement of an alliance. Successful alliances went on for 25% longer than those without such a function. In addition, extra value came from the ability to form more alliances and attract better partners. They suggested that the role of the function included knowledge management, external visibility, internal

WHAT WINNING ALLIANCES LOOK LIKE   49

coordination and legitimacy as well as alliance assessment and an ability to sort out problems quickly.

Becoming an alliance partner of choice. *Accenture Outlook* **point of view (2000)**[33]: in an early and brief discussion about alliance brand, Accenture looked at a range of 'premier alliance builders' from different industries. Without suggesting the organisations created so much value because of their alliance capability alone they highlighted that the financial returns from these premier alliance builders were 1.5 times that of competitors. Citing Pfizer, BP Amoco and Intel as well as IBM and Starbucks among others they sought to find out what it takes to get an alliance reputation. They suggested four sources: unique corporate assets; alliance track record; alliance management skills (over the alliance lifecycle) and promotion of the alliance brand to key stakeholders. Reinforcing my own experience and research Accenture confirmed that firms with a good alliance reputation are the first port of call for other companies searching for partners and emphasised that this reputation could bring about greater concessions from partners because of higher belief in success. Accenture also suggested that 'partners of choice' demonstrated consistent excellence in three areas: speed, performance discipline and partner focus where they add additional value back to their partners beyond the agreement terms.

Survival of the Fittest. Extending the Enterprise. **Deloitte 2004**[34]: following research conducted with Economist Intelligence Unit and Deloitte itself, Deloitte suggested that operating as an extended enterprise meant companies needed to be effective in three core areas: managing the alliance portfolio, creating alliances and managing alliances. The most successful firms were noted as the IT firms mentioned earlier but also GE, Nike, Walmart, Toyota, BP, Coca-Cola and Nokia among others. Enhanced with my research, having joined the firm, Deloitte reported that a key indicator of success was not just having alliance managers or a dedicated function it was also where that function sat in the firm and how much exposure it had to the core business and the ability for it to execute, not just facilitate. Successful organisations had processes in place to monitor alliance performance with poorly performing alliances addressed quickly. Hurdle rates and performance targets are set high in leading organisations whereas in poorly performing organisations it is too easy to create an alliance. Leading organisations enable collaboration through policies, processes and rewards, actively addressing cultural and other challenges. Less successful firms encounter road blocks at a personal, company and extended enterprise level.

The State of Alliance Management. ASAP 2002[35]: this report was drawn from a survey response of 150 members of ASAP. It suggested that over 30% of stock market value was brought about from alliances. Results indicated that alliance success was correlated with alliance experience and not necessarily complexity. There was an increased urgency in this field to be seen as a partner of choice because firms were becoming more selective in their partnering activity. Successful firms used a wider range of tools and techniques including alliance databases, joint evaluation tools and standard selection approaches with alliance metrics. Intranet and other knowledge transfer practices were used reinforcing the point made by Dyer *et al.* above. In addition, the successful firms had trained alliance managers who operated within an alliance department and were able to exchange experiences with each other, again reminiscent of the Dyer *et al.* findings.

IDC and Gartner are global research firms who have offered reports on alliances, mainly around sell-with alliances in the IT sector. Their findings reinforce much of the work above, although it is expensive to access the reports and reproduction is not allowed.

From the research above it all looks quite straightforward, just make those investments, sort out a few things around the organisation culture, invest in a bit of training and that's it, the organisation has a successful alliance programme offering great rewards with compelling returns on investments! Well, not quite, there are a number of forces challenging alliance success. The next chapter highlights how difficult alliances can be in practice.

## CHAPTER 5

FORCES CHALLENGING ALLIANCE SUCCESS

ALLIANCE FAILURE RATES

Despite the growing forces for alliances, the majority of them fail, indeed in much of the research noted in the previous chapter there is also commentary about alliance failure. Failure in this instance is where the alliance has not achieved its objectives, either for one or all of the partners. Having undertaken detailed secondary research between 1997 and 2000 there were many surveys and reports suggesting a failure rate from 50% up to as high as 70%. A quick check on Google today will confirm those numbers have not changed despite the growth in alliance activity and better practice research available. In primary research with a panel of alliance experts operating across various industry and competence backgrounds it was confirmed that up to 70% of alliances are believed to fail[36]. Figure 5.1 demonstrates the primary research findings. Adapted initially from

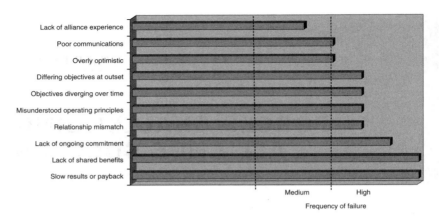

Figure 5.1 Reasons why alliances fail.

other surveys, it highlights the frequency of failure for each reason.

Slow results or payback tied into the dimension of being overly optimistic. When conceived, the partners often felt that the alliance would do wonderful things, yet much may have been glossed over at this honeymoon stage. Once it became apparent that results and payback would take longer, one or both organisations lost interest. In addition, lack of ongoing commitment was often cited, reiterating the importance of nailing down commitments from senior management in terms of the assets being provided. Lack of shared benefits reinforces the need for a win/win in alliances. Alliances or any other form of relationship, in particular buyer/supplier agreements are rarely sustainable if the benefits overtly favour one party. Even if a partner signs up for an unattractive alliance at one point, as soon as a better opportunity comes along they will be off, either as a whole firm or with their best resources.

Poor communications has a dimension of its own but implicitly this inability to collaborate is also the cause behind differing objectives and misunderstood operating principles as well. There are many examples of alliance creation activity where the partners had not thought through their objectives or stated them clearly yet these are issues that can be addressed very quickly and easily. Alliances also fail because of unclear operating principles. For example, in a sell-with alliance there were arguments over which partner was going to take the revenues, and who was responsible for a certain set of activities in an outsourcing alliance. As will be demonstrated in Part III, by using a simple task list and breaking down the key activities in an alliance and including a few well laid out ground rules about who does what and when, these issues get addressed early on.

Objectives do change over time for firms and that might hasten the end of an alliance, for example movement in a different direction or a maturing of a business or industry sector, as well as M&A activity. Reuters had to make some changes to an alliance with Compaq following the HP merger in 2003. This fundamentally shifted the priorities for HP and caused huge distraction to the teams on the ground as noted before when a change of control happens, productivity is lost, so the alliance stalled. The great Siebel and IBM alliance has some challenges ahead following Oracle's purchase of Siebel. Cisco and Microsoft are also finding their core business areas not enough to sustain revenue growth. As a result they are starting to see an overlap in areas such as networking, security and internet protocol (IP) communications, meaning they are likely to compete with their partners and confront each other in the market despite both senior teams reinforcing the collaborative nature of their relationship.

Culture is regularly cited as a reason for alliance failure although like alliances, culture means different things to different people. Clearly, cultural alignment has a large impact. This area is more about relationship compatibility and an ability to collaborate rather than culture per se with many other factors affecting success. Other relationship-oriented failures have included leadership styles, organisation structures, values mismatches and relative size of the partners. Reasons why alliances fail around relationship mismatch also include a lack of effective collaboration mechanics (e.g. rewards, targets) indeed existing rewards and targets may discourage new behaviours. For example, one client invested a huge amount of money in setting up a new alliance yet failed to realise that their key route to market (in-house sales staff) were encouraged with bonuses and targets to sell a competitor offering! Until this had been addressed the alliance went nowhere whereas afterwards it made several high value sales and both partners were very happy with progress. In another example, a services partner focused its staff on annual rewards schemes and liked to have intimate long-term customer relationships, not pressurising them into swift decisions. However, its technology alliance partner had a more aggressive approach to clients and was driven by quarterly earning targets meaning staff were motivated to close deals at the end of each quarter. The conflict in leadership style, values and rewards led the alliance to fail.

Small nimble firms may get very frustrated about the need to engage 20 people from one global corporate and yet still not get an answer. Time to market is sometimes a key driver for an alliance and a reason why firms go externally yet many large corporates are still much slower than an SME would like. It is important to condition smaller partners to be tolerant and help them understand the way decisions are made and the time it takes to execute in large enterprises. Also having a clear partnering process with stage gates and decision points indicates both internally and externally where the parties are at. One of the key operating metrics introduced at one firm was around time to partner. Partnering decisions could be delayed and often prospects were still in talks one year after first discussions. With a clear consistent process, around 99% of all partnering decisions to proceed or not were made in days or weeks. Incidentally, most 'ideas' were quashed early on for various constructive reasons, enabling staff to retain a focus and third parties to mitigate their time invested in the proposition. This improved relations with prospects because they also got constructive feedback on why the proposition did not prove attractive to the organisation at that time.

Exercise 10: Alliance failure

Look back to any failed alliances in your organisation. What have been the underlying causes and why? Is there a trend or common set of reasons you need to investigate further?

While there is much research on alliance failure, the named examples given are quite limited. There have been numerous alliance failures in recent years; however, many do not make it into the public domain for obvious reasons. Examples that have gone public include:

R&D, sales and marketing alliance: in the pharma bio tech industry the stakes are high. Successful alliances can take many years to evolve and deliver, then all too soon the 20-year patent runs out and competitors destroy the alliance profitability. This is also a field where the big organisations like Pfizer, Glaxo and Eli Lilly ally with the small bio techs who help keep their pipelines full and act as bets on the future. The small bio tech benefits from the funding, reach and brand of the big players. Its no surprise then that there are often big fallouts because the alliances can make or destroy the bio tech player. Dow Jones[37] reported 'Australian biotechnology company Biota Holdings Ltd was seeking damages of up to $326 million from GlaxoSmithKline PLC for allegedly failing to market Relenza, the world's first influenza drug. In another case that mirrors Biota's, U.S. biotechnology company Gilead Sciences Inc. was seeking to end a licensing agreement with Roche Holdings AG (RHHBY) for influenza pill Tamiflu, alleging that the Swiss drugmaker poorly marketed the drug and miscalculated royalties.' Reasons for failure were cited as potentially poorly drawn contracts, lack of relationship continuity in such lengthy alliances and changing priorities.

Sell–side alliance: BT and MCI in their Concert alliance, then AT&T in the second Concert alliance. This example was actually a joint venture but the principles of failure are similar. The underlying alliance strategy was questionable as it affected BT's ability to compete, and there were possibly too many assumptions over customer habits and country regulations changing. The partners had different value systems and execution was stifled with conflicting leadership styles and operating policies.

Buyer and supplier alliance: British Airways and Gate Gourmet; the airline found itself in dispute with its caterer in 2005 and consequently saw between £35 m and £45 m in lost revenues as well as untold reputational problems with its customers and other partners[38]. Could it be that an aggressive price and cost saving focus from BA affected the ability for its partner to make a profit which subsequently triggered action by Gate Gourmet that then led to the high opportunity costs for BA?

Buyer and supplier alliance: the UK Government Department Child Support Agency and EDS have been roundly criticised for their activities which have cost the taxpayer some £450 m[39] and the CSA chief executive his job. In another project failure on tax credits, EDS recently paid compensation to the Government of £71 m having already lost the contract to a competitor[40]. These are two examples of a host of public sector IT projects that have been brought into question in recent years which should perhaps have been more collaborative alliances but were treated like arm's length supply deals. The Parliamentary Office of Science and Technology (POST) published a report in July 2003[41] with their thoughts about why these projects (alliances) fail. Their top reasons included:

1. Lack of project linkage with organisation priorities and measures of success
2. Lack of clear senior management ministerial ownership and leadership
3. Lack of engagement with stakeholders
4. Lack of skills and approach to project and risk management
5. Failure to understand the supply industry at senior levels
6. Proposals driven by price rather than long-term value for money or business benefits
7. Not enough attention on effective development, launch and management implementation
8. Inadequate skills and resources to execute the total delivery portfolio

Sales, marketing and branding alliances: Disney has had problems in recent times with some of its alliance partners, notably Pixar, the animation geniuses behind *Finding Nemo* and *Toy Story*. Disney enjoyed significant rewards from the marketing, distribution and licensing and Pixar felt hard done by when success followed success. Most recent reports suggested that the alliance will end in acquisition by Disney of Pixar. Disney may also be hit hard when its 10-year alliance with McDonald's ends in 2006, with the possibility that McDonald's may seek a more opportunistic approach to future alliances and seek promiscuity with Disney and its increasingly attractive competitors. The Rank Group also suffered in negotiations with leading suppliers when it started losing market share and selling off its assets in the mid-1990s, meaning it was a less attractive marketing and promotion partner for some big FMCG brands.

Using the personal brand of individuals in marketing alliances can be high risk but also high reward. Nike is delighted with its relationship with Tiger Woods among others, as is T Mobile with Robbie Williams today. Not so West Bromwich Building Society (WBBS) with their Brum Brum product after some well-publicised alleged racist comments made in 2004 by Ron Atkinson, the football pundit, with whom WBBS had a high profile marketing alliance. It got worse for WBBS as their other partner in the marketing alliance was MG Rover, the car company that went into receivership in 2005! Barclays is apparently happy with its sponsorship alliance of the FA Premiership but Vodafone recently ended its sponsorship of Manchester United citing greater opportunities at a European level with Champions League football. Was it a coincidence then that at a similar time Manchester United suffered major change on and off the pitch with reputations put at risk because of factors such as change in ownership and bad press around player behaviour?

OTHER FORCES CHALLENGING SUCCESS

Mitigating well-known causes of alliance failure is a major challenge to address in building successful alliances. Other forces that even prevent alliances get off the starting blocks include those shown in Figure 5.2 and discussed in further detail below.

Internal M&A or build pressures can be a challenge. If you only have a hammer, all you will see is nails and this is a major barrier to alliances. For example, when the dominant force advising the CEO is his M&A advisor who has a team of corporate financiers twiddling their thumbs, is it any wonder that M&A is the preferred option over alliances? Similar principles apply to organic growth, although one reason why firms might use alliances is because the assets are not available internally or perhaps capacity is already stretched.

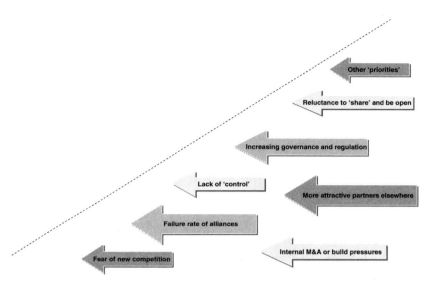

Figure 5.2   Forces challenging alliance success.

Other priorities are an often cited problem. Part of the challenge is that senior management don't always understand the significance or importance of alliances, both in terms of value creation benefits or value destruction in terms of reputational or financial risks. Constant communication about performance and alliance contribution is therefore crucial as shown in Part II when considering the alliance infrastructure needed for success.

Partnering implications cause many firms to fear they will create new competition by sharing ideas or information, and worry about losing staff to partners. These issues can be addressed through legal agreement although the psychological aspects get addressed by building trust and mitigating the threat of opportunistic behaviours as described earlier. Being unable to control partners is also a fear for many organisations especially those with autocratic leadership. There are many operational risks in working with third parties including being exploited, losing strategic flexibility, experiencing interruptions to supply, lack of continuity in resources from a third party, confidentiality leaks, and the possible loss of intellectual property rights as well as the risks of losing core competences and future advantage. The risk of losing core competences will generally come about because of one of two reasons: short-term cost cutting targets, or a view that something is not core when in fact it is at the time, or shortly afterwards[42]. Look back to the start-up of Microsoft for just one example of how IBM missed an opportunity. IBM considered the future was in hardware not software and so decided to outsource its operating system to Microsoft. The rest as they say is history!

Much work has been carried out in the area of asset specificity as a part of transaction cost economics. Asset specificity refers to when the assets in a transaction or alliance have a higher value to that particular transaction or alliance than if they could have been used for other purposes. Examples include equipment designed to make only one product, a small number of employees having knowledge for a bespoke system that is business critical, or perhaps a location that enables advantage to be achieved for some reason, such as lower transport costs or unique traffic passing through. This means that to some extent, these aspects are locked into any deal, and if offered out to a third party, but not included again at the termination of the alliance (ceteris paribus) it could mean major problems for the partner, either in renewing with or replacing the other partner. Outsourcing buyer/supplier alliances are a good example where this might happen. This leaves one partner in a strong position to leverage the relationship and is an example of why exit strategy should be considered early on in the alliance creation process.

Increasing governance and regulation is a challenge as well as a positive force. Firms may feel threatened by the amount of disclosure required under the Combined Code, OFR or Sarbanes

Oxley for material relationships and assess an alliance as being too much of a reputational or financial risk. This is primarily because of the lack of control and trust in much early stage alliance activity and so in-house delivery might be favoured. Failure of a material relationship that affects the business may ultimately result in a director being jailed. OJEU regulations have long been seen as a potential barrier to effective collaboration in public sector procurement-led initiatives. The regulations are, however, changing and the policy setting bodies are making efforts to enable greater collaboration and innovation. Whether the local procurement teams and legal advisors can change their behaviours is open to question. Without changes to the way they are targeted, rewarded and motivated, the likelihood of swift change is low. While the OJEU regulations may hamper innovation and collaboration during the tender process, some of the adversarial behaviours exhibited by the supplier facing teams do little to enhance cooperation and delivery of mutual benefit.

Despite using partnering and alliance terminology it may be just an excuse to achieve a lower price. As a result some prospective partners with very attractive assets may not wish to engage in tenders and the alliance may not happen with the best partner. For example, one specialist SME was engaged in alliance discussions with a large blue chip company. The end user HR department wanted a close-knit relationship with its potential talent management 'partner' seeking innovation, flexibility and attractive solutions to help make them a better employer; however, the purchasing department joined in and focused on price. Purchasing drove the final process and decided to e-auction the opportunity as well as state strict contract terms that stifled innovation. The blue chip customer may have got a lower initial price for the outsourced service but the HR department will not have an innovative collaborative alliance or the best partner's resources delivering a business critical service for it, which may affect its ability to hire the most talented staff in the future, thus affecting future competitive advantage.

More attractive and experienced partners elsewhere are threats for organisations without a positive reputation and results from alliances because of the growing 'pool' of potential partners to choose from. Risks and opportunity cost in the alliance also occur when one partner dictates how the other partner does something instead of specifying what needs to be done together. This usually comes from a dominant partner who is not prepared to share and learn or from an inexperienced or apprehensive partner. It is a sign of an organisation that might not be able to collaborate. Building on this point, someone once said 'we have met the enemy and it is us'. Put into context, Doz and Hamel argued that alliances frequently failed because of internal deficiencies, and there is an irony that companies enter alliances because they are not fit enough to do things alone, but the same lack of fitness causes the alliances to fail as well[43]. The authors then presented a brief checklist to enable organisations to look inside first to prevent failure, and Spekman among others also proposed similar questions without necessarily providing all the answers. The questions have been adapted and represented in Table 5.1. It is a hint of what needs to be addressed before looking out for partners.

The forces pushing for alliances mean the available pool of potential partners is growing. The rewards from success can be very attractive and leading organisations generate powerful returns from their alliance activity. Conversely, the forces challenging alliances mean that failure is a high probability, and with that comes serious consequences which might put the organisation at risk. Yet in comparison with M&A, and organic growth, alliances have many greater attractions.

In the same way that organisations will need to study possible allies, prospective partners will also look more closely at them. A typical problem in alliances is the excitement in rushing off to create an alliance without the organisation itself first having the ability to partner. This gives rise to both reputational and financial

Table 5.1 Pre-alliance readiness checklist.

Consider all the questions below and reflect on how your organisation might respond

Does the organisation have a strategic architecture and do the people understand it?	Is the organisation ambition rich and resource poor, or the reverse?
Are the organisation's managers driven to do more with limited resources?	Does the organisation's people know how to collaborate and do the system of rewards encourage collaboration internally and externally or pit one against another?
Is the organisation capable of commitment?	Can the organisation and its employees respond quickly when the game changes?
Does the organisation communicate well internally and externally?	Does the organisation learn as a group and are there mechanisms in place to learn from alliance experiences?
Do the organisation's policies and practices encourage continuity?	Do the organisation's managers have enough motivation to provide continual value in their alliance activity?
Does the organisation have appropriate alliance experience?	Does the organisation culture and values support and reinforce alliance-like qualities?
Does an alliance infrastructure support the alliance efforts?	How well does the organisation select and negotiate with potential partners?
Is the organisation perceived as a good alliance partner?	Does the organisation have something of value to offer partners?

risks including loss of future value or competitive advantage, for example if an asset is given away, future core competence lost or the wrong partner chosen. As a result firms need to get smarter about how they pick and choose their alliance partners, as well as how they present themselves as a good partner with which to work. Some organisations are doing that right now. They are designing in processes and using tools to speed action, help reduce risks and increase the probability of success. They are also investing in their people and creating a better infrastructure to transcend single individuals and embed knowledge across the firm. However, many firms don't know where to turn and as with any nascent market offering there are some good and less good avenues to follow. Organisations need to place their alliance bets carefully and consider partners which already have a reputation and identity for successful alliances. The final chapter in this part of the book therefore introduces the importance of brand and reputation and brings out the meaning of alliance brand, before moving into Part II which addresses how to develop and build alliance brands.

## CHAPTER 6

ALLIANCE BRAND

*T*he last chapter expressed that to achieve success from alliances firms need to think about building their credibility as a partner, reinforcing their capability to partner and demonstrating a desire to work with potential partners. Two words initially stand out that sum up what is needed: reputation and brand.

REPUTATION IN CONTEXT

A 2004 survey of some the world's leading CEOs and organisation leaders[44] said that corporate reputation is a more important measure of success than stock market performance, profitability and return on investment. Only the quality of products and services edged out reputation as the leading measure of corporate success. Some of the survey feedback suggested well-known recent corporate scandals, which had driven the wave of new governance legislation touched on earlier, had heightened the importance of a strong reputation. Some went so far as to say that more than 40% of a company's market capitalisation was represented by its brand and reputation.

Another article asked the question whether a company's reputation can affect its business results and the answer was that reputation is the firm's most valuable asset[45]. Indeed, in Part II Chapter 10 looks closely at identifying and protecting the attractiveness of the organisation's assets and demonstrates how it can use them more effectively in alliance activity. Partner selection and management carries enormous financial and reputational risks. For example, it was reported earlier that BA had £35m–£45m of direct financial losses from its alliance dispute with Gate Gourmet. What is less clear is the ongoing reputational impact it has suffered both with its customers who choose not to travel with BA in the future, or its suppliers and partners who may look closely at some of the underlying causes of the dispute. Partners may choose to increase their negotiation starting point to price in the greater risks, or perhaps choose not to deal with BA in future.

Dr Charles Fombrun is the founder of the Reputation Institute and one of the leading scholars in the study of corporate reputations. Through his research and writing, he has encouraged empirical measurement and valuation of reputations. In 1999, he introduced the Reputation Quotient (RQ) survey instrument with the market research firm Harris Interactive. The RQ is designed to uncover six underlying dimensions of corporate reputation: emotional appeal, products and services, financial performance, social responsibility, workplace environment, and vision and leadership. The RQ instrument has been used to measure the public reputations of visible companies around the world since 1999. The results of research measuring public perceptions of companies have been widely published and demonstrate how benefits can accrue to companies from having positive reputations, including increased sales and business growth, an improved ability to recruit talented employees, increased investor confidence in the company and stakeholder loyalty. Companies that topped RQ surveys conducted in 2004 in the UK were Virgin Group (1), Sony (2), Body Shop (3), Microsoft (4) and Tesco (5).

In his 2004 book *Fame & Fortune*, Dr Fombrun and his co-author Dr van Riel examined how the top companies in RQ surveys conducted in five countries differ from a comparison group of rivals. In particular, they describe four key principles that winning companies demonstrate:

- **Distinctiveness:** strong reputations result when companies occupy a distinctive position in the minds of resource holders
- **Authenticity:** strong reputations arise when companies are genuine
- **Transparency:** strong reputations develop when companies are transparent in their dealings and communicate in ways that increase their visibility and enable them to engage others
- **Consistency:** strong reputations develop when companies focus their actions and communications around a core theme

From a consumer perspective it has been said that a negative corporate reputation can have serious consequences including boycotting a firm's product or services or not investing in their shares[46]. Sixty-five per cent of UK consumers were likely to take this sort of action and top targets in 2004 were said to include McDonald's and Shell. Gerald Ratner made a disastrous gaffe in public in the early 1990s when he suggested his products were of poor quality and as a result his store's reputation was sunk and could not recover, losing millions in the process.

> **Exercise 11: Reputation**
>
> Consider what organisations have a great reputation in your view and what it is about them that causes that reputation?
>
> What organisations have a poor reputation and why? What has been the impact on their business as a result?

BRAND IN CONTEXT

Like alliances, there are challenges over the definitions surrounding reputation and brand, and how they relate to each other. At a simple level, brand suggests 'what a firm stands for' whereas reputation is 'what a firm gets'. David Taylor, named as one of the 50 leading marketing thinkers by the Chartered Institute of Marketing (CIM), stated[47] that a true brand has the characteristics highlighted in Figure 6.1, which suggests reputation is a subset of brand.

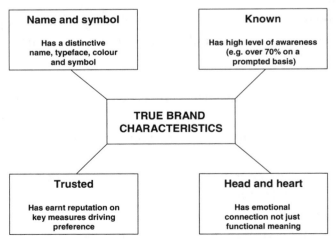

Figure 6.1　Characteristics of a true brand (reproduced with permission).

Taylor stated that the business benefits of building true brands are compelling and went on to list examples such as Häagen Dazs where 46% of users said they always bought that brand and were unlikely to switch, and 41% would go elsewhere if their store did not have it[48].

Bringing it back to the core business purpose, Rumelt[49] argued that competitive advantage could normally be traced to one of three roots: superior skills, superior resources or superior position. Position in this context is associated with brand (as well as size or scale), and once in a good position it is usually defensible. Blackett[50] reinforced this point when he described successful brands as being able to 'charge a premium, command higher volumes and achieve greater security of demand'. To reiterate the research from Accenture stated earlier, they said that premier alliance builders with alliance brands achieved returns 1.5 times greater than their competitors[51]. Taylor went on to talk about the brand being an organisational blueprint for value creation where the customer experience to be promised and delivered against needed careful definition[52]. Brad VanAuken suggested something similar in 2003 when he said that brand was 'the personification of an organisation or its products and services . . . the promise a company makes'[53].

Reiterating the challenges around brands, negative perceptions can cost firms business affecting advantage, and bad press can impact industries or sectors. An example is that following the collapse of Enron and then Andersen when the accounting and audit sector took a series of blows to its image. Research[54] carried out in 2002 highlighted that brands that deliver on their promises would get loyalty from 78% of consumers. However, those who break their promises suffer with 85% of consumers likely to try another brand and 75% sharing that bad experience with someone else. Put another way, Paul Davies, Director of Procurement Excellence in the Police Service (PEPS), has a saying that sums up this aspect neatly: 'marketing activity without operational excellence equals customer rejection'.

ALLIANCE BRAND; A TIMELY INITIATIVE

The importance of reputation and brand, and how it can affect the creation or destruction of value is now understood. Earlier chapters also covered the operational aspects of successful alliance performers and addressed how firms need to get smarter about how and whom they partner with, basically looking for those organisations with an alliance brand. Organisations also need to become alliance brands themselves. But what is an alliance brand?

Alliance brand means an organisation has **'a positive reputation and results from its alliance activity'**. This is a good starting point to help distinguish the good performers from the bad; however, it does not provide enough clarity. Categories of alliance brand therefore include:

- **Leading alliance brand:** 'stands out in its field as the partner to work with, delivering on its promises and creating superior value for its customers, partners, shareholders and other key stakeholders from its alliance activity'.
- **Emerging alliance brand:** 'demonstrates positive results for its customers, partners, shareholders and other key stakeholders from its alliance activity; however, may not have the optimal reputation for its efforts'.
- **Laggard alliance brand:** 'has a strong reputation; however, this does not always translate into positive results for its customers, partners, shareholders and other key stakeholders from its alliance activity'.
- **No alliance brand:** organisations without a positive reputation and results from alliances and likely to be of higher risk and lower reward than organisations with an alliance brand.

This segmentation can be demonstrated more effectively in Figure 6.2.

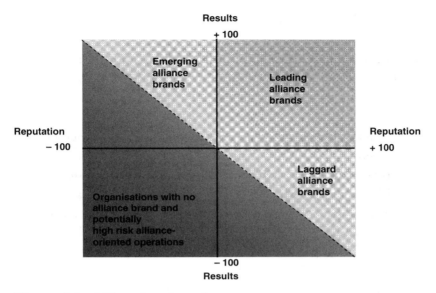

Figure 6.2 Alliance brand matrix.

Leading alliance brands enjoy great results and an excellent reputation as highlighted above. But what does this mean in practice? Tangible benefits include the following:

- **Faster time to better results and greater value:** leading alliance brands make decisions more quickly and the time taken to create value is reduced without sacrificing quality of the solution.
- **Lower risks of partner and alliance failure:** leading alliance brands have better qualification processes and undertake more comprehensive due diligence on their alliance initiative as well as partner prospect.
- **Lower costs of partnering and higher ROI:** despite making greater investments in alliance infrastructure leading alliance brands target those investments more selectively. By avoiding 'spray and pray' activity they get higher, longer returns

from the chosen alliances regardless of whether the goals are cost reduction, revenue growth, innovation or other metrics.

- **Improved relationships internally and externally:** by having clarity on tasks, clear roles and responsibilities with suitable rewards and motivators in place leading alliance brands are able to satisfy stakeholders and avoid unnecessary disputes and conflicts. Being part of a winning team is also more conducive to better relationships than being part of a losing team.

- **Improved staff skills and knowledge retention:** leading alliance brands have an effective infrastructure that supports development of alliance professionals and is underpinned by effective technology systems that aid knowledge sharing and information protection.

- **Governance friendly and transparent processes:** leads to lower operational and compliance-based risks especially for listed firms.

- **Increased investor attractiveness:** as a result of delivering great results and standing out from the crowd leading alliance brands appeal to investors who want to achieve attractive returns from their investments.

- **Increased alliance brand attractiveness:** having achieved the reputation and results leading alliance brands become enormously attractive to partner prospects. As such they get first option for new alliance opportunities in their markets and can increase the leverage from their assets in what becomes a virtuous circle.

In helping organisations understand their alliance brand positioning and the respective strengths and areas for improvement in their alliance activity an alliance brand audit can be undertaken. The audit looks in detail at the outputs in terms of reputation and results as shown in the alliance brand matrix in Figure 6.2. It also addresses the inputs affecting alliance performance as demonstrated in Figure 6.3, which is an extract of a summary from an alliance brand audit.

Element	%	RAG status
Strategy and direction	61%	AMBER
Core competences	61%	AMBER
Strategic choice	52%	RED
Asset attractiveness	56%	RED
Collaboration	56%	RED
Governance	51%	RED
Alliance infrastructure	60%	AMBER
	58%	RED

Figure 6.3   Alliance brand audit input results.

Areas addressed as part of an alliance brand audit could be one part or all aspects of the value chain where alliances are used. When undertaking a full alliance brand audit, output results are based on reviewing available financial and nonfinancial information, and reputation feedback is provided by the firm and obtained objectively, for example from customers, partners, industry observers and compared against stated strategic goals. The inputs are reviewed against over 200 questions and high performance characteristics held in a proprietary software tool derived from ALLIANTIST VIP Map shown in Figure 6.4. Part II is devoted to building alliance capability by using the VIP Map.

Exercise 12: Alliance brand audit (quick test)

ALLIANTIST alliance brand audit quick test is in Appendix 1 and online at www.alliancebrand.co.uk. It addresses the inputs to alliance brand. If you have not already completed it then please consider it before delving into Part II. It will take around 10 minutes and give a good insight into where to prioritise building alliance capability.

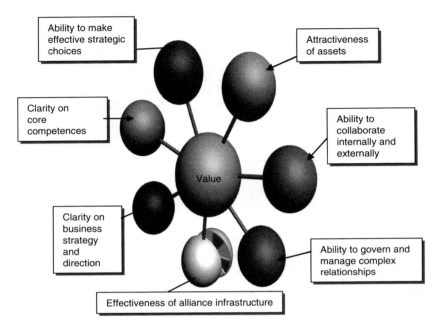

Figure 6.4   ALLIANTIST VIP Map.

EXAMPLES OF ALLIANCE BRANDS

Alliance brand is an evolving model with its standards set high to ensure improvements in performance to improve the current 70% failure rate and give organisations a better chance of future success. As such there are few good examples to draw from; however, many firms do exhibit characteristics of alliance brands and specific examples of great approaches are presented in Part II.

In terms of organisations that demonstrate consistent leading alliance brand performance, the archetypal performer is Cisco. It manages to score highly across all dimensions of the VIP Map and has enjoyed attractive rewards from its alliance activity for many years. Its reputation as the partner to work with in its field has been assured for some time. In 2005 Cisco had revenues of some

$24bn, much of which was driven by partners. It has clarity on its strategy and core competences which are the manufacture and provision of network and communications services that transport data, voice and video globally to homes and offices. CEO John Chambers has a leadership style that reinforces the importance of alliances and collaboration and this pervades the organisation with appropriate recruitment policies, rewards and incentives to drive performance. He sees alliance strategy and business strategy as interdependent. Alliances are led from a similar level as M&A and organic growth. There are clear criteria to help decide whether to make, buy or ally on new initiatives. Cisco's business model firmly emphasises alliances across the value chain in particular down-stream with a comprehensive channel sales infrastructure and a strategic alliance programme underpinned with significant invest-ment. For example, there is over 200 staff in the strategic alliance function and they deliver a compelling return on investment. Cisco's alliance infrastructure enables all parties to understand their value and importance, and the role that partners play is clear because of the way the programme is structured and partners are managed. A leading edge technology system exists that enables partnering success and improved productivity including intranet and extranet access as well as online training with certification and testing for qualified partners and their staff. Its governance is not only strong to adhere to Sarbanes Oxley legislation, but it also takes the opportunity to drive increased performance from the way it measures and monitors alliance activity. Alliance initiatives have to pass strict return on investment criteria and are subject to scrutiny by high-level sponsors and other interested stakeholders.

Reuters used to be a laggard alliance brand for its client facing alliances, promising much with its great reputation but not deliver-ing enough positive results from its alliance activity. However, in 2000 it made strides into alliance brand status by first investing in a UKI and US alliance programme then architecting a global alli-ance programme which changed the way it dealt with many of its partners. Positive results flowed shortly afterwards. It has got greater clarity on its strategy and direction, divested noncore activity in recent years and considers alliances at a more strategic level than before. There are tools, policies and procedures in place that aid alliance initiatives and Reuters has got much smarter about the way it promotes and engages in alliance activity. There are simple but effective systems that support the alliance resources in place. V. Balasubramanian (Bala) is senior vice president and now leads Reuters' Global Alliance Programme. Bala and his team oversee some 500 alliances and report into the sales channel alongside the delivery resources responsible for sales and alliance execution. While revenues derived from alliances are starting to grow at Reuters, the aim is to build it to 20% of Reuters turnover during the next couple of years. Global alliances with organisations such as Accenture on reference data will help meet this target and increase profitability for Reuters, enabling increased investment in the alliance infrastructure to help take it firmly into leading alliance brand status in the coming years.

SEEDA is a good example of an emerging alliance brand, in particular the Enterprise Team who are responsible for successful alliance initiatives such as Enterprise Hubs, Enterprise Gateways and Sector Consortia across the South East of England. As a relatively young regional development agency funded by public money it has a number of challenges to overcome. These include allocating its resources wisely with most of its actions open for public scrutiny. It has to balance the need to remain commercially focused and engage with private enterprise while working collaboratively with a large number of other public sector partners who may not have the same goals and objectives. Greg Ward, Head of Enterprise, manages to maintain that balance. His operations team, led by Julie Kapsalis, have delivered impressive results in the alliance activity although they have not yet gained a strong alliance reputation from those endeavours hence the emerging alliance brand position. They have clarity on their strategy and direction, and a clear core competence in commercialising, launching and managing value creating programmes with their extended enterprise of delivery partners. One of the Enterprise Team's strengths is a constant desire to improve and build on current practice, working closely with their partners on mutually beneficial activity. They continue to invest in their people, and develop the processes tools and systems to improve their results further which will give them leading alliance brand status in the near future.

Alliance brands are not just important for large organisations. An example of the partner who stands out in the chemical dispensing solutions market is Brightwell Dispensers who exhibits many leading alliance brand characteristics across its value chain despite being an SME. A small independent designer and manufacturer of dispensing equipment Brightwell has a partnering ethos throughout the business and is well known in its industry. The chairman, Neil Pybus, and the managing director, Stephen Woolmer, recognise the importance of relationships with key alliance partners and buck the norm for many entrepreneurial businesses who may lack trust and so desire control in everything. Brightwell has various initiatives in place to aid collaboration and reinforce the importance of partners to its success both internally and externally. These include initiatives such as a strategy that explicitly values how partners fit within its business model, clear ownership of alliances by relevant managers and holding partner award ceremonies alongside relationship building initiatives. Brightwell has close upstream alliances with key partners to aid design, development and supply, and works on numerous exclusive innovations with some of the largest organisations in the world where it is prepared to share in both risk and reward. It also focuses solely on the dispensing equipment rather than the consumables and offers an own branding service which enables it to ally with carefully selected in-country partners on the downstream sales and marketing activity.

GETTING RESULTS, REPUTATION AND ALLIANCE BRAND STATUS

The organisations noted above and others like Eli Lilly, Tate & Lyle, HP, BT and IBM have each achieved their alliance results and reputation in different ways. However, there are some common themes which when combined with the earlier research and past experience mean that achieving an alliance brand can be to some degree 'scientifically' prescribed. Alliance brands are not built overnight, however, indeed some of the leading performers have taken many years to get the results and reputation they have now. But there is now a clear way through and it is as easy as one, two, three; three critical success factors. The three critical success factors (CSF) are inputs for winning with alliances and gaining an alliance brand as demonstrated in Figure 6.5.

- **CSF 1 – Having a capability to partner:** without being capable of partnering itself, the organisation stands no chance of building meaningful and valuable alliances. Part II sets out how to achieve a capability to partner by following ALLIANTIST VIP Map.
- **CSF 2 – Having the right partners:** having a capability to partner is not enough. Without the right partners supporting and working with the organisation its alliance efforts will be made in vain. In Part III ALLIANTIST ICE Map is introduced to aid organisations in their search for the right partners.
- **CSF 3 – Having effective relationship architectures:** even having the right partners in place may not guarantee success. If the architecture that underpins the relationship stifles collaboration, and perhaps fails to offer appropriate safeguards or rewards for each party then the alliance will fail or not reach its potential. Also in Part III the ERA Map highlights how organisations can build effective relationship architectures to support their alliance activity.

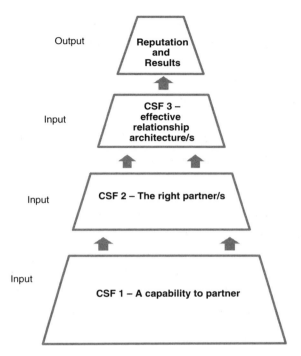

Figure 6.5   Steps to achieving an alliance brand.

Clarifying critical success factors

Jack Welch, the leading business guru originally behind GE, was an advocate of setting the output target (e.g. number one or two in an industry) then focusing on the inputs and letting the outputs take care of themselves. This approach has inspired the philosophy behind the modelling of the CSF above and the maps and models presented in the book. CSF analysis has also become much abused where suggestions of tens or hundreds of CSF might exist. By following the definition of CSF proposed by Rockart[55] in his *Harvard Business Review* paper of 1979, that just doesn't make sense. Rockart said that CSF are:

■ A – 'The limited number of areas in which results, if they are satisfactory, will ensure successful competitive performance for the organisation. They are the *few* key areas where things must go right for the business to flourish. If results in these areas are not adequate, the organisation's efforts for the period will be less than desired.'

■ B – 'Areas of activity that should receive constant and careful attention from management.'

As a final point to reiterate on the three CSF and their underlying components is to note they have been developed since 1997 following intensive focus in this field at both an academic and, more importantly, a practitioner level, having felt the pain of failure and tasted the sweetness of success. Following the maps, tools and techniques that underpin the three CSF will help lead you to greater success more quickly in the future without the need for so much pain.

DOES YOUR ORGANISATION NEED AN ALLIANCE BRAND?

At the opening to Part I there were some probing questions to consider. Having presented the research and background to alliance brand there are a couple of key questions outstanding. Does your organisation need to do better with its alliances and does it need an alliance brand? Not all organisations need an alliance brand, nor do they all need to get to the same level of maturity as each other. The starting point for the journey towards an alliance brand is also likely to be different for many organisations. To put this into a useful perspective, consider the hypothesis tree in Figure 6.6 for leading alliance brands.

The assumption is that the organisation has already tested positive for the subhypotheses 1.1 and 1.2. Given the earlier discussion

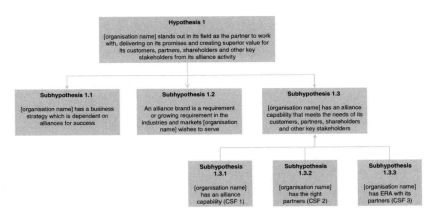

Figure 6.6 Leading alliance brand hypothesis.

in the book of the forces pushing for change it would be surprising if an organisation's strategy didn't include alliances and the markets/ industries it serves didn't see alliance brand as a requirement now or in the future. The focus then for the next two parts of the book becomes subhypothesis 1.3, which addresses the three CSF, and when proved true will mean hypothesis 1 is positive and a leading alliance brand is achieved.

PART I SUMMARY

*P*art I has looked at value and advantage, then undertaken a fairly detailed primer around alliances and their growing importance on business success. The forces pushing for alliances as well as those challenging their success as shown in Figure 6.7 have also been discussed in some detail.

The rewards for those organisations that can execute well are now clear. The risks and threats for poor delivery or failure to meet commitments are also understood. These threats can potentially cost directors of firm's their liberty and compromise survival of the organisation. The benefits of the organisation having a good reputation and being seen as a trusted brand are known, and the consequences of a negative image are also pretty apparent. With the pool of potential partners increasing there is greater choice yet until now there has been little to help easily distinguish between a good partner and bad one. There has been no uniform mechanism from which to help 'get inside' the prospect without major

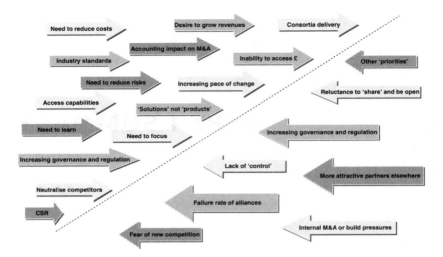

Figure 1.0 Forces for and forces challenging alliance success.

investment in due diligence, or indeed to help the better alliance organisations stand out from the crowd. The concept of high performing alliance organisations has now been framed to help them stand out in the future by introducing alliance brand.

In turning to Part II the book takes the first step towards building an alliance brand by addressing CSF 1, having a capability to partner, and demonstrating the detail and tools that underpin ALLIANTIST VIP Map.

HAVING A CAPABILITY
TO PARTNER

*T*he last chapter stated that there were three critical success factors (CSF) for winning with alliances and gaining the all-important reputation and results that lead on to alliance brand status and the start of a virtuous circle of increasing rewards. This part introduces CSF 1 which is 'having a capability to partner'. Like many things in life, achieving CSF 1 is made easier by following a map. ALLIANTIST VIP Map sets out the value inflection points (VIP) which are specific areas where organisations either create or destroy value from their alliance activity. While the map is not necessarily the territory, and each organisation has its own specific set of characteristics, the VIP Map will aid the journey. At its most basic, the VIP Map is a comprehensive checklist to address before embarking on alliance activity. At its most effective it will guide the review of internal alliance capability and that of partners to help positively transform VIP elements that are not yet optimised and adversely affecting alliance success.

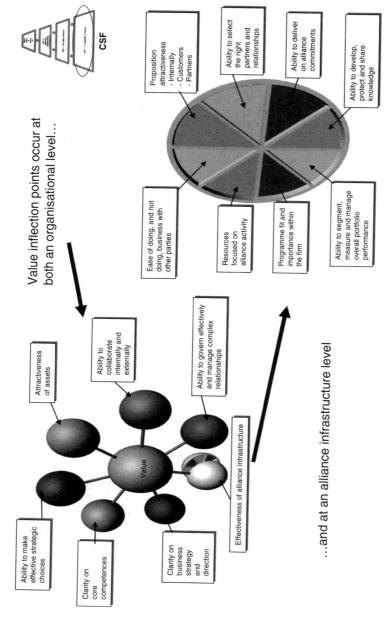

Figure II.1 ALLIANTIST VIP Map breakout.

As intimated earlier, it is not just elements at an alliance infrastructure level that affect value, indeed organisational level elements are a major cause of success or failure. As such, the VIP Map addresses two levels and each VIP is inextricably linked to the others as shown in Figure II.1. Chapter 7 starts the process by reviewing clarity on the business strategy and direction.

CLARITY ON STRATEGY
AND DIRECTION

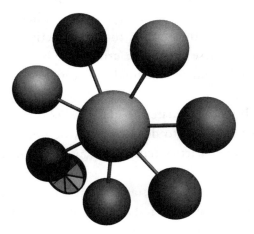

*I*f you don't know where you are going, then any road might lead you there. As such organisations need to have an understanding of firm strategy and goals in order to help determine whether the business can create value, and if alliances will add to or destroy that value. Ben Gomes-Casseres, one of the leading alliance academics, advocated putting strategy before structure in one of his masterful articles[56].

THE IMPORTANCE OF CLARITY ON STRATEGY AND DIRECTION

There are many definitions of strategy and some were touched on in the first part of the book. Put simply, 'strategy is about the direction of an organisation towards clear goals and the effective allocation of its resources and assets towards those goals'.

Resources and assets include those available within the firm and accessible from the extended enterprise through alliances and other relationships. A good strategy will not only communicate clearly what the organisation does, but will also state what the organisation does not do as regards its execution of the strategy. Porter talked about trade-offs where the provision of one thing would mean less of another[57]. He and others have also raised the importance of how the sum of the firm's activities creates value and advantage. These points are crucial for both the firm and its partners as well as other stakeholders because:

- An inability to articulate the strategy and direction of the firm may leave it unable to demonstrate where it will create value and why other parties (customers, partners, investors) should support it on the journey.
- Everyone needs to understand where they fit in. An inability to articulate what is offered and not offered may leave partners confused about whether they should collaborate or compete with the firm.

Alliance brands have clarity on their strategy and direction. Having clarity on it may be somewhat easier for an SME. Consider

Brightwell Dispensers. It has a clear strategy for the design, development and manufacture of high quality innovative chemical dispensing systems into hygiene and cleaning related markets. It does not sell consumables or the chemicals that are dispensed from its systems. These are sold by its partners and customers who know Brightwell will not compete with them. By collaborating closely with its key suppliers, customers and strategic partners, Brightwell designs and develops solutions to meet the end user needs. Relating it back to the value disciplines from Part I Brightwell's main discipline is on product leadership tied closely into customer intimacy and its choice of partners complements that philosophy. It is not the cheapest provider in its markets and will not buy business for the sake of revenue growth. However, through its customer focus and pioneering designs which offer superior value over competitors, this strategy has helped Brightwell become the leading independent supplier of dispensers in Europe and a growing force on the broader international stage. Brightwell's employees know the overarching strategy and are able to articulate it clearly in a neat 30 second elevator pitch when asked.

Having clarity on strategy and direction is of equal importance for large enterprises, however, sometimes can be much harder to achieve. For some firms it is quite straightforward and examples here might include BP, BA and Cisco. However, for firms like BT and Reuters it is somewhat more complex as they have multiple activities and at times boundaries blur. The problem arises when partners and prospects don't know whether to collaborate or compete, and even if they do collaborate are still unsure whether it will turn into co-opetition or outright competition at some point in the future.

BT is a leader in its field and has articulated eight strategic priorities as noted in Part I. The challenge is that these priorities are so high level it is not easy to determine how prospective partners fit into that strategy unless they are already very close to the organisation, and even then clarity is sometimes lacking.

Co-opetition was explained earlier in the book and will be covered again in more detail later in the governance chapter but in simple terms BT also has circumstances where it both cooperates and competes with its partners. In certain areas such as ICT outsourcing solutions it also has multiple partners such as HP, CSC and Accenture where those partners also compete against each other. Without effective communication, clear rules of engagement and strict opportunity management BT could frustrate these alliance partners, and confuse staff who sell the solutions, as well as its customers, about the various offerings. BT operates a strategic partner centre of excellence in order to address these factors as well as ensure it optimises its activity with its strategic alliance partners.

Reuters is a good example of a large global enterprise with clarity on its strategy and direction, although this has not always been the case. It had tremendous success in the 1980s and 1990s and much of its information services strategy involved the provision of complete solutions itself. It even used to make its own computers because external providers could not keep up with the growing information speeds and customer demands. Implicitly, if not explicitly, Reuters has operated a customer intimacy value discipline underpinned by product leadership and innovation. It has worked closely in customer/supplier alliances with its Focus Group Accounts (top 26 customers) for many years. During the late 1990s Reuters saw itself more as a technology solutions company. It attempted to move into services consulting, technology integration and outsourcing, investing in business process software firms among others and generally moved outside its traditional heartland of delivering information services. However, the basis of competition then changed to be far more 'price' focused and speed as well as cost became a key issue in the markets in which Reuters serves. It faced disintermediation from new entrants and increased competition from established players like Bloomberg. It had lost sight of how value was created and its real purpose was becoming less clear to all stakeholders. It had thousands of products in its portfolio, many of which overlapped, and its dominant upstream suppliers and partners also saw the organisation as an easy touch, with many using it as a profitable reseller or influencer route to the end customer. While its customer-led 'intimate' strategy was admirable, it caused distractions and confusion across the organisation.

In 2006 Reuters is a different organisation. Following its very public challenges, Tom Glocer, the CEO, has led the successful Fast Forward transformation. He has had some very difficult choices and took tough decisions that should have been addressed before his tenure, indeed Michael Porter said that the unwillingness to make choices is one of the biggest obstacles to a winning strategy[58]. Reuters has slimmed down and refocused for growth in its core business of information services. It has gone back to basics, divesting noncore businesses like Instinet and outsourced huge parts of its operations including IT field services, distribution, logistics, internal CIO functions and basic data management processes. In another bold move it has also sold its key route to market for distribution of its information, Radianz, to BT who are considered better placed to build and grow that capability with Reuters in an alliance for the future. Reuters has started acquiring new information services capability such as Telerate and built a global alliance programme to collaborate with complementary partners. Its website[59] succinctly states: 'Reuters' goal is to be the information company our customers value most, by offering indispensable content, innovative trading services and great customer service.' It then goes on to state quite clearly its focus and direction which will enable it to expand its addressable market from £6 billion to £11 billion per annum and move up the value stack in terms of providing increasingly profitable products and services. A section on the website is also devoted to the roles partners play in helping Reuters execute its strategy.

Despite being in different industries with sizeable revenue differences, Reuters' new strategy parallels that of Brightwell in its principles of focus, intent and positioning for growth as well as where partners complement its strategy execution. As a result, both Reuters and Brightwell have far greater clarity on the types of alliances and partners they need for success. They are then better able to articulate the benefit for those partners by working with them, as well as have clarity on the overall proposition for the end user.

PITFALLS TO AVOID

A lack of clarity on strategy and direction causes problems more frequently than one would imagine, especially for large organisations operating in maturing industries that are under continual pressure to deliver increasing returns to shareholders and extend their scope accordingly. Examples of problems to be avoided in this area include:

- **Allying away future advantage:** without a crystal ball this is a difficult one to avoid as no doubt IBM will testify from its first experience of working with Microsoft when it didn't think the future was in software. Despite the current pressures, for example on driving out cost which have led to outsourcing, it is important also to remember that a set of outsourced activities, even if not an obvious major affect on competitive advantage in the short term, will still contribute to the execution of firm strategy and may lead to increased or decreased value in the future.
- **Chasing bad revenue or being led by others:** no matter how well intentioned, the risk of being drawn into an alliance to purely solve someone else's problem is a common issue. It could be that the organisation's assets are temporarily attractive to a prospective partner and they see the organisation as a Trojan horse. In one example at an organisation the alliance

partner (A) had effectively taken over the majority of its partner's (B) UK sales team relegating (B) products and services to second place negatively affecting (B) revenues and margins.

- **Frequent changes in strategy and direction execution:** this situation causes problems when an organisation has stated its intention to focus on a particular product or service and use partners to complement its offering. However, it then decides that it needs to grab some of the complementor revenues to help fill gaps in its revenue pipeline. A common example in the technology industry is software vendors partnering with systems integrators and committing to take (say) no more than 15% of the services revenues for their own in-house team. The rationale is that the in-house team need to stay abreast of evolving client needs and make sure that the product is integrated optimally by the partners. However, when licence sales start to dry up that 15% share of services revenue increases and the partners see less of the integration work despite having invested in help to create the market. Unless previously understood and agreed through the rules of engagement (e.g. in co-opetition circumstances) companies that are seen to be collaborating one minute then competing the next in the same area are to be avoided.

- **Changes in leadership or control:** changing organisation objectives is one reason for alliance failure. The underlying cause of many of these failures is from a change in ownership or leadership where a new broom sweeps clean. The new leader has a different perspective on the strategy and direction of the firm, which will subsequently affect the role current alliance partners have in the future success. As such, watch out for firms in trouble, likely future acquisition targets for a competitor, those who follow the fads for a short while, and those who have a history of revolving doors at the top. While not necessarily to be avoided, go in

with eyes wide open and get clarity on the alliance exit
strategy.

■ **Missing the product lifecycle position:** it is important to
understand that a product or service has a lifecycle and during
that lifecycle there are different partners and alliances required
to help execute the strategy. Allying with the wrong partners
at the wrong time may leave the firm with a failed strategy.
Geoffrey Moore's work including *Crossing the Chasm*[60] gives a
great insight into how best to solve these challenges specifically
in the IT industry but his methods also have useful applicabil-
ity to other industries as well.

ACHIEVING CLARITY ON STRATEGY AND DIRECTION

Does your organisation (or one that is being considered as a
partner) have clarity on its strategy and direction and demonstrate
alliance brand characteristics in this regard? Table 7.1 outlines the
key questions that will help determine whether this element of the
VIP has been achieved.

If the answer is No to any of the points in the table then consideration needs to be given to what the implications might be and
how the organisation can overcome them. Solutions might be as
simple as setting out clear ground rules on how certain partners
work with the firm, such as who leads or provides which products,
or clarifying the roles and responsibilities that alliances have in
relation to the strategy. Addressing the issues from the test above
and then initiating a communication campaign to the key stakeholders is a sensible exercise. Completing the basic template in
Figure 7.1 will help clarify the strategy and direction as it relates
to the role of alliances, but may also be useful if clarification is
needed for other stakeholders such as employees, customers, suppliers and investors.

Table 7.1   Testing for clarity on strategy and direction.

Question	Answer Yes or No	Evidence or comments
Can employees succinctly communicate the strategy to other stakeholders such as partners in an elevator pitch or a one paragraph statement?		
Are the metrics for strategy success, SMART – specific, measurable, attainable, relevant, and timescale – oriented such that all stakeholders understand them – whether financial or nonfinancial?		
Is the organisation clear on the role current partners play to complement and not conflict with the organisation strategy and direction?		
Can the organisation's partners clearly communicate the strategy back and tie in how their strategy complements it?		
Do all the stakeholders agree on what the organisation stands for in terms of primary value discipline, i.e. product leadership and innovation versus customer intimacy and solutions orientation versus operational excellence and cost leadership?		
Has the organisation got a history of collaborating with its partners and not competing with them on		

Table 7.1 *Continued*

Question	Answer Yes or No	Evidence or comments
alliance initiatives (except in clearly specified co-opetition issues, e.g. activities outside the alliance)?		
Is the portfolio of products and services offered by the organisation itself clear to all stakeholders?		
Are the markets and industries served by the organisation clear to all stakeholders?		
Do the majority of the firm's overall revenues come from the core products and services in the markets and industries noted above?		
Does the strategy and direction or its execution remain stable to the extent that it does not negatively affect key partner relationships?		

HOW TO ENSURE THE STRATEGY AND DIRECTION CREATE VALUE

It is important to have clarity on the strategy and direction of the firm before commencing alliances. What is less clear is whether the organisation strategy and direction are likely to create value and advantage in the first place. As such there may be a need to

Stakeholder Name/ type	Key messages	Why they need to know	Failure to clarify means	How important is it	What media is used	When
Joint go-to-market partner	We offer outsourcing solutions – our competence is networking and comms – we have desktop and server mgt alliances to complete the stack	Avoid confusion about who does what	Competing in the alliance or gaps in capability	High Medium Low	Website Newsletter Conference Webinar Marketing collateral	One-off Daily Weekly Monthly Quarterly Annually Other
	Our target market is FTSE 100 firms with international presence	So we align target markets and client groups	Potentially conflicting priorities	High Medium Low	Website Newsletter Conference Webinar Marketing collateral	One-off Daily Weekly Monthly Quarterly Annually Other

Figure 7.1 Template for communicating clarity on strategy and direction.

understand more about the external environment and the opportunities and threats that exist so a quick tour on the key principles may prove helpful. External analysis is well covered in the literature on business strategy and financial modelling and there are a number of well-known tools and models to help determine whether the proposed strategy and direction (and product portfolio) are likely to add value. Most of these and more are all covered in great detail in the book by Fleisher and Bensoussan entitled *Strategic and Competitive Analysis*[61] and include:

- **SWOT analysis:** principally helps identify the internal Strengths and Weaknesses of the firm, as regards what it can and cannot do, and from an external perspective, any Opportunities and Threats that might suggest what it should do in the future.
- **PESTLE analysis:** this helps frame industry and macroenvironment characteristics from a Political, Environmental, Sociological, Technological, Legal and Economical perspective.
- **Porter's 5 forces:** Porter's framework helps consider the industry in terms of

(a) The impact current competitors (rivals) have on the environment

(b) The threat of new entrants

(c) How powerful the current suppliers might be

(d) How powerful the current customers (buyers and route to market) might be

(e) What the impact is from substitute products or services

■ **The Valuenet and PARTS:** from an alliance perspective this work by Brandenburger and Nalebuff[62] around co-opetition is a useful addition to the framework introduced by Porter. Customers and suppliers are similar to the above, and competitors also include the substitutes noted by Porter; however, complementor activity needs to be noted as well. Part I suggested that a complementor relationship is possible if customers value your product or service more when they have that complementor offering as well. PARTS stands for Players, Added value, Rules, Tactics and Scope.

■ **Scenario planning:** taking account of the findings from above, plausible scenarios can be constructed based on assumptions to conduct best, worst and likely case scenarios.

There are some key questions the organisation should be asking about its strategy and direction while using the frameworks above to guide the external analysis. These include the questions shown in Table 7.2. Firms with an alliance brand are clear on the answers to these questions.

External analysis and clarity on strategy and direction is important to help create value. In itself, however, it is not enough to ensure the firm does create value and advantage. All the activities that the organisation and its extended enterprise of partners execute will also determine the success or failure of the strategy. Internal analysis is therefore crucial to determine what the firm does versus others, both in terms of where it adds

Table 7.2   External analysis-based questions.

Question	Answer	Evidence or comments
What is the basis of competitive advantage and creation of value in the core industries and markets served? (why does the organisation win or lose business over others)		
What are the key industry challenges and opportunities facing the organisation over the next 1–3 years?		
What specifically is it that customers value about the organisation's products and services over other alternatives?		
Is that likely to change in the near future and if so why and what can be done about it?		
What dependencies does the organisation have today across its supply chain on partners and alliances for success with those products and services?		
Is that likely to change in the near future and if so why and what can it do about it?		
What complementary or new products and services should the organisation be considering either to make, buy or ally to sell to its existing clients and markets?		
What new clients and markets can the organisation sell its existing products and services to either by going direct or through alliances with others?		

real value and where it can seek help from other parties to do it more efficiently or effectively. Chapter 8 looks at how internal analysis and clarity on core competences can help the creation of value.

CLARITY ON CORE COMPETENCES

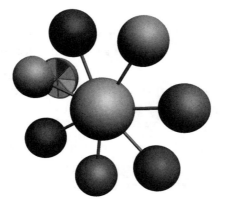

*I*n industries with few obvious opportunities and significant threats, the external focus will not be the only source of competitive advantage and potential for achieving value. Jay Barney[63] argued that some firms are able to generate high levels of profit and advantage in competitively trying industries by also looking internally to their strengths and weaknesses. Certainly given the macroeconomic challenges and limitations on growth in mature industries, focusing internally has been the main way of retaining profitability for organisations like BA, Reuters and others in recent years. This internal analysis, the resource-based view of the firm (RBVF), seeks to understand the relationship between the resources, assets and capabilities of the organisation and, when combined, whether they are capable of meeting its strategic goals.

THE IMPORTANCE OF CLARITY ON CORE COMPETENCES

Part I saw Porter and others suggest that it was the total activities undertaken across the firm and with its extended enterprise that created value and advantage. Stalk, Evans and Shuman reinforced that it is how the organisation chooses to compete as well as where it competes that will determine success. However, if organisations don't have the depth and breadth of assets they need for execution of the strategy it is unlikely to be successful. Not all these assets need to or indeed should be held internally if they can be accessed via alliances and other types of relationships, reinforcing why having a capability to partner (CSF 1) needs to become more of a core competence for many organisations.

There are, however, key attributes that are the primary sources of competitive advantage, underpinning core competences and therefore need to be held by the firm in order to differentiate it and compete effectively, yet firms struggle to identify them. In addition, given all the forces pushing for alliances and the need for many organisations to produce results quickly, there is a danger those firms will underinvest in or ally away a core competence or key attribute that may not directly create advantage today but could do in the future. Failure to leverage a core competence may also mean suboptimised value with missed opportunities for developing new products or accessing new markets. Conversely, for those that address this area effectively and get to understand where superior value is created now and in the future, they will be well positioned to build advantages early or compete well in hitherto untapped markets and industries at a lower risk than through complete diversification.

Some business tasks and activities are considered 'hygiene', i.e. they must be done but add no overt value. Consider the analogy with personal hygiene. Having a shower every day and being seen (or smelt) as clean yields no value or differentiation yet failure to respect this process will soon find the individual losing value and reputation. The difference in business is that firms can get others to do their hygiene tasks although they still need to be done to a suitable standard! As a result many hygiene tasks and business processes around back office management have been allied away, and so have many business critical tasks that are considered noncore competences but still remain central to the creation of value and advantage. As with much business language core competences can be interpreted many ways so it is important to understand what it means from this book's perspective.

DEFINING CORE COMPETENCES

Hamel and Prahalad sought to identify what differentiates the successful organisation from the unsuccessful. The two authors are probably the best known proponents of the competence-based view of the organisation, thanks to their 1990 *Harvard Business Review* article[64], and best selling book *Competing for the Future*[65] which brought out the concept of core competence to a mass audience. However, this concept actually emerged much earlier, with readings going back to 1957 from Selznick[66] and 1959 from Penrose[67] and it is more deeply understood than many would guess.

Hamel and Prahalad defined a core competence as 'a bundle of skills and technologies that enables a company to provide a particular benefit to customers'[68]. The authors argued that businesses needed to develop foresight about the future in order to be successful, and in so doing presented a number of questions as shown in Table 8.1. These questions serve as a good introductory test to help bring some clarity on core competences, but do not go as far as needed to make a real difference in practice.

In practice the definition proposed by Hamel and Prahalad is not very specific and a much deeper understanding is warranted for effective internal analysis. Indeed much of the writing of Hamel and Prahalad has been criticised by other authors, including Treacy and Wiersema who say that 'suggesting that Walmart's

Table 8.1   Questions for market leadership now vs future.

Today	5 to 10 years in the future
Which customers are you serving today?	Which customers will you be serving in the future?
Through what channels do you reach your customers today?	Through what channels will you reach your customers in the future?
Who are your competitors today?	Who will be your competitors in the future?
What is the basis for your competitive advantage today?	What will be the basis for your competitive advantage in the future?
Where do your margins come from today?	Where will your margins come from in the future?
What skills or capabilities make you unique today?	What skills or capabilities will make you unique in the future?
In what end product market do you participate today?	In what end product markets will you participate in the future?

success stems solely from its logistics competency . . . pushes the concept of core competences too far'[69]. *The Witch Doctors*[70] book also undertook a constructive critique of many management theories including the central tenets of Hamel and Prahalad's views about having a business built around core competences.

Coyne, Hall and Clifford[71] presented a more complete definition of core competence as: 'a combination of complementary skills and knowledge bases embedded in a group or team that results in the ability to execute one or more critical processes to a world class standard'. Deeper thinking about competences, with more concrete academic backbone and empirical value, is presented in the book entitled *Competence Based Strategic Management*[72], edited by Heene and Sanchez. Heene and Sanchez suggested (core) competence be defined as 'the ability of an organisation to sustain co-ordinated deployments of resources in ways that promise to help that organisation to achieve its goals'[73]. These authors went further as well, explaining quite clearly that their concept of competence attempted to integrate and incorporate essential 'dynamic, systemic, cognitive and holistic aspects of organisation'[74]. The use of 'resources' in this context also meant resources within the firm (firm specific) and resources outside of the firm (firm addressable). Where firm addressable resources are used this brings out the principle of 'competence alliances', linking one firm's competence to those of other organisations. Durand[75] broke down 'competence' into ingredients:

- Standalone assets (artefacts, intellectual property, brand, software, machinery, buildings etc.)
- Cognitive capabilities (individual and collective knowledge and know-how, skills and technologies)
- Processes and routines (coordinating mechanisms that enable the company to operate, combining the actions of individuals into collective functioning)
- Organisation structure (facilitating or hindering change)

■ Behavioural and cultural dimension (shared values, beliefs, rites and rituals)

ALLIANTIST has a definition of core competences that seeks to build on all this work as well as past practical experience and is proposed as 'a combination of complementary skills, assets, processes, routines and knowledge attributes embedded in an organisation that are integral to its success and yield a competitive advantage'.

It is also useful to understand what core competences are not. They are not the individual components or attributes such as individual skills, equipment, capital or intellectual property in a stand-alone capacity. It is only when the key attributes fuse together and become embedded that they yield real advantage. Organisations generally only have one or a few core competences. Long lists of supposedly core competences will probably mean that the organisation has a good list of attributes and components to build on but has not yet identified its true core competences.

As will be seen shortly, Reuters has two clear core competences, one of which is the 'gathering and reporting of international news'. It does this better than anyone else in the world and it is the combination of the attributes shown in Figure 8.1 that enable the company to achieve it.

Crucially, Reuters has embedded that core competence in the organisation. It transcends individuals, who move on, and there are attributes which feed into it that are delivered by alliance partners, for example some of the additional secondary research and IT systems management.

EFFECTIVE INTERNAL ANALYSIS

Having a definition of core competences helps indicate what components and underlying attributes the organisation should be

Figure 8.1   Example of the underpinning attributes of a core competence.

looking for but there is a need to go further to understand exactly which of these attributes creates value and advantage. As intimated earlier, one of the key problems for internal analysis is that it is difficult to identify which attributes and components create real advantage and therefore need to be held internally from those that do not, and so could be accessed from others (for example) through alliances. To do this it is necessary to get deeper in order to ascertain where the strengths and weaknesses are inside the organisation.

The internal analysis review process in Figure 8.2 is one example of how to conduct deeper more valuable analysis. Use it to help inform on core competences and for current and future strategy decisions alongside the external analysis conducted in Chapter 7.

Discovery

Having now understood that value and advantage are brought about from the sum of the activities undertaken, a few core competences are what differentiates the organisation against others and

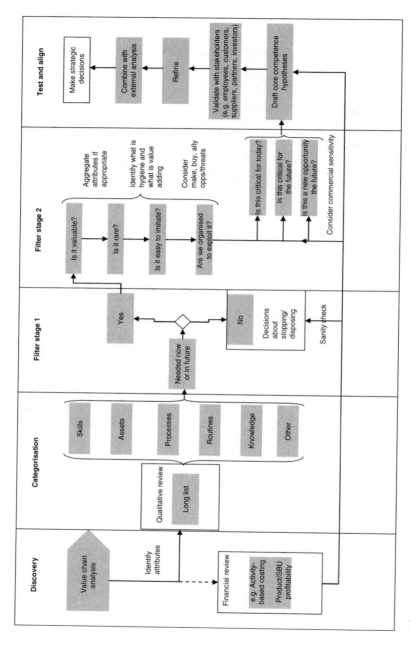

Figure 8.2 Internal analysis review process.

it is likely that some key attributes are the things that add real value underneath those core competences. It is important therefore to produce a list of the things that the firm does and has in order to bring its products and services to market and manage them over the lifecycle. This would include any existing partner/third party activity. One could just produce a list of the activities a firm undertakes, but things could be missed and interdependencies forgotten. As such, Porter's value chain[76] is a useful framework to build on. The primary purpose of the value chain is to disaggregate all the relevant activities to enable identification of costs and existing or potential sources of differentiation.

The value chain concept and core competence analysis helped transform one failing project late in 1999 into a very successful alliance for Reuters and its partner Fujitsu, which is still going strong in 2006. Having been asked to take on a project that was in post-tender negotiations for outsourcing Reuters' UKI IT distribution and logistics function, it was quickly evident that this scope of work held little attraction for prospective suppliers due to its trend of diminishing volumes, increasing costs and high risks. As such Reuters looked at the rest of the value chain to see whether there were other areas of value or assets it could offer prospective partners. In a brief workshop of about two hours a series of related value chain tasks and services were identified that were capable of being executed by others which could offer increased value to suppliers and give them greater reason to take on the less attractive logistics and distribution activities. However, this additional work introduced a much higher risk, putting much of the UKI revenues at risk (some £500m per annum). After selling the revised business case to the UKI board the team went back to basics and crafted a far more collaborative alliance opportunity, which became known as Project Aragon, instead of a more traditional arm's length outsource transaction. The simplified value chain is shown in Figure 8.3.

The increased value for the partner became clear. By working with Reuters in this enhanced capacity it would get physical access

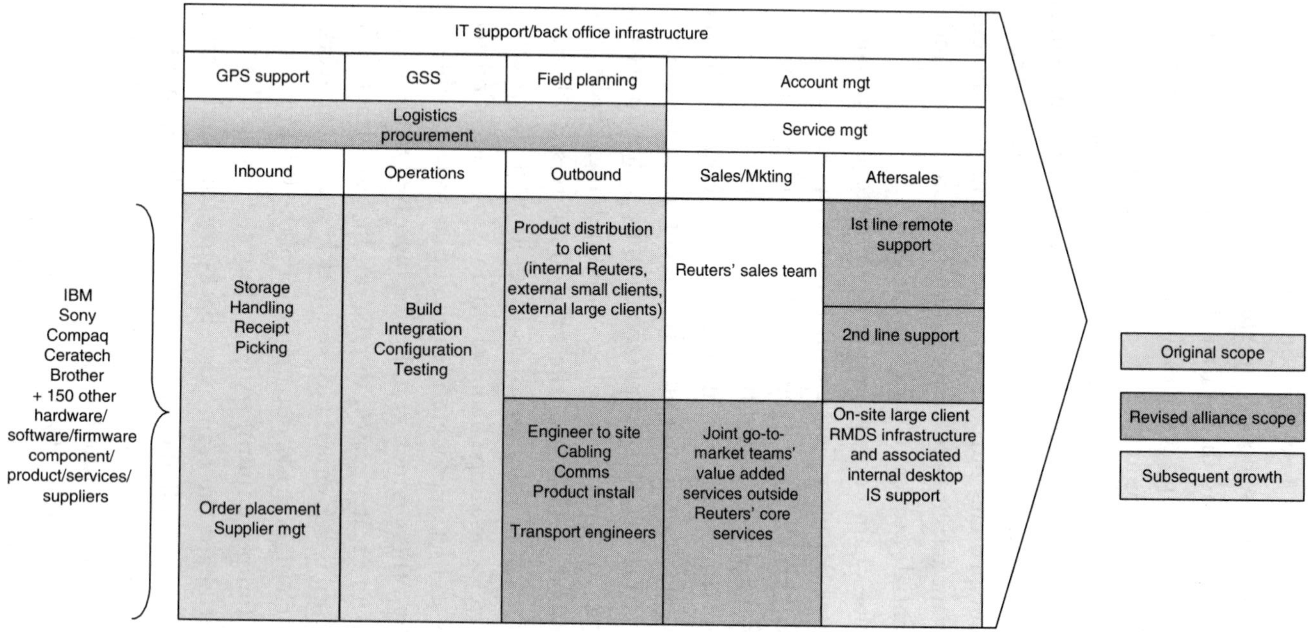

IT support/back office infrastructure

GPS support	GSS	Field planning	Account mgt	
	Logistics procurement			
			Service mgt	
Inbound	Operations	Outbound	Sales/Mkting	Aftersales
Storage Handling Receipt Picking	Build Integration Configuration Testing	Product distribution to client (internal Reuters, external small clients, external large clients)	Reuters' sales team	1st line remote support
Order placement Supplier mgt		Engineer to site Cabling Comms Product install Transport engineers	Joint go-to-market teams' value added services outside Reuters' core services	2nd line support
				On-site large client RMDS infrastructure and associated internal desktop IS support

IBM
Sony
Compaq
Ceratech
Brother
+ 150 other hardware/software/firmware component/services/product/suppliers

Original scope

Revised alliance scope

Subsequent growth

Figure 8.3 Simplified value chain scope for Project Aragon.

to Reuters' clients, actually going on site and gaining the chance to use Reuters as a key route to market. It had a captive and warm audience because the client had already sourced Reuters' products and would likely need complementary services such as hardware, software and other IT support which were no longer being offered by Reuters. The clients got a great benefit because they could access best of breed IT services as part of a one stop shop. Reuters benefited from the enhanced customer service, increased cost savings and better focus on its core competences. As part of the new alliance roadmap there was also an opportunity for the partner to win a share of Reuters' internal desktop and related IS business, and a large carrot of managing Reuters' largest clients on-site IT infrastructure. Five years later the alliance remains a great success with Fujitsu working even more closely with Reuters on a greater suite of products and services.

There are problems with value chain analysis, however. For example, the degree to which you break down tasks, and where to assign activities in each case, especially in large organisations who might have multiple value chains for different parts of their business. The advice is not to get hung up about this point and unless the organisation is looking at a specific alliance initiative, as with the example of Project Aragon, find out which parts of the business are performing well versus their potential, and start there. Like most portfolio analysis, it does not always matter where something is put in the framework to start with, the key is usually identifying it and then analysing its implications. It should broadly follow process flow, but the basic principle is that activities should be isolated and separated where they have different cost drivers, have a high potential impact of differentiation and represent a significant or growing proportion of cost. In addition to the qualitative observation and insight that arises from value chain analysis, quantitative and financial reviews can also be undertaken using methods such as activity-based costing and product or business line profitability.

Categorisation

As a result of undertaking value chain analysis or using similar techniques, a long list of activities and attributes can be created. These are then categorised into the various 'buckets' such as assets, skills, processes, routines, knowledge and other. Another benefit of producing this list is the transparency it gives to how attractive the firm's overall assets are, which is the subject of Chapter 10.

There is a danger of producing lists just for the sake of it but the important thing at this stage is to get the information down on paper as it quickly gets filtered in team discussions, especially when an external facilitator is constructively challenging the findings.

Filter stage 1

A quick analysis of the attributes to determine if they are needed now or in the future helps filter unnecessary activity. Separate consideration can be given to whether the attribute should be stopped, disposed of, or amended in any way to add some value in future. If there has been any financial analysis undertaken a quick sanity check can reveal whether there are cost savings or profit improvements, increased risks or other opportunity costs before taking final actions.

Filter stage 2

Jay Barney[77] stated that critical conditions must exist in order to generate value and advantage, and they are that the attribute or competence be scarce, and that it also be valuable. It goes therefore that for sustained advantage, the attribute or competence must remain scarce and remain valuable. In 1996[78] Barney presented a framework for analysis that addressed the issues around resource scarcity, value and sustainability. Called the VRIO, it asks four key questions which can help determine whether the attribute is a strength or a weakness. Adapted from that work, consider the following questions:

1. **Value:** Does this attribute/combined set of attributes enable the firm to respond to external opportunities and threats, and is it something that customers will value and be prepared to pay for over other alternatives?

2. **Rareness:** How many competitors or potential competitors already possess these attributes? In essence this test looks at how much of a premium might be charged depending on availability elsewhere.

3. **Imitability:** Do firms without this attribute face a cost disadvantage in obtaining it compared to firms that already possess it? This test seeks to understand how long any advantage might be before others imitate it and affect (say) the ability to premium price.

4. **Organisation:** Is a firm organised to exploit the full competitive potential of its attributes? A key test to determine whether the firm can actually take advantage of any VRI attributes is whether the structure, leadership, culture, processes, routines etc. are enabling or disabling the creation of value from the attribute/combined attributes. Firms are usually structured around products, geographies or customer groups. This might work well; however, in large companies with different profit and loss account owners, politics, bureaucracy and competing pressures it might be that the firm's key differentiating attributes are locked down in one division and not easily accessible to other parts of the firm meaning loss of value.

Table 8.1 represents the value creating potential associated with the VRIO outputs[79].

Table 8.2 VRIO framework outputs.

Is an attribute or combined set of attributes:

Valuable?	Rare?	Costly to imitate?	Exploited by the organisation?	Competitive implications	Economic performance	Strength or weakness
No	–	–	No	Competitive disadvantage	Below normal	Weakness
Yes	No	–	↑	Competitive parity	Normal	Strength
Yes	Yes	No	→	Temporary competitive advantage	Above normal	Strength and distinctive competence
Yes	Yes	Yes	Yes	Sustained competitive advantage	Above normal	Strength and sustainable distinctive competence

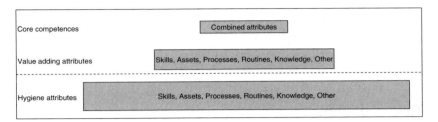

Figure 8.4 Hierarchy of attributes.

While an attribute may not yield any VRIO and be a weakness, it could still be a hygiene activity and therefore essential for the firm to operate effectively. A useful way of presenting the outputs from the exercise is shown in Figure 8.4. By identifying the attributes that are hygiene versus value adding the firm can start to think about whether it should be holding those attributes in house or accessing them from external parties.

Having filtered the attributes to find the top VRIO attributes the organisation can then determine whether it is critical for advantage today and the future. Consider the following questions:

1. What will happen if the organisation were to stop investing in this attribute (especially the hygiene/weaknesses)?
2. How critical is this core competence likely to be to gain advantage in the future and why?
3. By holding this core competence what position is the organisation able to adopt in its broader industry value chain to drive industry or market change that others cannot do, or at least cannot do without us?
4. What new product or market opportunities might arise as a result of looking through a core competence lens instead of a focus purely on geographies, customers or product sets?

Having gone through a fast track version of this process, Brightwell Dispensers has now identified at least one, if not two, new opportunities to take its current core competence of dispensing equipment design and development into adjacent markets with relatively low risk and possibly high return.

Test and align

Having completed the tests above, the organisation will get a good idea of what its core competences might be. However, rather than act in an academic or theoretical vacuum sitting in a workshop risking 'group think', it is important to test those findings with a wider group of interested stakeholders. There is a threat of leaking commercially sensitive information at this stage so consideration needs to be given to what is communicated especially if the findings mean significant change might be proposed in the future.

It was stated earlier that Reuters has undergone significant changes over the past two years. One of the inputs into that transformation programme was the findings presented to the board after a core competence review project. Led by the strategy team with help from the global alliance team, Reuters ran a review process using some of the tools above and some recent analysis work on its potential core competences. Some 15 senior executives from across the organisation came together in a half day workshop with an external facilitator to help maintain focus and remain objective. After some heavy debate creating long lists and then filtering them, the workshop concluded with five core competence hypotheses to test. Key customers, investors, suppliers, employees, joint ventures and alliance partners were selected to test the findings. The feedback was very illuminating and along with the other external analysis produced, helped make compelling proposals to the board about what Reuters should do in the future. It was no surprise then a few months later when Tom Glocer announced the Fast Forward programme and a movement away from numerous areas where Reuters had not been able to create sustainable advantage and ongoing value. It was going to refocus on information services and divest noncore operations as well as seek alliances in certain key areas internally and externally. Its core competences were considered to be around:

- The aggregation, cleaning, tailoring and global distribution of real and nonreal time information
- The gathering and reporting of international news

THE CHALLENGES OF INTERNAL ANALYSIS

Barney did recognise that his framework had limitations if used in isolation, in particular the threat of change coming in an unpredictable and rapid manner, hence why this book proposes that it is complemented with other forms of internal and external analysis. The ALLIANTIST hybrid model outlined above is not scientifically perfect; there are also other tools which seek to help the process although none has the complete answer. Klein and Hiscocks[80] proposed a set of tools to aid the competence analysis process but the authors also stated that the degree of ambiguity around definitions and lack of consensus in this field meant the platform upon which they proposed their methodology was somewhat 'loose' and therefore subject to misinterpretation.

Another challenge in using this or any other form of subjective framework includes leadership influence and how the leaders perceive the world around them. Take the example of two large insurance companies with very similar target customer profiles. One firm believes its core competence to be around customer relationship management and is very protective and exacting of the way in-house staff engage with clients on the phone from the first point of contact, over the lifecycle of the relationship. The other firm chose to outsource its call centre to India in an alliance and focused more on driving out cost of operations in order to try to lower premium costs and win business on price. Who was right? The answer is that both could be right or wrong! Going back to the value disciplines and the organisation goals, one firm's leadership had focused it strategy more on cost leadership and the other on customer intimacy so both had differing views on what their core competences were. The Indian call centre was actually just as focused and perhaps better staffed with graduates whereas the other firm's call centre suffered from high churn and low educational standards. Arriving at the right conclusions quickly with internal analysis is not easy; however, it can be very valuable if done well.

Another big issue in core competence and internal analysis is accessing the information in the first place. Large firms can spend months and hundreds of thousands of pounds attempting to define their core competences because of the inability to access appropriate information upon which to undertake effective analysis.

WHAT HAPPENS NEXT

After undertaking the internal analysis, the organisation will understand whether it has attractive core competences, a need to develop existing ones, build or acquire new ones, outsource distractions or perhaps bring in missing or weaker attributes. Developing or changing attributes and competences can have major implications and depending on what needs to change, it can be achieved quickly or sometimes take many years. Durand presented a competence continuum[81] which has been adapted as shown in Table 8.3.

Table 8.3   Competence addressing and change continuum.

Easiest change/quickest time ←				→ Toughest change/longest time	
Stand alone assets	Cognitive capabilities	Structure	Strategy	Routines and processes	Culture and identity

Before rushing ahead and developing new competences internally, the decision-making process for what to have in-house or to access externally is the basic foundation for make versus buy versus ally and one to be addressed in the next chapter on strategic choice.

## CHAPTER 9

ABILITY TO MAKE EFFECTIVE STRATEGIC CHOICES

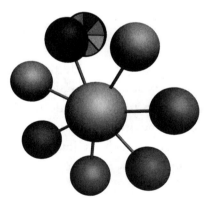

ALLIANCES ARE ONLY ONE OPTION

Alliances are not the only option to create value and execute strategic goals. While the forces for alliances are increasing, it would be foolish to automatically assume they are the correct option

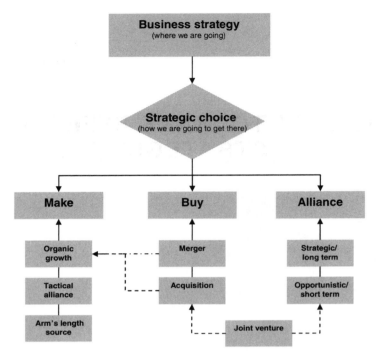

Figure 9.1   Strategic choice hierarchy.

every time. At a macro level alongside the alliance 'ally' option, internal 'make' options exist, and then also the merger and acquisition (M&A) option exists to 'buy.' Underneath that level further consideration needs to be given to arm's length sourcing and potential hybrid variations such as joint ventures as shown in Figure 9.1. Alliance brands have a joined-up approach to strategic choice.

STRENGTHS AND WEAKNESSES OF OTHER OPTIONS

There are strengths and weaknesses with each option and depending on the internal environment and external analysis undertaken previously, the decision on option may vary. Some of the merits and risks for each option are briefly explored below.

Make

- **Control and ownership:** in Part I the forces resisting change included a reluctance to cede control and let go of ownership. In some cases it is sensible to build internally, for example if it is to capture or develop a value adding attribute which is embedded in a core competence and will affect the creation of value. There is also much more control of timing and speed of change or implementation, although it is useful sometimes to have external pressures driving internal change, for example in shaking up a stale area, or bringing fresh ideas.
- **Rewards and risks:** if no external partner is engaged then the organisation gets all the rewards that go with the initiative. However, they also pick up all the risks and liabilities which could mean expensive initial investments and no ability to hedge or share any downside. Additional risks of internal build projects is that sometimes they lack an external rigour and objectivity which comes with the engagement of another party where focused questions get asked of each other early on.
- **Variations on executing the make model:** as well as pure internal build it is possible that goods and services may need to be sourced from other parties to help execute the project. Consideration should be given about the merits of arm's length traditional procurement versus tactical alliances where there may be enhanced collaboration and some minor investment in success/failure by the supplier. Examples could include sale or return policies instead of typical transactions, and collaboration on value engineering costs out of the supply chain for mutual benefit. In selecting this submodel, questions to ask include:

(a) What extra value can be gained by collaborating and seeking a risk/reward relationship with the supplier? Answers could include financial gain and risk mitigation.
(b) What value and rewards might the organisation sacrifice by collaborating and sharing some of the spoils?

Buy

The M&A option satisfies many CEO egos and sometimes it should be questioned whether there are other valid reasons given the probability of success is so low from this option. Joking aside, there are strengths in this option when it is done well and for the right reasons. These include:

- **Immediate access to benefits:** whether it is to access products, markets, industries, core competences or other assets, acquiring them through M&A is usually quicker than building internally and ownership is also assured. If there are external regulatory issues or delays in closing then alliances might be quicker although ownership is lost. Well-priced and effective acquisitions could amount to a lower total cost and quicker time to benefit than building in-house. However, depending on the type of transaction, significant value can be lost through poor integration, management distractions and the risk of key competences and assets walking out the door.
- **Neutralising threats:** as with alliances, M&A can neutralise competitive threats although M&A is a more permanent option than alliances. This generally comes at a price as well and the acquisition premium might not just be the obvious financial premium over a share price. It could also include the purchase of excess baggage which is not wanted and also slows down the synergy benefits being achieved.

For a much deeper insight into the issues surrounding M&A the book by Mark Sirower called *Synergy Trap*[82] is a worthwhile read.

BRINGING IT TOGETHER IN A COHERENT FRAMEWORK

Companies that have an ability to make effective strategic choices have the people and processes responsible for each choice aligned, they know when to use each option and are consistent in their application. Cisco as a leading alliance brand is a good example to draw from. They are disciples of Geoffrey Moore[83] in their approach to make, buy and ally decisions and generally look to acquire future leaders early in the technology adoption lifecycle and seek alliances to build complete solutions and expand the addressable market. The overall decision-making framework is owned at a senior level looking across all the various choices.

Getting to this stage of coherence with the approach to making strategic choices is not easy, certainly in large companies where the responsibility for the make, buy and ally execution may be led and owned by different teams. Take the example of SmartAlex Plc (not its real name) a large organisation who had a corporate M&A team reporting to the CEO, and an alliance team that was on the fringe of the business. The M&A team had the ear of the CEO so it was no surprise then that this organisation preferred to acquire if it could not develop internally. Sadly the business wrote off hundreds of millions in failed acquisitions and investments. That does not mean that alliances would have been the better solution in every case, but without the option being explicitly and objectively discussed, the strengths and weaknesses of each option cannot be compared. Consider the questions in Table 9.1 to see if your organisation might suffer similar problems to SmartAlex Plc.

Table 9.1 Making effective strategic choices.

Question	Yes/No	Evidence/comments
Do all options for strategic choice get considered before key decisions on investments or strategy execution are made?		
Does the choice process include consultation with the key representatives from the make, buy, ally fraternity?		
Is an objective decision-making criteria and framework used to aid the choice process?		
Is the decision-making framework owned by a function in the business that can look objectively at the strengths and weaknesses of each option?		
Are there examples across the firm where past choices have proved to be correct? If so have lessons been learnt from them?		
Are there examples across the firm where past choices have proved to be incorrect? If so have lessons been learnt from them?		
Does the organisation monitor trends and activities in the industry regarding how its competitors, customers and suppliers execute their strategy?		
Most organisations have a natural preference for make, buy, ally – is it clear what your organisations preference is and why?		

If any questions have been answered with a No, consider the implications in light of the opportunity costs and risks that might arise from just one failed strategic initiative. Lost market share, increased costs, compromised reputation and credibility, and market valuation drops are just a few examples of what might happen by making the wrong choice. While there is no panacea and each firm will have its own idiosyncrasies, there are some common factors to consider when thinking about the best choice. Building on the previous two chapters the factors are both internal and external and highlighted in Figure 9.2.

Each factor can be considered and scored relative to the specific options being considered. The depth of the analysis should reflect the significance of the risks and rewards as a percentage of the organisation value. Scoring can be weighted on a spreadsheet in a semi–scientific manner using the template in Figure 9.2 as a guide, or with key executives debating the factors around flip charts and whiteboards using simple decision criteria such as SFA which means:

- **Suitable:** is this option consistent with the organisation goals and objectives?
- **Feasible:** is the organisation in a position to execute in terms of funding, resources, addressing competitor responses and so on?
- **Acceptable:** is it likely to deliver satisfaction for key stakeholders, meet financial goals and risks and so on?

If appropriate each factor can be subjected to analysis by specialist staff, for example the financial aspect might only have input from the accountants, in addition to their separate financial modelling for each option. In terms of the quantitative financial modelling it is not proposed to go into any detail here because there are a multitude of useful books around and most organisations have an excess of good number crunchers to call on. If only it were the

Project name:
Review team member:
Date of analysis:

	weighting	Make — in-house development	Make — arm's length purchase	Make — tactical alliance	Buy — merger	Buy — acquisition	Ally — joint venture	Ally — strategic alliance	Ally — opportunistic alliance	Showstoppers/other comments
Internal factors										
Mgt commitment to option										
Fit with strategic goals										
VRIO impact on key attributes accessed										
Attractiveness of financial rewards										
Attractiveness of non-financial rewards (e.g. brand)										
Emotional significance of investments (qualitative)										
Financial whole life costs of option (quantitative)										
Opportunity costs of option										
Financial risks of option										
Reputational risks of option										
Need for control										
Need for ownership										
Availability of internal resources										
Ability to integrate and execute effectively with current resources										
Baggage and distractions to be encountered										
Implications at exit/end of life										
Sub total 1		0	0	0	0	0	0	0	0	
External factors										
Option availability/possible targets										
Industry maturity, volatility and attractiveness										
Product/service maturity, volatility and attractiveness										
Speed and pace of change										
Competitive forces implications										
Opportunity costs of option										
Regulatory and legal impacts										
Customer demands and perceptions of option										
Investor demands and perception of option										
Other stakeholder demands and perception of option										
Impact on existing partner portfolio										
Likely competitor responses										
Sub total 2		0	0	0	0	0	0	0	0	
Total		0	0	0	0	0	0	0	0	

Figure 9.2 Factors to consider for effective strategic choices

same for alliance professionals! The only comment worth adding is that it is useful to prepare headline financials for each option before making selections, then drill into deeper analysis once the options have been short listed or a decision been made. In some circumstances there will be 'showstoppers' that come out and preclude further analysis of a particular option until they are resolved. Examples might be a lack of senior management commitment to an option, or the inability to access a desired asset externally, i.e. if there are no potential M&A targets. Having the output scores from the spreadsheet is useful, but not in itself the goal. Going through the process is the important factor and explicitly considering each point will bring a greater awareness of the issues. Findings and learnings can then be used for making more effective strategic choice decisions and providing input into future activity, for example negotiations with alliance or M&A candidates.

The previous three chapters have expressed the importance of clarity on strategy and both the external and internal perspective, and the need to consider both aspects carefully when making strategic choices. It can be seen that a one size approach to strategic choice does not fit all, and organisations that are not joined up in their approach to this area risk sizeable value destruction if the wrong option is chosen. Having conducted the analysis the organisation is well placed to have a good idea of the attractiveness of the organisation as a partner, and the assets it might offer to prospective players going forward. The next chapter looks closely at how to bring about maximum value from those assets.

## CHAPTER 10

ATTRACTIVENESS OF ASSETS

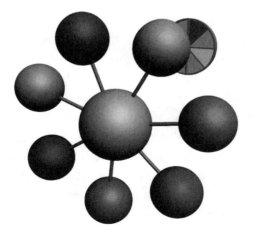

USING ASSETS EFFECTIVELY

Part I said that assets are what you access in alliances and the organisation will probably implicitly if not explicitly look for those partners with the most attractive assets to meet its needs. It makes sense therefore that without any attractive assets itself it is unlikely that prospective partners will see the organisation as the partner to work with in a specific area. Just as in selling a house, there is a need to make sure that its assets are presented in an optimal light to encourage interest. However, with alliances, organisations cannot get away with cheap and quick makeovers to mask problems like those seen in houses on the TV property shows!

Experience suggests few organisations optimise the way they use their assets in alliance activity and they rarely have consistency in their approaches. This could leave value on the table for the alliance partner at a cost to the organisation, or a missed opportunity for the alliance overall. Just because alliances are about close collaborative relationships with other parties it does not mean assets should be given away without getting something valuable in return.

Being associated with a company in a certain fashion can bring significant benefits. Take the example of firms like Siebel, Oracle and other leaders in the software industry who demonstrate alliance brand traits in this aspect of the VIP Map. Clearly they have attractive assets in the products and services they provide and the strength of their brand name. However, by offering a structured alliance programme they can also 'sell' their brand asset and network of relationships, as well as access to specialist resources and so on for large sums of money. To be a top tier partner might cost millions of pounds in terms of marketing development funds, committed people investments, joint R&D and so on, yet the return on those benefits is considered very attractive for the partners as demonstrated with the Siebel and IBM example in Part I. By having tight control over the sales and marketing messages and the way they work with certain partners their alliance programme becomes a huge asset in itself. Cisco is another example. It operates an alliance programme similar to other IT vendors and has strict criteria on investments and paybacks on alliance initiatives to the extent that it can get partners to contribute a disproportionate

ATTRACTIVENESS OF ASSETS 137

amount of assets in joint engagements. Reuters is another that can punch above its weight, not just because of the strength of its brand name, but also because of some of the other assets it has, such as valuable routes to market and strong relationships with some of the most attractive and wealthy clients in the financial markets.

Looking at a simple example from a basic supply alliance perspective, it might be really important that the supplier can present the customer as a case study or key partner in their portfolio to help them win other business. If the customer just concedes this 'brand' asset without getting something in return, or reciprocal benefit, value is lost, especially if it sets a precedent that affects other supply relationships. Imagine letting all suppliers or customers use the term strategic partner in their relations with your organisation. It dilutes the real value of the attribute when a true strategic partnership arises and may have implications on the assets offered to other partners in terms of physical resources and support infrastructure. Having a pound coin for all the tenders issued by buying companies seeking 'strategic partners' when in fact all they want is a lower price, would make someone very wealthy! Suppliers see through this abuse of language nowadays too and the whole exercise becomes a waste of a potentially valuable asset. Many suppliers see great value in some customers and therefore invest in strategic account management teams for key customers. The principle is also valid for supplier relationship management, a growing activity on the supply side of business. However, to do it effectively the buyers need much more clarity on the value and importance of certain relationships and should consider carefully what assets they invest in each type of supplier management activity.

Taking another example in a joint go-to-market alliance, one of the partners wanted access to a particular group of clients and by creating an alliance used the other partner's sales force as its introductory route to market. What value should be placed on the 'route to market' asset, and how is that value arrived at? Typical negotiated approaches might reflect a value exchange being sharing of a small commission on sales made; however, this fails to take into account the real costs of the asset and timing of benefits received by each of the parties. Consider the questions in Table 10.1.

Leading alliance brands answer Yes to each question. If your answer is No to any of the questions in Table 10.1 then consider

Table 10.1   Asset optimisation checklist.

Question	Yes/No	Evidence/comments
Does the organisation have a clear idea of its assets?		
Have all the assets got valuations placed on them?		
Does the organisation have a good understanding of what might happen if certain assets lost their value?		
Does the organisation have effective policies and processes in place to optimise the use of assets and mitigate the risks of value destruction from loss of assets in alliance activity?		
Does the organisation make distinctions on what assets may/may not be available to certain alliance partners?		
Does the organisation revise the value of its assets to reflect their worth to prospective partners?		
Are there examples that demonstrate the effective use of assets in alliance activity that serve as positive lessons to draw from?		

the implications shown in Figure 10.1: ALLIANTIST asset optimisation window. It is based on the same principles as the well-known Johari window. The implications could include asset leakage causing suboptimal alliance returns, and asset loss resulting in ongoing loss of advantage and reducing business results.

Reputation risks and issues also increase without effective controls around who does what with the assets as well. One firm had numerous complaints from its customers because some of its 'partners' were not well qualified and failed to execute effectively. There was also unnecessary channel conflict among some of the partners. There were no real quality controls or due diligence for selection of partners in place which compromised the overall reputation of the firm as well as left bad feeling with some of its better partners. By crafting a simple partner programme and introducing controls around partner selection, effective ground rules to mitigate channel conflict, standards on marketing terminology and tiering of partners it was able to weed out the poor performers to build better relationships and results with those that remained.

Figure 10.1 ALLIANTIST asset optimisation window.

LEVERAGING ASSETS

So how can organisations move into alliance brand territory to optimise and leverage their assets effectively? 'Value' was expressed earlier as the overall price paid or investment made for the benefits gained in return. It stands to reason therefore that organisations should want to communicate the total benefits of these assets to increase their value and use them more effectively in alliance activity for its and other stakeholders' benefits. The process to help achieve this is set out in Figure 10.2.

Figure 10.2   Asset leveraging and management process.

IDENTIFYING ASSETS

From an alliance perspective an asset could be defined as 'anything that a partner or customer might seek from your organisation and value accessing to aid delivery of its own goals'. Taking this interpretation further assets can take three broad forms: physical, intellectual and identity related as shown in Figure 10.3. The linkage with the attributes identified during the core competence and internal analysis work can be seen here and that activity will prove useful in considering how to leverage the assets in working with others.

Identity related assets include alliance brand. Once built this asset enables the firm to raise the bar on its other assets valuations given the greater probability of alliance success, lower cost of business and increased confidence partners can have in firms with

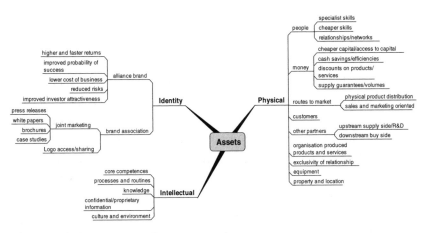

Figure 10.3 Asset mind map example.

alliance brands. Access to the traditional organisation or product brand itself may be very important for certain firms to enhance their own identity although it should be reiterated from earlier statements that end customers are getting wise to the limitations of just 'logo sharing' alliances which have little substance underneath. This is particularly true for those firms that might have strong brands but are not always great at executing alliances. At best these great brand firms are laggard alliance brands where they might fail to deliver good results from time to time, and at worst they could be a huge liability and financial risk for partners.

Consideration is also needed for the other physical and intellectual assets which can provide a material contribution to the partners and the alliance. These include the obvious people, plant and property, but also less obvious extensions such as risk controls and operating practices, customers, relationships and networks, and routes to markets. One firm had failed to place a value on access to its customers or the physical infrastructure in place to facilitate that route to market. Many of its partners had a great time exploiting the asset leakage, offering nothing of value in return.

Following a review, new policies and conditions were put in place to change how some of the channel and go-to-market alliances would work in future. One alliance partner contributed a further $500k in additional value to the firm immediately in exchange for more consistent access to some of these assets as well as improved sharing of the alliance benefits in the future, which amounted to a much greater bottom line contribution. It also set a positive precedent for future alliances in that organisation. Nonprofit firms also have assets to offer their alliance partners, for example in accessing key relationships with local or highly regarded leaders, helping organisations being seen as associating with good causes and perhaps conducting award ceremonies that also help raise profiles.

ASSESSING VALUES

Valuation tools now exist for many physical assets. Independent valuations can be achieved on property, people and equipment relatively easily by comparing against others that are freely available and seeking specialist help where appropriate. But what if alternatives don't exist and comparison is difficult? Should one just look at the net book value or a replacement cost as in traditional accounting valuation and take a proportion of that for use in negotiations? Perhaps this might work and is certainly to be considered when arriving at valuations. However, by using the VRIO principle again it can alert to opportunities for increased value. Consider the VRI from a customer or partner perspective, and ask:

- **Valuable:** does this asset have a value to others and will they be prepared to pay or reciprocate something of theirs to access it?
- **Rare:** assuming it has some value, how valuable is it? Can it be accessed by working with others as well or do you have a scarce asset that could be worth more than first thought?

- **Imitable:** by understanding whether it is easily imitated or substituted you can get an idea of what alternatives might be available and how long you might have leverage before it starts losing its value.

Having asked these questions the organisation can get a good idea of what premium if any can be placed on the assets. Just as with acquisition premiums, where firms pay over the listed share price for an organisation, we might call this the alliance premium, where firms give and get more than they would in strict arm's length transactions. A simple example and really little more than good sourcing behaviour under the right circumstances is the movement from a multiple supplier situation to the focus on one supplier partner. In exchange for (say) exclusivity, increased volumes, a longer-term framework agreement, better access to internal customers, the supplier might offer a premium benefit in the form of lower costs, better management team, greater innovation commitments and so on. Organisations have got to 'give to get', and this means packaging its assets well at the beginning and offering commitments. Sadly many organisations and old style purchasing departments do not do this well when they issue poorly specified tenders, don't offer up valuable information and guard against making even basic commitments like a share of the spend. Effective purchasing professionals now have good marketing and selling skills too.

The Rank Group Leisure Division used to tender the build of each new leisure venue separately and prospective suppliers had to complete tenders for each build. This meant suppliers had no ability to plan for the long term or bring about improvements by investing in their operations just in case they didn't win future builds. Yet there was a bigger capital investment programme in place that highlighted just how many Odeon cinemas, Mecca bingo halls and Grosvenor casinos Rank was going to build over the subsequent three years. Rank's unused yet attractive assets included specialist resources to jointly engineer better solutions, longer-term supply agreements, exclusivity guarantees and a commitment to help suppliers reduce their cost of business, not least by not needing to tender for each build. In taking a more holistic perspective and identifying who the key suppliers were Rank worked with them in a collaborative alliance capacity for mutual benefit using these assets in negotiations. One example was with a seating manufacturer where Rank helped them access these additional assets and in return they were able to get cheaper funding from their bank to invest in new production machinery and provide resources in joint R&D. As a result the total cost of seating dropped by over 30%, yet the supplier improved its margins and other upstream suppliers like fabric and foam suppliers also got benefits from assured supply and the ability to use Rank as a case study in their discussions with other customers.

Valuing brands and brand association is now far easier as well with the advent of brand valuing models and indexes from specialist firms like Interbrand and Brand Finance. The emerging accounting conventions are also seeking to bring much greater transparency from intangible and intellectual assets. Consider Jeff Bezos, CEO of Amazon, when asked how he could justify an investor's share ownership when the market value was around US$13bn yet the book value was under US$2.5bn. His response was that the additional value came from its assets around brand, customers, technology, distribution, e-commerce expertise, a great team and strong company values around serving the customer[84]. In future these statements might need to be backed up by independent valuations to arrive at transparent total market values especially if the postponed OFR or similar legislation is introduced.

CONDUCTING ASSET RISK ASSESSMENTS

Having identified the assets and sought to place values on them, however rudimentary, consideration also needs to be given to the

Asset	Risks from alliance activity	Probability of risk occurrence 1 = low, 9 = high	Impact from risk occurrence 1 = low, 9 = high	Risk priority (probability × impact)	Actions to be taken
Brand	Partner abuses our brand and our reputation suffers leading to lower share price	3	9	27	Effective qualification of partners, standards for use on our brand, legal safeguards
Key staff	Poaching by partner leading to loss of current skills, potentially new competitor meaning lost sales/margins and share price erosion	3	7	21	Identification of key staff going into alliance, ensure they are well motivated, legal safeguards with no poaching expressed in agreement backed up by transfer fees policy contingency
Strategic partner	Misuse of partner terminology leading to shared liabilities	5	3	15	Clarity on the meaning of partner in legal agreements, tiers of partners to protect value of asset in partner eyes

Figure 10.4 Template for risk assessment.

risks from allowing others to access those assets. The increasing financial or reputational challenges and consequences from alliance failure were written about in Part I. Risk analysis needs to be conducted for each alliance as will be seen in Part III; however, there is a need to set out a risk framework that looks across the asset base regardless of alliance partner. To build on the examples above, thought needs to be given to the implications of awarding exclusive contracts for either sales or supply-based activity. Implications of offering the brand and other assets as well as confidential information or key intellectual property also need to be weighed up.

Again, looking to keep it simple, the framework template in Figure 10.4 offers a useful starting point for an internal workshop. The scoring is useful to help prioritise activity, but the key thing is to capture the risk in the first place then look to mitigating or eradicating the risks with targeted actions.

Having identified the key risks and issues, proactive action can be taken around protecting assets and optimising their use before and during alliance activity. The measures might amount to introducing basic safeguards added into each contract, conducting more effective due diligence during alliance selection, or a host of other interventions such as improving the way staff are managed and motivated and restricting access of some assets to a limited group of partners.

SETTING THE FRAMEWORK FOR USE AND MONITORING ITS EFFECTIVENESS

It is important to set out ground rules, or offer frameworks that assist staff in the way they go about alliance activity and ensure continuity in the event people change. If set up well this framework can also be a key marketing tool to help drive up quality, increase interest and stimulate greater investment from partners in the way that firms like Siebel, Cisco, IBM, Eli Lilly and others have done. Some organisations created a simple 'menu of benefits' with two page guidelines that limited uses of assets to certain tiers of partners in exchange for their specific investments. In other organisations they have crafted more detailed policies and guides to help staff consider how far they can go in their alliance negotiations.

Having rules allows them to be broken from time to time and there are always exceptions, although to be determined only by senior management intervention, not a maverick alliance manager! In one organisation it created a clear set of criteria for what was to become 'strategic relationships'. After its approved introduction the firm had only a handful of formal 'strategic relationships' who were able to access key assets such as dedicated strategic relationship managers, board-level stakeholder sponsors, key client introductions and so on. Shortly after having the programme in place two things happened. One positive point was that one slightly miffed important but not considered strategic partner increased its investments into the firm to achieve the new heightened status, mainly to remain in board view alongside a key competitor. The second positive point was that missing criteria were captured because a board director took a greater interest in the programme because it knocked out another partner from the top tier. He felt that the criteria needed amending to also reflect what he called the 'balance of trade' because the partner was also a competitor and the fear was that by relegating them to a lower tier they might be encouraged to compete more heavily against the organisation in the future. The criteria were amended and the partner joined the new ranking.

Alliance brands manage access to their organisation's assets to bring about greater value for the organisation and increase its attractiveness in alliance activity. Those assets need to be identified first and then valued as well as a risk assessment undertaken to understand potential consequences of their being accessed by others. Restricting access is not necessarily a bad thing as it can drive up demand. One only has to look at parallel examples such as the product launches of gadgets like iPod and XBox 360 to see the value from restricting supply and stoking demand. Having conducted the exercises in this chapter it is possible to go back to Table 10.1 and answer Yes for each point with confidence that the firm is going to leverage and optimise its assets for future alliance activity.

The next major challenge is to understand the importance of collaboration both internally and externally and how it affects successful alliances. That is the subject of Chapter 11.

ABILITY TO COLLABORATE INTERNALLY AND EXTERNALLY

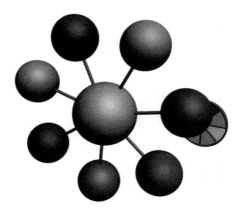

COLLABORATIVE CULTURES

The *Concise Oxford Dictionary* defines collaboration to be quite simply 'work jointly' and this sums up the essence of an area around alliances that regularly destroys value for business rather

Table 11.1 Comparison of culture characteristics.

High performing collaborative cultures	Circle the point on the continuum that best represents your organisation in each characteristic	Low performing noncollaborative cultures
High expectation and results oriented with transparency in performance	10 9 8 7 6 5 4 3 2 1	No expectations with ambiguity in performance
Favours calculated risk taking	10 9 8 7 6 5 4 3 2 1	Favours no risk taking
Proactive and decisive	10 9 8 7 6 5 4 3 2 1	Reactive and indecisive
Trusting by default (innocent until proven guilty)	10 9 8 7 6 5 4 3 2 1	Distrusting by default (guilty until proven innocent)
Power is based on expert knowledge	10 9 8 7 6 5 4 3 2 1	Power is based on seniority
Organisation pursues broader holistic purpose that espouses the importance of other organisations (positive sum messages)	10 9 8 7 6 5 4 3 2 1	Organisation pursues selfish motives that imply or suggest no other organisations are needed (zero sum messages)
Relationship-based cross-boundary working where differences are cherished	10 9 8 7 6 5 4 3 2 1	Transaction-based silo-oriented working where differences are manipulated
Rewards and recognition encourage teamworking	10 9 8 7 6 5 4 3 2 1	Rewards and recognition encourage individual working

	Scale	
Consequences and accountability are team oriented	10 9 8 7 6 5 4 3 2 1	Consequences and accountability are individual oriented
Engagement is made early, information is shared and communication is open	10 9 8 7 6 5 4 3 2 1	Engagement is made late, information is withheld and communication is closed
Roles and responsibilities are clear, the environment favours constructive dialogue and working as a team	10 9 8 7 6 5 4 3 2 1	Roles and responsibilities are unclear, the environment favours destructive dialogue and working as a group of individuals
Governance and controls facilitate and support teamworking	10 9 8 7 6 5 4 3 2 1	Governance and controls stifle and compromise teamworking
Alliances are conducted based on relationship building and collaborative negotiation	10 9 8 7 6 5 4 3 2 1	Alliances are conducted based on transactional tenders and adversarial negotiation
Disputes are solved by discussion and arbitration	10 9 8 7 6 5 4 3 2 1	Disputes are solved by threat and litigation

than creates it. If only collaboration were that simple in practice; sadly few firms demonstrate effective alliance brand traits in this element of the VIP Map.

The forces pushing for collaboration are evident as described earlier. Indeed, back in 1993, John Byrne wrote about the move towards collaborative attitudes rather than competitive. He said 'Atomistic, Darwinian competition is increasingly seen for what it is: out of step with current realities. More and more, companies are seeing that "we are all in this together" and global strategic alliances, joint ventures, and partnerships are flourishing as never before.'[85] Teaming, communication and collaboration are very important yet speak to many people about why alliances fail, and a word heard more regularly is culture. Culture has a major impact on alliances in terms of how it affects an organisation's ability to collaborate. Successful collaborative cultures found within leading alliance brands build on characteristics which high performing cultures exhibit. Does your organisation exhibit both high performing and collaborative characteristics? Assess your organisation against the comparison of characteristics shown in Table 11.1.

Once completed add up all the individual results. Few firms score 140 points; however, firms with a more collaborative culture and alliance brand will generally score over 100 points and not have any individual score below 5. Reflection on each characteristic in Table 11.1 will give some insight into potential strengths and weaknesses of collaboration in an organisation's cultural makeup. This exercise also can be used in helping assess partner fit as discussed in Part III.

FACTORS AFFECTING COLLABORATION

Going a little deeper, if culture is loosely defined as 'the way things are done around here', it is necessary to identify what factors are

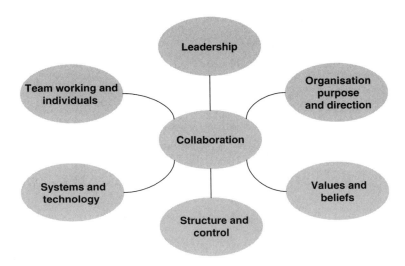

Figure 11.1   Factors affecting collaboration.

important for successful collaboration and then understand the way they are currently 'done' in the organisation. That will help determine whether each factor enables or disables collaboration and what might be done to correct it for future success. Figure 11.1 highlights the factors that affect collaboration.

Leadership

In his book *Organisational Culture and Leadership*[86], Edgar Schein argues that leadership and culture are two sides of the same coin and that culture begins with leaders who impose their own values and assumptions on a group. Powerful and charismatic leaders who have carved an imprint on their organisation with their values and beliefs include Jack Welch at GE, Michael Dell at Dell, John Browne at BP, Terry Leahy at Tesco, Anita Roddick at the Body

Shop, Richard Branson with his Virgin companies as well as Margaret Thatcher and Tony Blair in the way they have led their country in recent times. But what makes a great leader and how does it affect the ability for an organisation to collaborate? Warren Bennis and Robert Townsend wrote about leaders displaying various traits summarised as congruence, consistency, caring and competent[87]. Review the statements in Table 11.2 to see if your organisation (and alliances) has good leadership.

Individuals who score more than 24 points can be considered as strong leaders with the organisation's or alliance's resources right behind them. Leaders who don't demonstrate these traits and score poorly will unlikely have the complete backing and support of their organisation or alliance team. The environment in which people work under poor leaders will be more like the low performing noncollaborative culture expressed earlier where leaders garner no respect and the firm cannot collaborate effectively internally let alone externally. For example, at one organisation going through major change there was a great emphasis on cost reduction and downsizing with policies put in place to manage expenses. However, the board continued to fly first class taking their partners on trips, and generally showed little interest in driving down their personal expenses. This behaviour was not lost on the workers who lost a great deal of respect for their leaders and failed to collaborate on many of the other cost reduction initiatives.

Leaders who score highly are able to motivate and persuade stakeholders to stretch themselves and can bring the organisation to work together. In addition they are also likely to have a flexible style of leadership and management recognising that there are times when stamping and shouting are required and times when a more diplomatic approach would be better served. There are times when decisions should be made democratically, and some circumstances when leaders need to make them unilaterally. A real skill is being aware when to use each one. This comes with experience and is not easily taught.

Table 11.2 Leadership qualification.

Statement	Yes ↔ No	Evidence/comments
Our leaders have an absence of arrogance and keep their personal goals in check as well as ensure that the higher purpose and goals of the organisation prevail.	5 4 3 2 1	
Our leaders are good communicators who demonstrate intelligence and an ability to articulate the issues quite succinctly, preferring to communicate face to face rather than through other mediums.	5 4 3 2 1	
Our leaders can also follow, are good coaches and listeners, as well as being comfortable, giving credit to others and taking the blame when things don't go as planned.	5 4 3 2 1	
Our leaders live the values of the organisation and walk the talk, demonstrating support to others and no mercy for behaviour that compromises the relevant values and beliefs.	5 4 3 2 1	
Our leaders are good at their job and through their competence, consistency and ability to trust in others have earned staff trust and respect.	5 4 3 2 1	
Our leaders value collaboration and encourage alliance working across organisation boundaries internally and externally.	5 4 3 2 1	

Organisation purpose and direction

Earlier chapters have already explored the importance of clarity
on the purpose, strategy and direction of the firm in some depth
but it is worthwhile reiterating its importance as it relates to collaboration. For investors, employees and other stakeholders such as
partners it is important to understand the purpose and strategy so
they can choose whether to support and follow the organisation's
direction. Many individuals choose to join organisations on the
basis of its purpose and what it does, for example admiration for
the purpose of the Body Shop, the NHS and nonprofit organisations such as the Red Cross or Oxfam. In a similar vein, others
choose not to join firms because of their purpose and typical
examples might include tobacco manufacturers and life science
organisations. It is the same with organisations who may want to
be aligned with another organisation's purpose and direction and
seek out that firm for an alliance. On the other hand one organisation may not wish to work with another on the basis of that
organisation's broader motives and purpose being incongruent
with their purpose, or perhaps conflicting with the espoused values
and beliefs.

Values and beliefs

Deal and Kennedy advised that 'values are the bedrock of corporate
culture and provide a common direction for employees guiding their
day to day behaviour'[88]. Strong values in successful companies such
as alliance brands are ubiquitous, easy for everyone to understand and
tune into, and enable motivation for employees to work together in
a consistent fashion toward the common cause. Values and beliefs
include things like the work environment, how people are treated
and engage each other, attitudes towards quality, ethics, and customer service as well as the characteristics noted in Table 11.1.

Many organisations now express their values and beliefs on their websites and in other corporate material. BP, the oil company, has a clear set of values stated on its website and highlights the importance of external relationships as well as performance, people and capability along with health, safety and the environment. It makes the point about '*Mutual advantage:* to conduct our business on a long-term and sustainable basis, founded on relationships that are mutually advantageous and capable of enduring beyond a single transaction.'[89]

Quick and useful ways to ascertain the values and beliefs of an organisation in practice as opposed to those espoused in corporate material include understanding the following aspects:

- How staff are measured and rewarded. For example, if a company states customer or partner satisfaction is an important value yet only measures staff on financial indicators that might send a different signal. Leading alliance brands like Cisco back up its values around customer service and partnering with extensive satisfaction metrics for staff and a part of the reward scheme is based on meeting those targets.
- How staff are treated and empowered. For example, if a company's values espouse trust and speed in decisions yet simple actions take weeks to address, and there are layers of forms or committees to navigate, then the opposite might be true. Many organisations now also have spyware on their computers and operate CCTV inside, perhaps for valid reasons but it might betray the values message.
- How partners and external parties are treated. Some firms now hold award ceremonies and special prize givings as well as the more typical annual reviews and appraisals. Energis, the telecoms company acquired by Cable and Wireless in 2005, held special awards for suppliers that delivered exceptional service. Mike Crone, the Director of Procurement, called it the ABCD awards; Above and Beyond the Call of Duty. This is a neat initiative that

sets out how much Energis valued its suppliers and helps the leading parties stand out from the rest of the crowd, with that behaviour aiding them favourably at contract renewal time.

While strong and clear values are important, there can be risks, for example if they prevent change when change is required maybe because old values and beliefs compromise future organisational goals. An example of this can happen if mature organisations need to partner, when in the past they had been vertically integrated and dominant in their fields. It is sometimes difficult to shake off that past heritage and accept that others may have better skills, ideas and ways of working.

Change takes time and needs to come from the top. What more can your organisation and its leadership do to help install the appropriate values and beliefs and remove those that stifle collaboration and alliance success?

Structure and control

Organisation structure can have an impact on performance and affect collaboration. There are numerous ways to organise businesses all of which have been extensively written about and these include centralisation, decentralisation and a hybrid form. In addition, organisations can be organised around customer lines of business, geographies, product groups and, rarely, core competences. Many individuals now have matrix management environments to contend with where they might have a functional home (e.g. marketing) and a geographic reporting line (e.g. United Kingdom). There are strengths and weaknesses in each approach and some are better for collaboration while others are worse depending on where the organisation is at a point in its lifecycle and its strategic goals. The key elements to consider around this for collaboration effectiveness are:

- How aligned the goals and priorities of the different reporting lines are in practice and how they relate back to the organisation purpose
- Where the primary reporting line is for staff and how their performance is valued and measured
- How decisions are made on paper and in practice, and understanding where the political power lies
- Who owns the profit and loss statement, has the budget for investment and might get fired in the event of failure (there are many people who come forward for credit in the event of success!)

A major element in the success of leading alliance brands is having their alliance resources close to the customers and partners. This is discussed in more depth during the chapter on alliance infrastructure when programme fit and importance is also addressed.

Systems and technology

Systems that reflect the cultures and values can be formal and informal. Formal systems backing up collaborative cultures will include consideration of the way the company communicates, and how people are recruited and remunerated, especially in terms of bonuses and incentives. Technology has helped solve many communication problems but it can also create issues as well. Receiving and responding to 50–100 emails a day as well as trying to do the day job is not easy! Email and instant messaging can be a pain, but as trust builds between individuals there is less need to send formal written communication, and there are other technologies such as Microsoft Sharepoint that are better for teamworking and can act as repositories of knowledge to reduce the amount of email exchange and individual desktop filing. There are also other new and exciting technologies coming onto the market that help improve collaboration and communication especially for remote workers and groups who need to interact in different locations, a common feature of alliances. Webinars, virtual whiteboarding and teleconferences are all tools in the bag that should be considered depending on alliance goals. These can demonstrate compelling returns on their investment as long as they get used in the right manner. Many organisations have invested in technology such as Customer Relationship Management (CRM) yet failed to leverage it, either because of failure to deal with the broader changes needed in other areas such as training and change management, or because the system itself failed to meet the user's needs. Intranets, extranets and shared systems for reporting, filing and managing information are all useful for improving communication and offering greater transparency in activities. In ideal circumstances teams that need to collaborate will co-locate but this is just not practical for many alliances, such as international ventures or where equipment and other assets are located separately. Having effective technology and systems is only as good as the people using them and this is where some fundamental issues around collaboration emerge.

Teamworking and individuals

Alliances are basically about individuals and teams, and how they collaborate and communicate together can determine the success or failure of ventures. As such it is useful to understand how individuals are motivated and demotivated and what affects their behaviour. Maslow, Taylor and others have written at length about motivational theory and individual behaviour from a scientific and theoretical perspective, so this is more an observation of past experience of what works and fails in alliance practice. In basic terms, employers seeking collaborative cultures want employee commitment to the values and purpose of the organisation and high performance behaviours with a team orientation towards delivery of their respective goals and objectives. Employees generally want attractive pay and rewards, job satisfaction, honest and open communication with an opportunity to learn and grow. Leading alliance brands demonstrate real strength in this area. Figure 11.2 outlines the subcomponents that impact individual and teamworking success. Bear in mind this area is challenging when the individual is an employee. It can prove even more difficult when allying with other organisations that may have different approaches towards their employees and create conflict when brought together.

Individual makeup

When looking at individuals, it is normal to understand their capability to execute, perhaps judging by their knowledge, skills, attitude, personal drivers and experience. This aspect is discussed in more depth in Chapter 13 when looking at the specific resources focused on alliances. There are other facets which also affect individuals such as whether they are driven towards goals or away from failure. Threats might work for some staff and incentives may work better for others. In addition, it is useful to try to ascertain the underlying profile of a character. There are many techniques for doing this including Myers Briggs and other personality type tests as well as a good technique for assessing style called Kirton Adaption-Innovation (KAI)[90]. This framework gives an understanding of the source and implications of an individual's differences. It is used to provide insights into how that individual can use their own diversity and that of others positively. This knowledge can then be used in everyday life as well as in specific team situations to improve teamworking and optimise team structure given the nature of the alliance, environment and leadership style.

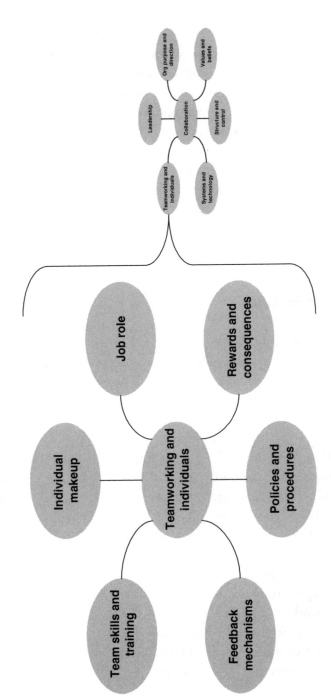

Figure 11.2 Teamworking and individual components.

Other well-known models include Belbin's team roles which look at the preferences individuals have and the type of team role/s they would best play. To ensure a balanced team it would have a Co-ordinator or Shaper (not both) for leader, a Plant to stimulate ideas, a Monitor/evaluator to maintain honesty and clarity, one or more Implementors, Team workers and Resource investigators or Completer/finishers to make things happen.

A very quick and simple (free) test is also to ask the individual what would happen if they were God for a day. Ask, 'what three things would you do and why?' Don't give any preparation time; look for fairly spontaneous answers within a minute or so. Having used it since 1999 in interviews, relationship building and to help understand personal drivers, it can provide a wonderful insight into the character and their frame of mind at that point in time. For example, if the responses come out as being quite selfish, e.g. 'I'll give myself a Prada handbag, a new Ferrari and money for life' (and that was a true response), then the organisation might want to reconsider whether that person is a team player and able to think more holistically! Personal circumstances outside work can also affect behaviour, and with individuals' stress levels increasing it is no wonder organisations are turning to niche solution providers like Whole Being[91] to help their staff become less stressed. Individuals and their national culture can also affect how organisations work together. For example, at a very stereotypical level, Americans can prove to be quite aggressive and keen to get to the finish line without worrying about the process or detail, whereas the Germans will adopt a more analytical and process-oriented approach which can mean fireworks when the two cultures come together!

Job role

The job role in itself can have a significant impact on successful collaboration. Factors to consider here include:

- How challenging the role might be and what the measures of success are. There is a need for stretch goals and targets; however, consideration needs to be given to whether the targets are relevant and achievable. If someone never scores goals they will soon become demotivated and despondent, but similarly if one is always scoring goals it can become a little boring and lose its excitement pretty quickly. Clarity on the measures for success is also important to avoid misunderstanding.
- How well defined the job role is and to what extent others also need to understand the job role as well. Ambiguity can lead to unhealthy gaps or overlaps in project teams and destructive behaviour. A simple way around this is to define the tasks required as will be seen in Part III, but also to consider using the RACI formula for job roles and tasks which highlights who should be Responsible, Accountable, Consulted and Informed.
- The move to matrix structures and multiple reporting lines increases problems of managing external or other pressures, affecting priorities with those of other matrix managers. This is a key issue in alliances as many firms still believe that staff can do alliances as well as their 'day job'. They cannot, at least not to optimum effect. When considering the resources for alliances it is essential to understand what other delivery pressures they might have and what percentage of their time can be devoted to alliances activity.

Rewards and consequences

What gets measured gets managed is an old saying but it is true. Take a close look at how staff are rewarded and encouraged to execute their role with the key metrics they report against, over and above the personal satisfaction of a job well done. As with successful alliances, staff may be more engaged and collaborative when they have 'skin in the game' as well. This could be either incentive (bonuses) or consequence based (salary at risk, or job loss), but with no reason to perform, many sadly don't and this is a common problem in organisations where staff are not under enough pressure or their position is so entrenched there is no reason for them to exert themselves.

One organisation was unclear why sales were not growing in a certain product area. Alongside some basic training issues the primary reason was because the compensation plan did not encourage staff to focus on that product with their clients. Another organisation was trying to drive out costs and improve efficiency in a certain area yet it was not initially prepared to motivate its staff or partners to help out. As a result nothing material happened until it looked at changing the scorecard and reward scheme, and offering a share to the suppliers. Rewarding for cost reduction is a little more difficult than for revenue or margin; however, it can be done once effective criteria around areas such as quality and baseline measures on aspects such as volumes are agreed.

Brightwell encourages its production and clerical staff through spot rewards and suggestion schemes to come up with bright ideas that might help make a difference, and they usually do. Back in the early 1990s the Rank Group held an enterprise and innovation award scheme. A winning UK proposal of treating some suppliers more as alliance partners and working on joint sales and marketing initiatives generated around £1 m per annum incremental cash for Rank in the first project and went onto transform the way it worked with many partners for mutual benefit in subsequent years. The reward for the individual was £5 k holiday vouchers and a weekend away which satisfied the winner and gave a great return on investment for Rank.

From an alliance perspective rewards and consequences can get a little more problematic to address because of dealing with other organisations that may not have the same drivers or motivators especially when the partners are of vastly different sizes.

During creation discussions in one recent alliance, it came to the subject of targets and rewards both for staff in the alliance team and those on its periphery. Despite the organisation expecting significant revenues over the alliance life, it hadn't considered the implications to the frontline staff that were to sell the alliance solution. Worse was to come, the partner had its sales staff motivated to sell a competitor solution! Until this area was addressed and resolved satisfactorily for both sides the alliance struggled to make headway. However, after it was sorted out, the common goals, joint measures and complementary reward strategy helped drive staff behaviour and the alliance went on to deliver towards its potential.

Ensuring that alliance rewards are congruent for both parties and all team members is essential for effective teamworking as well. Many times those who have other priorities act as a bottleneck on performance, and where rewards are incongruent it can spell disaster for some alliances. High flying sales staff in one organisation were motivated to sell large-scale outsourcing solutions and rewarded based on the anticipated revenue of the solution. They didn't care much about the risk and consequential impact to delivery quality or profitability post contract. The majority of their sales bonuses were paid fairly quickly after contract signature. A small amount of the bonus was held back to cover transition challenges but the amount was not enough to outweigh the initial approach that led to the series of problems. As a result various promises were made to customers by the sales staff which much lower paid internal service delivery colleagues could not deliver. It left the customer as well as the delivery team frustrated and the outsourcee facing financial loss on many outsourcing alliance agreements. By changing the way that the sales and delivery team collaborated early on, for example in solution design and due diligence, including having bid proposal qualification gates and making changes to the reward structure to encourage teamworking and a longer horizon on sales commissions, the organisation saw positive improvement.

Rewards can take many forms, from basic salary and share scheme financial benefits to increasing trends around flexible benefits to buy more holiday time, increase pension, health care and of course career development, promotion and learning. Job titles, cars and other status symbols are also important to some and schemes or ceremonies like the Energis ABCD awards also encourage performance. Corporate hospitality, training development and meeting senior company leaders are also attractive options to introduce as are special treatment clubs for top performers. The culture and environment will dictate much of this as well, for example at an aggressive IT sales recruitment firm the charismatic CEO used to drive a high powered expensive sports car and it symbolised success for many of his up and coming ambitious sales professionals. After moving home to be closer to the office he decided that a smaller car would suffice. However, what many staff saw was a removal of a symbol of success and found it quite demoralising. He quickly saw the effect on staff and now drives another high powered expensive sports car!

Michael Armstrong and Helen Murlis wrote the book called *Reward Management*[92] and suggested criteria affecting the design of incentive schemes should take into account that:

- It should be appropriate to the type of work being carried out and the workers employed
- The rewards should be clearly linked to the efforts of the individual or the team
- Individuals or teams should be able to calculate the reward they get at each of the levels of output they are capable of achieving
- Individuals or teams should have a reasonable amount of control over their efforts and therefore their rewards
- The scheme should operate by means of a defined and easily understood formula
- The scheme must be carefully installed and maintained

■ Provision should be made for amending rates in defined circumstances

As described above some people may work more effectively when considering threats and risks acting with 'away from' motivations. The introduction of individual or team-based consequences into rewards systems is therefore of merit in some instances to help focus behaviour alongside 'towards'-based incentives. Before introducing such measures, however, policies and procedures that enable success and training and skills development as well as the tools for optimal performance should be in place to help address gaps in capability and aid productivity.

Policies and procedures

Policies and procedures can take many guises from unwritten rules about working style and approval through to large manuals that take months to read and digest. Those that affect external collaboration the most, based on past experience, outside the communications, rewards and recruitment policies covered above, are the risk management and governance policies. Whether it is audit, compliance or legal functions, someone always has a bad story to tell about how an individual in one of those departments scuppered an alliance or compromised a relationship with noncollaborative tactics and behaviours citing internal policy as the excuse. That does not need to be the case. By building relationships, sharing the business and alliance goals at the idea stage, and understanding their motives and drivers, these functions can add tremendous value. Having worked with legal, audit and risk management on numerous alliances they generally act very collaboratively to help improve results and drive out risks. But they must be engaged early on before making decisions, not in some damage limitation fashion afterwards. Lawyers have a job to protect the company interests and it is no wonder they seek to guard company assets and transfer risks and liabilities to partners in legal contracts. However, by understanding their policies and involving them early as well as working closely with them around the commercial details instead of abdicating responsibility to them, better solutions prevail.

Team skills and training

Another area that is usually not formalised but evolves over time based on past values and beliefs is how teams work together. Individuals usually have knowledge, skills and experience that enable them to achieve their role as alluded to above in individual makeup. However, with more and more tasks being dependent on teaming, not just alliance activities, organisations need to consider whether their employees are adequately prepared for effective teaming. Consider the teaming skills that are shown in Table 11.3. Do the resources operating in alliances hold these skills?

Feedback mechanisms

Providing consistent and transparent feedback on performance can help improve collaboration although there are times when it is useful to have anonymous feedback. In addition to more formal traditional performance reviews and reporting through means such as scorecards, various tools and frameworks exist to aid this area and these include:

■ Individual appraisals and coaching, using both informal means as well as more formal 360° surveys to assess feedback from leaders, followers, customers, suppliers and colleagues whether internal or external. In administering them it is useful to get a balance on feedback, for example if someone wants to make

Table 11.3 Team skills checklist.

Team skill	Held Yes/No
Facilitation techniques and managing group discussions	
Ideas generation, for example brainstorming and mind mapping	
Constructive decision-making and options analysis, for example using qualitative methods like Ed De Bono's six thinking hats alongside traditional cost/benefit analysis	
Problem solving using tools such as cause/effect, SWOT and risk analysis	
Enhanced communication, both written and verbal presentation, as well as collaborative negotiation, listening and dealing with conflict	
International culture and language appreciation especially when undertaking cross-border alliances	
A sense of humour, because things always go wrong somewhere along the line!	

a criticism then they should also try to identify a positive area as well. This is not political correctness, more an effort to get people to think carefully about positive attributes that are all too easily left behind in the wake of negative reviews.

■ Team gatherings looking at best practice and lessons learnt from past activities. Cisco operates a best practice award scheme in its Strategic Alliance group for the best new idea that might help improve partnering success across the organisation. Reuters invited partners to share their practices. This helped build relationships as well as leverage ideas that could have mutual benefit.

As can be seen, collaboration can be a tough nut to crack and there are many factors that affect its success. Deloitte's People & Change practice identified five conditions that have to be present for individuals and organisations to successfully change. They resonate in this field of collaboration:

1. People must have a Purpose they believe in
2. There must be Role models adopting the desired behaviours
3. People must be given the Skills to change and succeed in the future
4. There must be Alignment of key reinforcing mechanisms
5. People must want to change

Alignment of the factors that affect collaboration is essential for success within an organisation. There should obviously be signs the partner can collaborate itself, and when the two partners come together there needs to be understanding of the factors and consideration of whether they can work well in practice as will be seen later in Part III. Tolerance and understanding of an external partner's culture, values and collaboration idiosyncrasies are actually more important than having exactly the same 'culture'. It should be recognised that on occasion differing values and ways of working within an organisation or across alliance partners may sometimes be useful depending upon the goals and objectives. For example, assertive new management and leadership through an outsourcing alliance could shake up a hitherto stale area and transform its results far quicker and better than could be achieved by rearranging the deckchairs internally.

This chapter concludes with a five step team exercise highlighted in Figure 11.3 to ensure that the factors affecting collaboration in the organisation are creating value not destroying it. This is a workshop–based exercise that should take two to three hours to execute steps 1 to 3. The first three steps can be done in parallel but are broken out for ease of understanding.

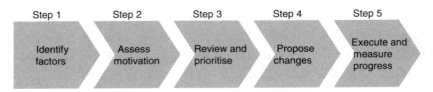

Step 1	Step 2	Step 3	Step 4	Step 5
Identify factors	Assess motivation	Review and prioritise	Propose changes	Execute and measure progress

Figure 11.3 Collaboration challenge exercise.

Step 1 identify factors

Work in small groups to identify the things that affect collaboration in your organisation. Use the factors from Figures 11.1 and 11.2 above as 'header flags' to place findings, spending no more than 5–10 minutes for each factor. If using flip charts then write the comments individually on sticky notes or similar so they can be moved around in later steps. If allocating factors to different teams ensure enough time to share the findings with the group and update as necessary with other observations.

Step 2 assess motivation

During this step consideration needs to be given to whether the factors identified are enabling collaboration. A simple way of considering this is to discuss each one briefly and have three columns to organise the findings as shown in Table 11.4 (assuming this was the flip chart on leadership):

Table 11.4 Leadership factors affecting motivation.

Motivating	Neutral	Demotivating
e.g. passion and drive	e.g. open door policy	e.g. always goes to the corporate hospitality with partners, never takes us

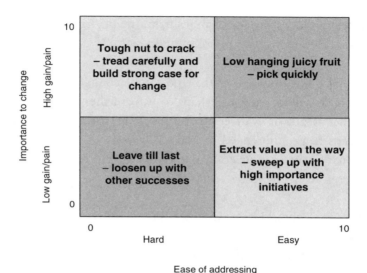

Figure 11.4 Factor priority matrix.

Step 3 review and prioritise

Ranking the findings will help ascertain the degree of importance. A simple but effective way of doing this is to allocate between 0 points (low importance) and 10 points (high importance) in terms of assessing pain or gain, and then a similar approach for ease of addressing with 0 points for hard to address and 10 for easy. This can then be mapped on to a simple 2 × 2 matrix as shown in Figure 11.4.

Step 4 propose changes

Assuming decisions are not made in the workshop session, formal proposals for change might need to be pulled together where key stakeholders are targeted for support towards change. In considering how to make changes from the priority matrix shown in Figure 11.4 consider the following:

- What is within your control and can be changed without reference to others except perhaps to inform them?
- What is out of your control but can be influenced, and who needs to be influenced to make decisions?
- What is out of your control and just cannot be influenced and therefore needs to be accepted?

Proposals should state what needs to change and why, and what the anticipated benefit is, for example higher revenues from alliances, more attractive alliance brand or even reduced staff turnover and greater continuity in initiatives. The potential opportunity costs should also be identified if things stayed the same, for example failed alliances, loss of reputation and increased financial risks. Some changes might not have a direct monetary benefit but wherever possible financial indicators should be used to help demonstrate the impact on the business and any return on investment, financial, reputational or even emotional. Removal of the demotivating factors should be a priority before reinforcement and change to the neutral or motivating factors.

Step 5 execute and measure progress

As with any good change programme, an action plan with clear goals and objectives should be installed along with a communication programme and governance body to measure and report on progress. It should be noted that bringing such factors into awareness for staff and agreeing to make changes or not can be the difference between them staying and re-energising, or realising it is time to move on to pastures new. Past experience suggests that either way all parties win in the end.

Factors affecting collaboration have been covered in some detail during this chapter, yet in reality it has only scratched the surface as regards the body of knowledge in the field of culture and collaboration. Making cultural change, for example to values and beliefs, may be tougher than in any other VIP Map element but leading alliance brands do what it takes for success. Without effective collaboration organisations do not stand much chance of winning with their alliances. Those that do embark on change and see it through successfully will have an edge over their rivals and take another step towards that leading alliance brand status and gaining their desired results and reputation outputs.

## CHAPTER 12

ABILITY TO GOVERN EFFECTIVELY AND MANAGE COMPLEX RELATIONSHIPS

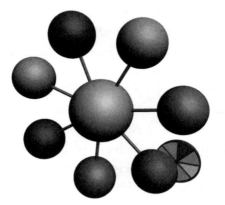

*H*aving an ability to govern effectively and manage complex relationships can help the organisation create value and differentiate it among its peers. However, being unable to demonstrate control and transparency as well as coordinate across organisation boundaries increases risks and may destroy value, especially where alliances are between competitors. There are two facets for consideration under this VIP that will be addressed in more depth and they are:

- The compliance and legislative implications around working with external partners
- The strategic and commercial implications of managing cross-boundary complex relationships

VIEW INCREASING LEGISLATION AS OPPORTUNITY NOT THREAT

Part I highlighted the increasing forces on organisations around legislation and compliance related activity. The Sarbanes Oxley Act 2002 (the Act) in particular gave rise to new legislation concerning internal control (section 404) and improved reporting about off balance sheet activity (section 401). For organisations that have material relationships with external parties this could represent a real challenge. However, for those organisations that embrace the principles of better control it is an opportunity to get greater transparency, increase collaboration and improve activities conducted across the value chain resulting in mutual benefit. At the time of writing, the Operating and Financial Review (OFR) had been shelved by Gordon Brown, the UK Chancellor; however, the principles within it will be reintroduced at some point, and the Combined Code will also get more teeth. Therefore governance around alliances needs to be improved sooner rather than later. Those that do successfully address it early will see alliance brand characteristics emerge, reaping the rewards of being a more attractive partner and less likely to cause financial or reputational risks for partners because of ineffective controls or reporting.

The implications from section 401 of the Act around disclosure of off balance sheet transactions include reporting any arrangements or obligations that might affect the future performance of the firm. Examples affecting alliances include reliance on key partners for sales and distribution, long-term supply guarantees with minimum volumes or exposure to assets that are held by one party, for example outsourcing key business processes or critical component manufacturing. Section 404 of the Act looks at the establishment and maintenance of adequate internal controls and the effectiveness of the controls for accuracy of financial reporting. This is an important point for those organisations that rely on partners because while activities can be delegated, including overseeing the relevant controls, compliance and control accountability cannot be transferred. Part I stated that organisations seek alliances with organisations that have more attractive assets such as core competences, or are better placed than them to execute, perhaps for efficiency and cost reasons. Typical partner selection should look at the capability and controls in place for (say) the provision of the product or service to the agreed quality, service and price standards. There should also be similar principles in place during partner selection due diligence for assessing the financial reporting and controls element to satisfy section 404 and the Combined Code as described in Part III shortly.

How compliant is your organisations alliance activity? Consider the questions in Table 12.1. If you can answer Yes to each question and, this must be stressed, provide sufficient evidence to back it up then your management, auditors and partners are likely to be happy and you are probably adding value from the way partners are governed and managed.

If the answer is No to any of the questions in Table 12.1 then it is likely your organisation is exposed to unnecessary business risks and could be failing to leverage opportunities that arise in each alliance. In Part III we address CSF 3 which is about having effective relationship architectures (ERA) underpinning each alliance. ERA facilitate

Table 12.1   Compliance and controls confidence.

Question	Yes/No	Evidence/ comments
Are material business risks associated with partner activity discussed and addressed with the board and other relevant senior management in a timely fashion?		
Do effective controls systems exist to keep management proactively involved and informed about significant business risks and issues arising from existing partner activity?		
Do processes and tools exist to aid the selection of partners who exhibit effective and complementary controls (e.g. internal audit assessment of partner controls during due diligence)?		
Do the controls and tools used in alliance activity align with the wider organisation risk management and controls frameworks?		
Does the underlying governance architecture associated with each partner/alliance reflect the value and importance of that partner/alliance as well as the relationship maturity and past performance of each party?		

alliance success and mitigate the risk of surprise or failure. Part III covers how to choose appropriate governance structures, build effective governance bodies, and look at the types of policies and controls that might be needed, for example dispute resolution and joint investment.

Figure 12.1   COSO ERM framework[93].

A broader risk and control framework is required for satisfying the legislative implications of the Act and to sit on top of ERA, above all alliance activity, improving both internal controls as well as the controls for partners. The COSO Enterprise Risk Management (ERM) framework as shown in Figure 12.1 is one such solution. This framework is used not just by listed companies; other public sector bodies like the NHS and small to medium size enterprises also use the framework's principles. It was created by the Committee of Sponsoring Organisations (COSO) which is a US-oriented voluntary association supported by the key bodies representing accounting and auditing professionals.

The Institute of Internal Auditors suggests this ERM framework supports value creation by 'enabling management to deal effectively with potential future events that create uncertainty and respond in a manner that reduces the likelihood of downside outcomes and increases the upside'[94]. The framework enables practitioners to consider eight components of risk management at both a strategic and tactical operating level meaning that processes can be managed consistently across internal and external boundaries as well as aligning them to a strategic level. The eight components are:

- **Internal environment:** looking back to the chapter on collaboration many facets about the organisation culture come out here including leadership, values, appetite for risk and how the nature of the internal environment affects risk.
- **Objective setting:** formally establishes the degree and tolerance for risk in the organisation and how much risk the board are prepared to accept in relation to achieving the potential rewards.
- **Event identification:** seeks to differentiate between opportunities and risks, where negative events are considered risks and may affect strategy achievement. Events can come about internally or externally, for example through alliance partner activity.
- **Risk assessment:** applies a financial impact and a qualitative grading and weighting to determine where the priority effort should be focused. Considering impact and probability is the usual approach to conducting a risk assessment, positioning findings as shown in Figure 12.2 using a table similar to that shown in Chapter 10 when conducting risk assessments around assets.
- **Risk response:** considers how best to deal with the risks identified. Measures include whether to monitor, accept,

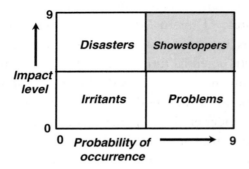

Figure 12.2   Risk assessment matrix.

remove, transfer or insure against certain risks, each option being considered against the risk culture and appetite established earlier.

■ **Control activities:** takes into account the policies and procedures for preventive (proactive) controls and detective (reactive) controls in use and needed, including the use of technology.

■ **Information and communication:** looks at the content, media and frequency of communication to the appropriate stakeholders both in the organisation and where appropriate with its partners.

■ **Monitoring:** assesses the extent to which the previous seven components meet the needs of the business and are effective in their operation. Ongoing and separate evaluations need to be considered, perhaps through the use of objective parties such as internal audit or external advisors.

Implementing the COSO framework will help align the alliance-oriented activities within the organisation and across its partners bringing about better governance, not least with the use of a common language. It will offer greater assurance for the financial reporting and controls activity, as well as helping identify opportunities for commercial improvement in the business and with its partners.

DEALING EFFECTIVELY WITH COMPLEX RELATIONSHIPS

Another major opportunity for commercial improvement and better governance is the way that complex relationships are managed. Failure to govern effectively across internal and external boundaries could give rise to significant risk and missed opportunities, especially if alliances include competitors or potential competitors. A complex relationship occurs when one party has multiple touchpoints with another organisation which address separate activities (for example, more than one alliance). Taking an example where the names of the parties have been changed this case demonstrates the value from managing complex relationships in a holistic fashion.

Jones Service industries had a complex relationship with Smith Global software where the firms dealt with each other across the following dimensions:

- **Customer to supplier:** Jones purchased significant amounts of Smith's software, having a global supply agreement managed by Jones global sourcing team.
- **Supplier to customer:** Smith purchased a relatively small amount of Jones's services and as a result was managed by a telesales team sitting within the small client function of Jones's sales organisation.
- **R&D partner:** Smith was considered a key technology partner for Jones and both organisations invested resources in innovation and new product development as evidenced in various successful collaborations. This alliance activity was managed by Jones technology partners programme.
- **Joint go to market:** both parties were also collaborating in customer facing activities, promoting not only the fruits of the joint technology development but also the broader offerings of both companies. This alliance activity was managed from the Jones client facing alliance office.

The R&D partnership was closely coordinated with the global alliance office; however, the other customer/supplier activity was originally managed in isolation. There was also another key dimension not actively being addressed; the competitive dimension. As Smith had grown and matured, its software started addressing vertical markets and moving into services potentially bringing it into competition with many of its partners, including Jones. This increasing risk and lack of communication internally led to asking some probing questions and identifying some issues around how Jones managed its complex relationships. These questions included those shown in Table 12.2. Consider them in relation to your organisation.

The answer for Jones in most cases was a firm No. As a result of these findings and other driving forces internally Jones introduced a more holistic approach to alliances and complex relationships. It introduced among other things a strategic relationship policy that led to better management of tier 1 (high value high importance) relationships. A strategic relationship manager was appointed from one of the dimensions to lead the overall relationship and coordinate with their opposite number at the other organisation as these partners needed to make similar commitments in terms of resources as well. The strategic relationship manager also had many interested parties to engage with internally. Board-level sponsors were brought in, along with cross-business planning and actions being introduced to raise transparency and look for opportunities to increase leverage, reduce risk and achieve mutual benefit. Alliance results and relationship health-oriented metrics were introduced as well. The benefits from the new programme were:

- Better understanding of the relationship by each interested party, and understanding of how the dimensions could be aggregated for increased mutual rewards including balance of trade and tit-for-tat implications if Smith or Jones decided to divest or invest in one or more dimensions
- Better leverage of the relationship resources and assets improving the ratio of value received to cost of business
- Lower risks and no surprises, including better trade-off management across the dimensions in negotiations with the partner
- Improved satisfaction for all stakeholders

Table 12.2   Complex relationship checklist.

Question	Yes/No	Evidence/comments
Is there a clear fit of some hitherto 'strategic' third parties with the organisation's future strategic direction?		
Has the organisation got awareness of its complex relationships where partners may also be customers and suppliers but especially competitors?		
Are there clear goals, objectives and measures such that success of complex or strategic relationships could easily be measured and reported on to the board?		
Is there effective internal communication and leveraging of mutual opportunities across the whole complex relationship internally and externally?		
Is there a joined-up approach to the commercial and financial management of the relationship, for example with an overarching profit and loss statement and sole executive accountability?		
Has the organisation overcome a fragmented silo approach; not being reliant on personal relationships without supporting structure and process thus mitigating the organisation's exposure to potential divide and conquer routines from other parties?		

Hard and soft measures were introduced and reported on to the board regularly. Results-based measures looked at the operating performance of the various activities between the parties, as well as relationship-based softer measures addressing how the firms worked together. Hard results-based measures took into account typical value creation metrics, for example sales, market share growth, process improvement, product development and cost management. In addition given the competitive dimension Jones also measured potential value destruction, for example where Smith used competitor solutions instead of Jones, or where other party alliances were introduced in Smith's portfolio that might affect Jones's offerings. Jones also started gathering competitive intelligence around the development of Smith's new capabilities or strategic actions which might indicate 'tanks on the lawn' or increased threats of opportunistic behaviour in the future. Softer measures looked implicitly at the trust levels between the parties, the depth and breadth of the relationships and peer-to-peer activity, strategic fit, investments and commitments as signals of future intent, as well as basic aspects like invitations to events and corporate hospitality. All of this information was held in a secure intranet with access levels internally dependent on role and interest in the relationship, and relevant elements shared more widely and easily with partners through extranet access.

One major failing for Jones was that it could not get aligned around P&L (profit and loss) responsibility at a relationship level, so functions and local business units still had the final veto and on occasion acted opportunistically. As such, despite many of the great improvements above, the complex relationship architecture was still somewhat suboptimised. For sustainable success, there needs to be an overarching P&L or commercial responsibility held by the strategic relationship manager or alliance leader.

Becoming organised around relationships led to interesting issues because while Jones was now starting to collaborate internally and create value with some partners, despite the P&L challenges, other partners were unable to do the same and it became a competitive disadvantage for them.

In another example touched on in Part I, HP and BT formed a strategic alliance. The core alliance offers their joint clients organisational agility through the provision of transformational services that span IT infrastructure, applications and support, and network connectivity. The value of the relationship runs into billions of dollars per annum for each party. BT and HP were already working together in a number of other areas as customer or supplier and alliance partner too. This new strategic alliance, while focused on a joint go-to-market initiative also had two other significant workstreams attached to it. Both companies agreed to outsource key business activities to each other in a 'drink your own champagne' story which meant they also became the first case study for their go-to-market alliance activity.

This complex relationship clearly touched many parts of both organisations so some pretty special 'glue' was needed to keep all the parts focused and working towards the broader goals. Both HP and BT demonstrated commitment by appointing full-time high profile leaders to the alliance; Hugh Barton from HP was appointed managing director of the BT relationship and Chris North of BT was chosen as managing director for the relationship with HP. Chris recently passed on leadership of the alliance to Lucy Dimes. Lucy was formally Vice President of Channels and Alliances for BT, indicating the continued importance BT place on their relationship with HP. Each organisation has also invested significant sums in building Integrated Service Architectures to deliver seamless and unique customer service from point of sales engagement back into operational service delivery. The alliance has been running for two years now, achieving many successes and a compelling return on investment, not least with clients such as Hertz and First Group, alluded to earlier.

How BT and HP chose to architect their complex relationship and alliance management activity back into each organisation offers insights into the practical challenges that need to be addressed on the ground in large organisations. HP is primarily organised around business units responsible for service delivery, and geographies which are responsible for sales activity. As such HP is great at local marketing alliances; however, it is not 'alliance centric' when organising for success in complex relationships. Most of the resources sit in the business units and geographies meaning that Hugh and his small dedicated team rely on virtual resources. P&L responsibility is also held by the geography and business units meaning the alliance team has no real ability to change commercial terms or create innovative financial solutions. This means much of the managing director role is spent on relationship management and internal evangelising with those who hold the decision-making capability, in order to create the best environment in HP for success with the BT relationship. Clearly this is working given the successes mentioned above. However, one of the consequences of having virtual teams and little real decision-making ability is that the alliance leadership role can be stifled. For such a complex high value alliance you need a CEO type leader who is used to taking big decisions without the need to consult on every detail. It was no surprise therefore that after two years of successes, despite the organisational challenges, Hugh Barton chose to move on. It could have been easier and perhaps resulted in greater rewards for both parties had HP been able to organise its alliance team more like BT, which is reminiscent of the IBM Siebel case explored in Part I.

Chris North, and now Lucy Dimes, also draws on virtual resources of the wider BT but there are some crucial differences that affect the creation of value and how business is done. While BT have client focused account managers who open doors for the alliance, the alliance also draws from a large dedicated pool of alliance focused specialist sales professionals who report to Lucy. So once the account is opened, Lucy's team can have a far greater influence on success. In addition, Lucy has P&L responsibility for the alliance and can therefore address commercial and financial propositions without the need to align many other stakeholders. This enables the BT relationship team to be far more focused on client activity and driving sales success on their key go-to-market alliance. In terms of working together, both organisations have worked hard to align each organisation. Each has adopted principles expressed in ALLIANTIST ERA Map which is addressed in Chapter 16. Activities executed on the ground to aid collaboration between the two organisations include:

- Early alignment of behavioural and quality expectations of the teams, embedded in aligned sales engagement processes to aid joint working
- Getting both teams in front of the client together early in the sales process, regardless of whether it is a joint sale or one partner effects a prime contractor relationship
- Swift escalation in the event of problems or opportunities that need broader management action
- Alignment of compensation rewards and benefits such that the partners focus on the client need and not on potentially destructive arguments over revenue allocation or pricing strategy

As can be seen, working in global complex organisations and operating such a complex relationship are not without their challenges. However, with commitment and sponsorship from Mark Hurd (HP CEO) and Ben Verwaayen (BT CEO), as well as the energies and desire from both Hugh, Chris and now Lucy, and their teams, the relationship is well placed to deliver ongoing value back to each partner and its clients in the future.

Even if organisations are joined up around complex relationships and have effective governance processes in place, partners may still end up competing head on and threaten the overall relationship. This might happen with Microsoft and Cisco, for so long allies and close partners. As their markets mature and the ongoing drive for growth continues, both organisations appear to be bumping into each other in areas such as security and communications networking. As a result some observers have questioned whether that competitive behaviour is starting to adversely affect some of the relationship dimensions, not least because Microsoft purchased key technology from a competitor to Cisco[95]. One thing for sure is that both parties will be making complex relationship decisions of this nature with their eyes wide open and not operating in a silo-oriented fashion.

MANAGING RECIPROCITY

For those organisations that are able to get joined up and demonstrate leading alliance brand behaviours, not just in collaboration but in governance and coordination too, it can provide another key asset to use for value creation. Imagine the opportunity for increased reciprocity and potential to further embed relationship and alliance activity in a key partner organisation. Things to bear in mind in this regard where more eggs are put in one basket include:

- Each initiative should add value in its own right, and strength in one dimension or alliance should not necessarily mean the organisation allows substandard performance in another dimension. Unless otherwise agreed (e.g. to help learning) the partner should be capable of providing the other required services or products at least as well as competitors and substitutes.
- Business and operational risks should not increase as a result of further integration and cross-business engagement. They may actually be a valid form of risk reduction. For example, increasing a partner's dependency by buying their goods and services could positively affect their likelihood of them not competing against you, effecting a 'balance of trade' approach to business.
- Each separate initiative, alliance or relationship activity should ideally stand on its own legal and commercial footing. Having

master frameworks and relationship business plans may, however, be sensible for longer-term relationship activity and show strong commitment.

Jones, BT and HP are not alone in addressing complex relationships in a sensible manner and the principles presented above work well for most organisations, except perhaps those that need to maintain clear Chinese walls on certain competitive dimensions, and or have potential issues around anticompetitive trading or possible collusion threats. Legal advisors should be consulted before introducing any form of complex or strategic relationship management framework that could be interpreted as anticompetitive or aiding collusive behaviours.

To summarise, increasing legislation is pushing firms to adopt more effective governance and should be seen as an opportunity, not a threat. Those firms that demonstrate alliance brand traits with strong controls and collaborative behaviours will have an attractive asset to differentiate themselves against others who may just seek to meet the controls guidelines, if at all. Where complex relationships are in place, being joined up and acting more holistically across the value chain can also bring greater rewards and mitigate the risks of competitive threat and subsequent value destruction.

So far the VIP Map has addressed the elements that create or destroy value in alliances at an organisational level. The last organisational level element is the alliance infrastructure itself. Chapter 13 addresses the eight alliance infrastructure aspects that can make or break alliance success.

EFFECTIVENESS OF
ALLIANCE INFRASTRUCTURE

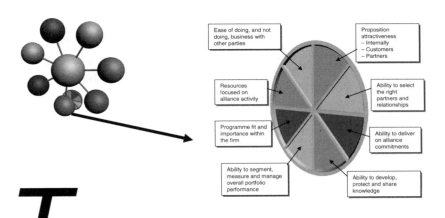

T his is the final part of the VIP Map – effectiveness of the
alliance infrastructure. Alliance infrastructure is the foundation for
a formal alliance programme and contains eight interdependent
elements which are:

1. Ability to segment, measure and manage overall portfolio performance
2. Programme fit and importance within the firm
3. Resources focused on alliance activity
4. Ease of doing and not doing business with other parties
5. Proposition attractiveness for the organisation and its customers and partners
6. Ability to select the right partners and relationships
7. Ability to execute on commitments
8. Ability to develop, protect and share knowledge

How explicit and mature these elements become in practice should be based on how dependent the organisation is on its alliances both now and in the future, and to what degree the organisation wishes to increase its reputation and results by building leading alliance brand characteristics. Consider the questions in Table 13.1 to assess whether your organisation needs to get smarter about its alliance infrastructure.

If the answer to any of the questions in Table 13.1 is Yes or you don't know, then the organisation's alliance infrastructure may need more serious investigation and investment before it can deliver optimal returns. Alliance brands take this part of the VIP Map seriously and invest for success. Many organisations seek quick wins and don't invest as necessary so fail to achieve the optimal rewards. As a further consequence, the better alliance staff will defect to organisations with alliance brands, or those who commit to build alliance brands, where their efforts can be valued more tangibly and their careers can progress more effectively by being winners.

ABILITY TO SEGMENT, MEASURE AND MANAGE OVERALL PORTFOLIO PERFORMANCE

One of the first tasks to undertake when building a formal alliance programme is to try to identify what is in the extended enterprise

Table 13.1   Fitness of alliance infrastructure.

Question	Yes/No	Evidence/ comments
Alliances have a significant impact on business success now or the firm commits to use alliances more strategically in the future yet the infrastructure is not effective		
Competitors are becoming active with alliances and the industry starts changing shape to the extent your organisation may be locked out from networks in the future		
Conflict starts arising with or among existing partners as a result of your organisation's actions		
There is never enough time or resources to meet promises so alliance results and organisation reputation are put at risk		

alliance 'portfolio' already. This means finding out about current alliances, their contribution, risks and the rationale for continuing their support. Many firms are not able to access key information easily which is a high risk, yet a good 'snapshot' picture of the portfolio can be captured quickly in a simply created database which will help inform future actions. Some of the questions to ask about alliance portfolio performance include those shown in Table 13.2.

If the answer to any of the questions in Table 13.2 is No then there are risks of value destruction, partner conflict and opportunistic behaviour. In addition there may be serious issues over financial reporting for listed organisations as demonstrated in the previous chapter. Alliance brands answer Yes to each question above.

Table 13.2 Understanding alliance portfolio performance.

Question	Yes/No	Evidence/comments
Is there a consistent understanding across the organisation about alliance terminology, role and the opportunities and threats vis-à-vis other relationships such as supplier, customer, channel partner etc.?		
Is there clarity on how many alliances the organisation has and needs, broken down by alliance type, value and importance?		
Can the value of the total alliance portfolio and its contribution in terms of overall business performance be easily measured?		
Can the contribution (financial and nonfinancial) and risks from each alliance be easily accessed and reported?		
Can the total cost (and ROI) from alliance activity be measured and reported easily?		
Are resources allocated to alliances and partners managed based on the value and importance of their contribution back to the firm strategy?		
Is basic information about alliances and partners easily accessible to key stakeholders, e.g. sponsors, contact details, scope and goals, and current performance?		
Can positive/negative trends in alliance and portfolio performance be quickly identified and addressed in relation to their impact on firm strategy and direction?		
Is there consistency in how alliance partners are able to represent their relationship with the firm?		

Identifying relationships

The strengths in looking across the value chain to address complex relationships have been highlighted in the previous chapter and similar principles apply in terms of assessing the overall portfolio. In building a portfolio, existing customers, suppliers and resellers should be relatively easy to identify because of the accounting transactions. Many organisations have already undertaken category sourcing campaigns or channel reviews in recent years which should mean that many details are already held. However, 'sell-with' joint go-to-market alliances or less formal but nonetheless important ties may prove harder to spot because revenues rarely flow between the firms and wider investigation may be necessary.

Collecting basic details such as what the relationship or alliance is for, its scope (products, geographies, markets, clients), who manages it internally and what contribution it makes will then help portfolio segmentation. A simple portfolio map might look like Figure 13.1, a high-level framework put together for one client that saw the benefit of looking holistically across its portfolio. In most organisations relationship portfolios will still be structured in a silo-oriented fashion by function, if at all.

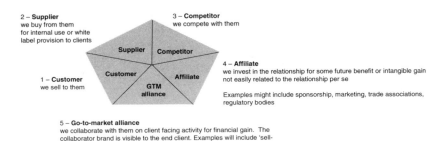

Figure 13.1   Portfolio map.

Segmentation

Categorising and segmenting partners based purely on financial metrics may miss key information which could affect achievement of strategic goals. For example, Cisco Strategic Alliances Programme takes into account the position that its products and partners play in the technology adoption lifecycle, as expressed in the chapter on strategic choice. In addition it seeks industry leaders for its portfolio and requires long-term investments in order to create breakthrough propositions in new markets as well as pre-empt competitive threats. Similar principles apply to segmentation across the portfolio but go-to-market alliances are more complex than other alliances and criteria to help construct a well-segmented portfolio mean two key factors need to be taken into account:

1. The **type** of alliances needed, in terms of what assets you want to access, to complement the organisation's assets and help address gaps in capability. The earlier strategy and core competence work will help answer this question as will answering questions such as 'what else does the customer need to purchase in order to get full benefit from our product or service?' This is the starting point for whole product modelling which is described in more detail on the section below on proposition attractiveness, and in much more depth in Part III.
2. The **value and importance** of alliances and partners. A simple way to determine this is to assess (a) and (b) below and plot them as shown in Figure 13.2.
    (a) How you measure value from a financial perspective; is it revenue, profit, cost or another metric that drives strategic goals?
    (b) What else is important nonfinancially? Some organisations have many weighted characteristics whereas others have just a few without weighting. Examples of aspects to consider include strategic fit, investments required, risks and

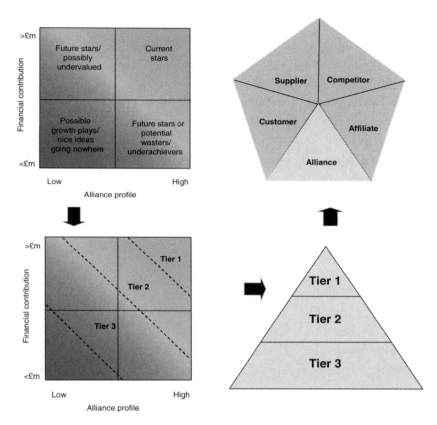

Figure 13.2   Value and importance mapping.

dependence, degree of integration needed, and partner brand value.

Some organisations have more or less than three tiers depending on their needs. The tiering is useful to help segment in terms of value and importance as expressed above, but it is also essential to help differentiate resources and allocate assets more effectively.

Being able to segment the alliance portfolio demonstrates a number of key strengths for the firm. These include having:

- A good understanding of the varying values and importance of each alliance enabling effective allocation of resources and assets into managing the alliances, restricting supply where appropriate to help stoke demand as well.
- Effective categorisation of the alliance types and volumes needed to execute the firm strategy, sending clear messages on portfolio fit and role to the partner community and other stakeholders. It also highlights opportunities for broader network alliances and better management of issues such as channel or partner conflict.
- An ability to use the segmentation and categorisation of alliances as an asset in negotiations, offering greater benefits for partners operating at higher levels.
- Strict criteria to help alleviate potential legal challenges from substandard 'wannabe' partners who fail to offer the right skills, capabilities and assets required to meet the threshold set by the firm.
- The opportunity to compare alliance activity across the firm value chain (e.g. supply side versus sales side) and look more broadly at the industry value chain dynamics to see where value might be migrating to and from.
- The ability to identify where leading practice occurs and share this more widely to ensure mistakes made by one group are not repeated by others.
- The opportunity for optimising alliance returns, and restructuring or even closing out ineffective relationships and alliances avoiding financial and reputational risks.

Brightwell, being a focused SME, does not need to characterise its few alliances in too formal a fashion but in essence it has design and development, supply and sales-based alliances. The alliance types sought by large organisations, like Reuters, Cisco and others, are more complex given the size and nature of its business. For Reuters, as described on its website[96], its 500 partners include content, channel, technology, service and supply partners. Cisco's channel partner alliance programme has even more structure and also looks at a partner's market access and position, the skills held and volume of resources available to pull through Cisco products. Table 13.3 highlights information from Cisco's website showing how it categorises partners. The website goes on to express the benefits available for attaining certain levels of performance and certification.

Table 13.3   Cisco channel partner programme structure[97].

Partner type	Comments
Cisco Registered Partner	Being a Registered Partner is a requirement of becoming a Cisco Certified Partner and/or Cisco Specialised Partner
Cisco SMB Select Partner	The Cisco SMB Select Partner designation is designed to recognise Cisco Channel Partners who have a focused business practice selling into the small and medium sized business market
Cisco Specialised Partner	The Cisco Specialised Partner programme allows organisations to develop its expertise in technologies, solutions and services. Specialisation is required in order to qualify for the Certified Partner programme.
Cisco Certified Partner	The Cisco Certified Partner programme integrates the technology focus of Cisco channel specialisations, flexible individual career certification requirements, customer satisfaction tools and pre- and post-sales support capabilities. Three levels of certification differentiate organisations and these are Gold (highest level), Silver and Premier

Not all firms are as structured as Cisco and Reuters although organisations like IBM, Siebel, Oracle and other large technology firms recognise the importance of structuring their portfolio effectively, because most have hundreds or thousands of partners, many of which actually underperform. Deloitte Consulting in the UK adopts a slightly different approach to sell-with and sell-through alliances. It has tight ties with a few vendor alliances such as Siebel and SAP (tier 1 partners) to help drive its system integration practice. Other alliances tend to be more opportunistic, based around meeting a specific client need and have little investment in proactive relationship building or market making initiatives. Part of the reason for this is cultural where the partner owners are keen to keep operating costs down and profits high on a short-term reporting basis. It is also down to Deloitte's elevated position in the client supplier model where it mainly pulls alliance business through rather than alliances pull business for it, so it is the dominant partner and can to some degree act how it pleases with 'partners'.

From a sourcing and supply alliance perspective, typical sourcing portfolio structures would look at the organisation spend and business risk as shown in Figure 13.3. Alliance candidates would generally be found on the right-hand side of the matrix where greater mutual benefit is likely to be had from working more collaboratively and under less adversarial conditions than traditional category and commodity sourcing behaviours.

Once alliances are categorised and reviewed (ideally reviewed by using ALLIANTIST PARA Map shown in Part III) it is possible to make proposals about investment, divestment or maintenance of alliances. An agreed action plan should be set against each alliance, to ensure the firm can further leverage the alliances it wishes to retain and grow, divestments happen professionally and new requirements are identified where there are gaps in the portfolio. This exercise should also look to the broader relationships in the overall portfolio, for example a customer might make a good 'go-to-market' alliance partner as well.

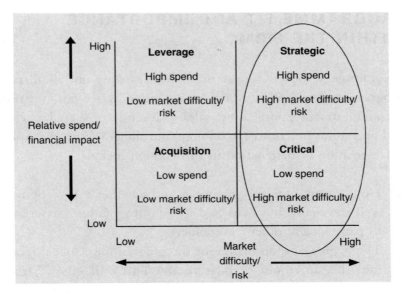

Figure 13.3   Typical supplier portfolio.

Information about alliance portfolios can get dated very quickly if not maintained, so regular alliance reviews and performance monitoring is essential. The depth of assessment and frequency of review should be determined by the value and importance of the alliance. For example, tier 1 alliances might have weekly or monthly face-to-face reviews and annual health checks from an independent advisor; whereas tier 3 alliances may just have bi-monthly reports submitted outlining performance for that period. Having taken the time to build a formal portfolio, effort should be made to keep the information up to date to enable effective reporting both in terms of governance and performance delivery. For some organisations this can be as simple as managing an Excel spreadsheet, whereas for others with large volumes of partners and high dependency on alliances, a more complex alliance management technology system may be required, which is explored in more depth later in this chapter.

PROGRAMME FIT AND IMPORTANCE WITHIN THE FIRM

Programme is used in a loose sense here because not all alliance programmes are explicit. Many are activities carried out as part of corporate strategy, purchasing, sales, marketing or shared services and operations functions and do not stand alone. Factors that affect value creation or destruction in this context include:

- How 'formal' the programme is and whether it is recognised well internally and marketed in a positive fashion externally to partners and other stakeholders.
- The degree of sponsorship for the programme. Does it report into the storeroom or boardroom? This will give a strong indication of the importance of alliances as viewed by senior management as well as how actively involved they get in areas such as sponsorship.
- How the alliance programme compares to other strategic choice activities such as the 'make' and 'buy' functions. For example, is the M&A team well established and does it have a close reporting line into the CEO while the alliance programme sits in a backwater somewhere without formal recognition? If the answer is yes then that also sends signals about what the preferred modus operandi is for the firm in executing strategy.
- The worldview and operating paradigm for the leadership also affects the degree of support for alliances. Leadership was addressed in the chapter on collaboration but if the CEO and her team have a background in M&A or organic growth then alliances may remain tactical or a poor cousin to the methods they prefer.
- The lifecycle of the organisation and its external environment will also have an effect on whether a formal programme is required and if its profile and importance need to be raised.

■ The profit and loss (P&L) ownership and decision-making authority of the programme.

Consideration should be given to the additional value gained from investing in and formalising an alliance programme, appointing an alliance programme director and raising its importance both internally and externally. It is clear from the independent research and past experience that leading alliance brands have dedicated alliance functions. Cisco, IBM, Eli Lilly, Reckitt Benckiser and others who exhibit leading alliance brand characteristics operate with dedicated alliance functions. This formality and infrastructure enable strong and positive messages to be sent inside and outside the organisation about the importance of alliance contributions to strategic objectives. Other benefits from formalising alliance programmes include offering a new career path for staff.

There can be challenges in constructing a business case for formalising alliance programmes. Moving from (say) a direct sales model to one including 'sell-with' and 'sell-through' is not just about the financial modelling of growing the revenue stream and incurring lower costs, it also involves a significant impact on the collaboration mindset and operating practices of the firm. Similar principles apply to other functions such as procurement where they will have a dominant operating paradigm that might not be congruent with collaborative alliance management. As such, change is likely to be needed in many of the areas identified in the chapter on collaboration.

One area for thoughtful consideration is where the alliance programme should sit and report in the firm hierarchy. Leading alliance brands have a very senior reporting line for their programme director, with many reporting to a board or executive member. In addition, it might make no initial sense to include strategic supplier alliances under a sales reporting line, but just giving it to procurement might also be wrong. Consider the existing reputation and results of the procurement function and the goals of the alliance programme. Are they congruent? For example, has that function previously operated in an arm's length adversarial short-term manner, focused on price reduction? If so then internal customers and external partners might well be concerned about whether procurement is the right home for strategic alliances, even if one of the goals is to reduce cost alongside (say) improving service. Similarly if introducing an indirect sales model or seeking collaboration with partners for the first time, is a direct sales channel function the right keeper of the alliance relationships? The answer could be yes and no in both instances; it depends on the leadership style, metrics for success and the other factors high-lighted in the chapter on collaboration. The take-away message is don't just 'tack' an alliance programme on to an existing function without carefully considering the implications.

Another important factor to consider around structuring alliance programmes is the structure and location of the alliance programme resources. Some of the factors affecting structure and control were discussed in the chapter on collaboration. There are three ways to design and position such a programme and these are:

■ **Centralised:** where the programme is owned and controlled from one function perhaps operating to consistent policies and procedures. It might leverage global scale and optimise resources although it may not always be close to its customers or swift in responding.
■ **Decentralised:** may mean the programme is a loose affiliation tying the alliance operation together, if at all. Strengths in this model are likely to be better local knowledge, faster response and a closer relationship with customers and partners, perhaps even co-locating with them. The downsides are that scale and learning may be compromised and synergy from other business units missed.
■ **Hybrid:** a more typical operating model to take the strengths of both the centralised and decentralised model is the Centre

Led Action Network (CLAN) where the Centre leads but has its resources distributed close to the customer. This is fine in many organisations although consideration needs to be given to issues around 'Centre Led'. In many devolved organisations the last thing they want is to be 'Centre Led' when they own their P&L and make decisions locally. At one organisation a FLAN was introduced to counter potential issues. This model was 'Federation Led' where a small hub of excellence was established in the corporate centre in a strategic capacity to develop and coordinate best practice as well as aid the business units and regions in their alliance activity. Decisions were still made locally by P&L owners although shaped considerably with the influence and alliance expertise from the small hub.

In terms of purely local alliance activities, a consistent FLAN programme across the regions and business units means leverage of expertise and aggregation of assets for mutual reward where appropriate. It also offers consistent terminology, shared experiences and enables cross-boundary measures, reports and league tables, highlighting opportunities, trends, issues and threats early in the cycle. Headcount would also be optimised as a result of sharing experiences, and having (say) one lead alliance manager for one global partner, rather than many, and internal measures and ratios (e.g. heads:alliances under management, contributed revenues:partner) could highlight performance issues quickly, from either the partner or internally.

The small support hub would aid execution and be responsible for facilitation, coordination and advising on best practice across the organisation, as well as identifying synergies that could be harvested from relationships within the other businesses (as outlined in the chapter on complex relationship management). Selection of the reporting line and operational home for the support hub will have a key influence on the success of any FLAN or CLAN structure as expressed above. Differing central group/

parent department objectives and incongruent operating philosophies could reduce buy-in and support from those it is designed
to help. It is also important to reiterate that the principles of the
FLAN mean that the decision-making power for alliance activity
would be with the federations and not in the centre per se, although
the federations and centre would ideally work closely together
with congruent goals relating back to the organisation's strategic
intent.

RESOURCES FOCUSED ON ALLIANCE ACTIVITY

At the start of 2006 alliance management has evolved considerably
as a discipline compared to just a few years before. However, there
is no formal qualification for an alliance practitioner although this
might change in the future with alliance trade bodies such as the
Association of Strategic Alliance Professionals (ASAP) looking to
formalise the discipline and offer types of individual accreditation.
Alliance accreditation has some merit, as without the appropriate
resources underpinning alliance activity, value will be destroyed
not created so more needs to be done in this regard. The jury is
out on whether a formal standalone alliance qualification for individuals will take off and if so how; at least in the short term, but
anything that helps raise the standards of alliance activity is to be
applauded. Companies want to do business with other companies
so the organisation should also receive accreditation, hence alliance
brand and an emerging model explored in the final chapter called
alliance brand index.

There are already many function and trade specific qualifications available for individuals. Does being a purchasing manager
with a CIPS qualification or a marketing manager with a CIM
qualification mean that that individual is well placed to create or
manage an alliance? Possibly not with that alone, valued as they

are in their particular fields. It is the same with strategy professionals, project management, sales, legal, accounting and operations resources too with their respective professional bodies. None
of those qualifications currently addresses the field of alliances in
a manner that would give a seasoned alliance director confidence
that that person could execute effectively in practice. Many
universities and further education establishments understand the
growing importance of alliances and have invested in creating
alliance-based modules as part of other courses such as masters
degrees and this is a positive step forward. Henley Management
College is a leader in this regard, and Leicester University, like
others, offers alliance modules as part of its distance learning
MBA.

Transferring from one primary discipline like procurement
into strategic alliance activity does not always end in success,
however. Take the example of Company A who were trying to
penetrate a new market with their software. It was determined
they needed to ally with an established player (Company B) to
gain access to clients and complete the product offering such that
it would be more attractive for clients to buy from them in comparison to others. The cost of entry for Company A was around
£1m, some of which needed to be spent with Company B in order
to integrate the offering. The market opportunity was worth tens
of millions in revenues per annum for both parties and would help
defend business in adjacent markets as well.

Company A decided it needed some help in selecting the right
partner and structuring the alliance. Procurement provided an
experienced negotiator who was interested in alliance management to support the existing strategy, sales and product specialists
in the creation team but things started to go wrong immediately.
In the partner selection process, his focus was more on using traditional competitive tendering techniques, for example using a
boiler plate procurement tender with adversarial terms specified.
Key information was withheld. In addition, when it came to

collaborative negotiation with the preferred partner, emphasis was made on cutting the investment costs of Company A into Company B, and little energy was spent on introducing more innovative mechanisms to ensure both parties were aligned on the bigger picture of revenue growth and market share. The credibility of Company A suffered as a result, the relationship between the two potential partners never recovered and the alliance failed before it sold its first proposition. The alliance team was disbanded and staff went back to their day jobs having missed a good market opportunity. In reflecting on why the relationship soured and the alliance failed it was interesting to note that not only did the procurement negotiator display inappropriate behaviours, the wider team also failed to manage the issues and there were structural factors that affected the organisation's ability to collaborate. These included misaligned objectives, for example procurement was measured on cost reduction yet this was a revenue growth alliance, and lack of organisation commitment to devoting resources to the alliance meant poor governance with staff having other priorities and no consequences in the event of failure.

Contrast that experience with a better one also involving a procurement professional. Company C had a poor reputation with its purchasing staff, internally and externally. Against the odds, it successfully negotiated a key client facing outsourcing alliance that involved cross-department teamworking led by purchasing. This successful integration of operations, sales, marketing, customer services and purchasing led to a feasibility study sponsored by the board into how the purchasing professional could add value to the client facing alliance relationships typically created by the sales and marketing teams. It was an area never before touched by anyone with a purchasing background. In order to improve the probability of success, the purchasing professional moved into the sales and marketing team, dropped the 'purchasing' job title and had a reward package that was congruent with the goals and objectives of the sales team. Inside six weeks, using experiences and practices redeveloped from her purchasing background she had transformed a poor performing alliance with a complementary player such that the annual joint sales target in one product area was hit inside the first quarter of her contribution. The feasibility study was deemed an early success so a formal programme was launched and it grew into a global proposition.

There are also many examples of success and failure when sales, marketing or other professionals attempt to engage in alliances especially when needing to collaborate on joint selling initiatives. Egos get in the way and arguments can arise regarding which organisation takes the revenue as it affects personal bonuses. There are some practising alliance professionals who suggest that direct sales professionals should not move into sales-based alliance management because the strengths that caused their success in direct selling would be their downfall in indirect sales alliances. But that is too much of a generalisation and a deeper understanding is required of the resources needed for success.

Getting SACKED is necessary for success

So what made the difference in the resources between the two cases above and what makes a great alliance professional? It is more than functional home, individual qualifications and the issues around collaboration that were addressed earlier although clearly these are very important. From an individual resource perspective it is about getting SACKED, which won't happen if the right capabilities are held! SACKED stands for Skills, Attitude, Character, Knowledge, Experience and Drivers as seen in the template in Table 13.4. Consider trying to complete the template based on your own experience before reading further.

It is also worthwhile to step back and see what alliance practitioners and the supporting cast need to do in practice as that will determine the SACKED backbone. To understand the tasks at a

Table 13.4   SACKED template.

Skills	Attitude	Character	Knowledge	Experience	Drivers

high level over a generic alliance lifecycle consider three key stages: Investigation, Creation and Execution. These stages make up ALLIANTIST ICE Map which will be discussed in more depth during Part III. The distribution and type of resources required for success will change for each stage of the lifecycle as can be seen in Figure 13.4, therefore the SACKED capabilities required will change as well.

There are four key types of resource for effective alliance delivery and alliance brands have this distribution of resources in their alliance activity. These are:

- Sponsorship
- Specialist support resources
- Alliance delivery resources
- Alliance management resources

Sponsorship

Sponsorship is an important role for alliance success, and it should have its own role definition or charter that a sponsor signs up to before taking office. Selection of a high profile effective and relevant sponsor signals importance and profile to the internal stakeholders and can get it off on the right track. At the Investigation

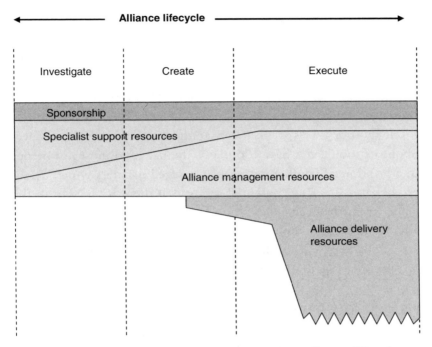

Figure 13.4 Illustrative resource distribution over alliance lifecycle.

stage sponsors harness internal resources and create the environment from which the alliance starts to emerge. They break down barriers and ensure the team remain focused on the task. During the creation stage a powerful sponsor can be a real asset in alliance negotiations with prospective partners. With the appointment of a strong sponsor, partner prospects can feel more confident in the alliance importance and sense a greater probability of success, encouraging them to invest more effort. In addition, a strong high profile sponsor on one side will increase the likelihood of a peer from the other side. Sponsors, with their strong communication and influencing skills are also useful to help overcome barriers and look laterally for solutions that evade the alliance teams on the ground. Sponsors will launch the alliance engaging in press and PR where necessary. During the execution stage sponsors from both sides will meet regularly both formally and informally and help develop trust and respect between the organisations. They will also take a strategic role leading major alliance governance reviews and assisting when disputes or issues require escalation internally or externally. Sponsors hold SACKED capabilities as shown in Table 13.5.

If sponsorship is weak it can compromise the whole alliance. Sponsors should not have too many alliances and must not be put in a position of conflict between sponsored partners which might erode trust. Question potential sponsors if there is no 'skin in the game' from them and they don't stand to gain or suffer from the alliance success or failure. One way of managing sponsors who repeatedly let the team down is to objectively measure and report on sponsor contribution as part of alliance reporting. Given their seniority it can be difficult to terminate poor performers. Changing sponsors surprisingly mid-alliance can send the wrong signal to partners, for example suggesting the alliance is now less important than it used to be. Good practice is to review sponsorship annually as part of a broader alliance health check and ensure that it still makes sense for all parties to maintain the same sponsors.

Specialist support resources

Depending on the type of alliance as well as its value and importance, a range of different support resources may get engaged in an alliance during its investigation, creation and execution stages. The teaming skills and collaborative culture behaviours reported earlier are essential for optimal alliance performance. Tasks that would be conducted at each alliance lifecycle stage might include a need for:

- **Investigation:** strategic planning, financial modelling and scenario analysis to help consider strategic fit, make, buy, ally

Table 13.5 SACKED capabilities for sponsors.

Capability	Evidenced by
Skills	Leadership, diplomat, strategic, analytical, great communicator, negotiator and listener. Excellent decision-making. Strong networker and relationship builder.
Attitude	Confident and objective. Focused on bigger picture and how the alliance will deliver to it. Results driven and someone who makes things happen. Teamwork is king. Longer-term mindset. Always available to help the team break down barriers and navigate obstacles. Doesn't get in the way of operational activity, and trusts the team to deliver. Curious and challenging but fair and consistent.
Character	Senior figurehead in organisation and ambassador for alliance both internally and externally. Well respected in relevant industry, likely to be an influential leader both inside and outside the organisation.
Knowledge	Intimate industry and company knowledge as well as good understanding of partner and target audience. Greater awareness of confidential organisation issues not yet evident to alliance team.
Experience	Would have been there and done it before, a successful business person with experience of how collaboration and alliances can make a difference.
Drivers	Strong vested interest in successful outcome, possibly with macro P&L accountability. Recognition and rewards of bigger picture success as opposed to alliance results per se.

implications, commercial impact and risk analysis. Solution and alliance design architects, both technical and commercial, would also aid the build of a business case for proceeding to the creation stage.

- **Creation:** commercial negotiation and technical designers to lead the alliance creation stage with both the sponsor and alliance manager taking a keen interest. Financial and tax advisory specialists would help shape the final commercial terms. Legal support would ensure that the company was crafting a suitable contract and managing its risk in accordance with the desired risk and alliance goals. Human resources support may be necessary to address staff transfer activity and construct relevant reward strategies to encourage alliance success. There is also merit in engaging support resources from groups such as audit and risk management to help both internal alliance design and also partner due diligence, especially if the firm is subject to compliance legislation described earlier such as Sarbanes Oxley. During launch there may be a need for marketing and PR support.

- **Execution:** specialist support has a small but nonetheless important role to play during this period. Support roles may include lawyers and accountants providing ongoing advice to the alliance manager around legal or commercial developments. Audit or a similar team possibly of independent advisors may also support the alliance manager and sponsor with programmed and periodic reviews. During renewal or termination it is likely that the commercial negotiators would reappear, although for renewal they would take much more into account from the alliance manager's operating experience with the partner than during the original creation stage activity.

The challenge in small and medium sized organisations is that they lack depth in some of these areas so one person or a small team has to take on multiple tasks which they may not be best placed to execute. There are also potential distractions that can take key executives away from their business as usual activity. In this case consideration should be given to external support because the consequences of failed or poorly constructed alliances (e.g. losing assets or carrying too much risk) can far outweigh any initial cost saving. The upside to a small team is that decisions can get made quickly and there are fewer cross-company conflicts to worry about.

In large organisations the problems can be quite different but require a similar solution through the use of external support. These organisations have a broader specialist skill set to call on, particularly for addressing high value important alliances although they may be drawn from roles where they have other tasks to focus on. That can sometimes also mean sizeable project teams, lots of personalities and competing priorities with multiple collaboration conflicts as shown within the failure case study described earlier in this section. The opportunity costs can be huge including delays bringing the alliance to launch, poorly structured agreements and damaged relationships affecting trust and productivity between the parties.

Alliance delivery resources

These resources are the ones that deliver at the pit face and either please or upset the end customer. Whether it is selling the joint go-to-market alliance products, delivering outsourcing services or assembling partner products in a shared factory, these people need to be alliance advocates. They need to be aware of and encourage support for the alliance goals and be motivated to see them come to fruition. Clients are tired of being sold the benefits of a great alliance and actually getting the delivery of products or services that don't actually fit together well in practice. So many alliances have failed to deliver the anticipated value to their

partners because of ineffective focus on these staff. The preparation and launch period of the alliance is a crucial time for
making sure that these delivery resources buy in and execute
well. Strong communications, marketing and PR are essential to
sell the alliance to these stakeholders, but of more importance is
giving them the tools and a reason to support it, whether that is
through changing job objectives, removing other tasks or addressing rewards and incentives more fully described in the chapter
on collaboration.

Alliance management resources

Sometimes described as superhuman, great alliance managers are
like hen's teeth. They are hard to find. This is not a part-time role
or one for failed sales staff, poor operations resources or ineffective
supply chain managers. Managing alliances can be similar to
running a business where the need for influence and credibility is
huge because the in-house delivery teams don't always have a
direct reporting line and many may work for the partner as well.
Alliance management should be considered a major challenge and
opportunity for an organisation's brightest stars with handsome
rewards on offer as a result. In this context the term alliance
manager means the lead person responsible for the performance of
the alliance after launch and charged with execution of its goals
and targets. They are measured on the alliance success, and rewards
would be based around alliance results and relationship health. The
SACKED capabilities are addressed shortly but prior to this it is
worth understanding the role that an alliance manager would play
over the alliance lifecycle for a fairly typical high value and important alliance.

Investigation: back in Figure 13.4 there is an emphasis on alliance
management resources participating in the early stages of alliance

investigation as well as driving delivery once created. This might not always be practical not least because an alliance manager may not have been appointed at this stage but the sponsor will possibly have someone in mind once the idea starts taking shape. At the earliest possible stage the alliance manager will get insight into the ideas and may have an important contribution to the business case. Delays in appointment and involvement will hamper buy-in and inhibit progress.

Creation: while the alliance manager will probably not lead at this stage their involvement is crucial to ensure shaping of the alliance solution and building of relationships with the partners as early as possible. In one instance the proposed alliance managers for an alliance could not see eye to eye yet the firms wanted to work together. As a result, early in the creation process the partner prospect replaced its alliance manager and progress continued more successfully. It also helps continuity and leads to a more effective handover from creation to execution.

Alliance managers also bring their own SACKED capabilities to add to the specialist creation resources and can keep their commercial negotiators focused on agreeing realistic terms and commitments that are attractive and sustainable for both parties. One firm failed to involve its alliance management execution team early on and as a result the handover was poor, the solution was not well architected for real execution and time to money was delayed by many months costing the firm dearly. The mindset the service and alliance management team had was one of 'not invented here', constantly looking for holes and operating more at arm's length with the alliance partner when closer collaboration was required much earlier than actually happened. An important point for organisations is to ensure that their partner prospects have an alliance manager in place during the creation stage as well rather than wait until an agreement is concluded, for the same reasons.

Execution: this is where the alliance manager can become the difference between success and failure. But success is not about one individual; it is about a team led from the front by the alliance manager under sometimes very difficult circumstances. Leading alliance brands are not dependent on one star alliance manager, mainly because of their overall alliance infrastructure, and the broader, deeper connections made with the partner organisation. If superstar financial fund managers leave, the business will go on although there may be some delay and inconvenience cost to accept unless effective succession planning and infrastructure is in place.

Alliance managers may have more than one alliance to manage causing a need to balance workload and potentially competing priorities. In this instance, like the sponsor, it is important not to have unhealthy conflict between the partners which might erode trust. A better option is to look at managing complementary alliances or broader networks where the partners can work together.

What does an alliance manager do in practice on a day-to-day basis? It is not all jollies and relationship management activity. Leading alliance brands will drive their staff hard to deliver results while maintaining the relationship health. If one or both organisations does not have a collaborative culture and the alliance goals of each firm are incongruent then that task will be daunting. Chapter 18 in Part III looks in detail at what it means to be an alliance manager responsible for delivery when in Phase 5 of the ICE Map. Alliance managers can be responsible for R&D, upstream supply, operations, marketing and sales-based alliances. Some of the traits differ but there are some common characteristics for success. Table 13.6 offers up the typical SACKED capabilities for alliance managers. Compare these with your earlier notes and see where there are areas for improvement.

This forms a fairly comprehensive but not necessarily exhaustive set of characteristics. Depending on the type of the alliance

Table 13.6 SACKED capabilities for alliance managers.

Capability	Evidenced by
Skills	Relationship management, strong communication, written and verbal presenting, effective negotiation and problem solving. Can manage conflict well. Good leader. Strong commercial acumen with strategic and operational skills. Change management. Good organiser, strong on process and control, able to multitask effectively.
Attitude	Results oriented, team player, hard working and determined to make a contribution. Decision shaper rather than just decision-maker, recognising a need to influence many parties. Open minded, inquisitive and prepared to support and challenge those around the alliance. Not afraid to take calculated risks. Focused on alliance delivery while bearing in mind the bigger strategic picture. Can play the long game while seeking quick wins on the way.
Character	Trusted by all, impressive appearance and highly credible across the firm also being a good alliance partner champion. Seen as an 'enabler' of success. A rising star or one who has already risen.
Knowledge	Deep company and industry background, strong understanding of partner. Good understanding of alliances theory and practice. May also be MBA qualified holding relevant industry qualifications such as CIM for marketing alliances, or CIPS for supply side alliances or perhaps a relevant engineering qualification.
Experience	Likely to have past failures to learn from as well as successes, possibly running own P&L. Past account/relationship management, project management and man management responsibilities.
Drivers	Rewarded on alliance success, measured by achievement of results and relationship health. Sees an opportunity for further personal growth with alliance success and satisfied stakeholders.

there will possibly be additional skills and experience required as well. For example, alliance management for a business process outsourcing alliance in a heavily unionised environment may also require knowledge of TUPE[98] especially if the specialist skills are not available from support resources. In large complex alliances and relationships such as that of HP and BT reported earlier, the alliance leader is more likely to be a senior executive like Hugh Barton with CEO and sponsor type qualities, supported by a number of alliance managers and other staff, operating like a mini business within a business.

How firms organise their resources in practice will be dependent on what they want to achieve from their alliances and how much investment they are prepared to put in the alliance infrastructure overall. For example, a leading alliance brand like Cisco has over 200 practitioners managing its strategic alliances across the globe and their efforts account for over 15% of Cisco's £24 bn revenues. It is one of the most profitable business units in the organisation with returns on investment much greater than most organisations could ever hope to achieve. Clearly part of that is because of using partners' capital and infrastructure in the joint go-to-market alliances, but it would not be achieved without high quality alliance professionals delivering on their tasks.

One of the other areas affecting success and failure in alliances is the resources focused on alliance activity in terms of capacity and number. Not only are the SACKED capabilities important, but the amount of resources devoted to alliances also makes a difference. Stretching an individual too far over too many alliances or having them responsible for other tasks as well will mean value is destroyed. Failure to align the supporting cast and sponsor as well will also end in failure. A little extra effort at the pre-alliance investigation stage in organising the resources effectively with the right players involved in the right numbers, at the right times with the right motivations, can go a long way. This is demonstrated in Part III using ALLIANTIST ICE Map.

Finally it is worth considering whether great alliance managers are born or made and how they can be developed. Much of what is expressed above in terms of character and attitude is learnt while still in short trousers although obviously the environment conditions behaviour over time as well. Leading alliance brands with large alliance practices will also offer bespoke in-house alliance training or seek external assistance to help develop key skills and knowledge. Other organisations may wish to develop through coaching from an alliance advisor and effecting knowledge transfer over time. A collaborative culture will also ensure drivers are focusing behaviour in the right direction. Simple recruitment techniques should look to establish the character and attitude of candidates regardless of their previous discipline, for example using some of the methods for analysing individual makeup, more fully explored in Chapter 11. Experience has proven to be an indicator for success as earlier research suggested that one of the reasons for alliance failure is a lack of experience. Therefore career opportunities should exist to grow resources into more demanding roles, for example initially managing lower tier alliances before growing into and beyond complex strategic relationships with high value and importance.

EASE OF DOING AND NOT DOING BUSINESS WITH OTHER PARTIES

What would your organisation's partners say about doing business with it? Is the organisation easy to do business with or a nightmare? Getting the balance right is crucial for value creation and avoiding value destruction as shown in Figure 13.5. Where does your organisation sit?

Imagine the following situation. One operating unit of a software organisation has decided that doing business with a systems integration (SI) partner prospect is too risky because of its poor

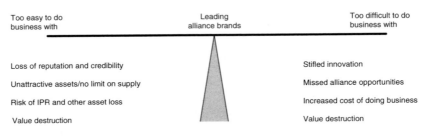

Too easy to do business with	Leading alliance brands	Too difficult to do business with
Loss of reputation and credibility		Stifled innovation
Unattractive assets/no limit on supply		Missed alliance opportunities
Risk of IPR and other asset loss		Increased cost of doing business
Value destruction		Value destruction

Figure 13.5 Balancing how to do business.

reputation and decided to qualify it out of future opportunities. What a surprise then that just a few weeks later the same SI organisation had the partner badge and won a piece of business on the basis of being an 'approved' partner. An end customer quickly complained about the SI partner not being capable and had concerns about its business intentions so the alliance was dissolved quickly. It turned out that the other operating unit of the software organisation had decided to let it deliver a piece of work because it was short on capacity and was not aware of the recent decision by the other unit not to award it an approval status. The SI partner clearly kept quiet as well. Albeit a low value alliance this is an example of one of the challenges about being too easy to do business with. Poorly specified partnering standards, lack of due diligence, consistency and ineffective communication across the organisation led to a temporarily damaged reputation for the software firm with an important client and increased cost as a result of needing to put the poor work right and recover the relationship.

On the other hand, making life too difficult for partners and prospects to work with an organisation may mean missed opportunities and increased costs. Picture the scene in trying to navigate a way around a large global organisation that fails to offer an effective central point of contact for its partner. It is hard enough to work out who to talk to in some firms if you work there let alone looking from the outside in! As a result partners may need to increase their resources and infrastructure to manage the alliance and relationship more effectively. This will impact margins which may in turn impact the rewards and benefits that get shared. It can also lead to the sort of divide and conquer routines and opportunistic behaviour discussed earlier when considering how to govern complex relationships. Some large organisations need 15 people in a room just to talk about an alliance task and still are not comfortable making decisions. No wonder alliances take years to get off the ground and decisions take months to happen in these organisations. Innovation and creativity may also be stifled or lost to competitors by having too much policy and too many gates to get through for new partner prospects where their proposals get lost in 'black holes'.

Having a well-structured formal alliance programme, effective governance and suitably skilled resources demonstrating the right behaviours is a massive step towards clarifying how to best work with partners but it might not be enough. So what are some of the other things firms can do to achieve the right balance in this area? Some firms prefer to be dealt with in different ways and having flexibility is a strength, although care needs to be taken that some standards are adhered to, for example in governance, reporting and allocation of resources as this is the root of CSF 3. ALLIANTIST ERA Map enables partners to achieve CSF 3 and build effective relationship architectures to facilitate alliance success and mitigate the risk of failure or surprise and is discussed in depth during chapter 16, with partner planning, which is Phase 3 of ALLIANTIST ICE Map.

Being an alliance brand, large volumes of partner prospects are attracted to the organisation because of its positive identity and reputation. As such alliance brands put in place infrastructure to help prospects navigate the organisation (or not!) as well as manage their own resources. External facing activities include the following:

- An alliance programme website linked to the organisation's home page with supporting collateral demonstrating the aims and purpose of alliances and how they fit the strategy and core competences of the company.

- An online partner qualification and registration capturing suitable prospect information and background to their interest in becoming a partner which can be screened inside 24 hours for fit. There may be a charge for some qualification and registration schemes assuming prospects pass a first screening. This can help demonstrate 'skin in the game' from the partner and mitigates the common problem of 'logo' hunters.

- Alliance brands will also suggest prospects pitch innovative opportunities quickly and succinctly. They have focused alliance proposal guidelines that express a need for the prospect to share their alliance proposition and demonstrate the market opportunity and suggest who will do what in the alliance and why.

- Clear processes and guidelines on decisions and timing of activities are essential. Offering prospects an idea of how long it takes to get through the process and what they can expect to do is good communication. Those organisations that fail to return calls or don't bother to offer feedback, good or bad, will signal how collaborative they might not have been in practice!

Internal facing activities include the following:

- Agreed policies and procedures for qualifying partner prospects in or out quickly. This might be a simple cursory glance for completeness and company fitness, then a quick test using a standard screening mechanism that demonstrates the value and importance, and fit within the portfolio using techniques described earlier in the portfolio section, before moving them onto deeper investigation or a polite no thank you.

■ Commitments to return calls and give feedback on why prospects' proposals are not going to be considered with feedback
on what they can do better for the future, if relevant.

■ Keeping a log of all proposals, prospects and incoming activity
whether unsuccessful or not for future reference and sharing
across the interested parties internally. Not least, this avoids
the example above of saying no in one part of the organisation
and finding it becomes a yes in another part, having to pick
up the pieces later. In addition it can also provide a useful form
of competitive intelligence to aid the business going forward
and prove a useful audit trail in the event of future problems
or questions from failed prospects.

Balancing the ease of doing business with others is tough, but
for those organisations that get it right it can really add value.
Partner newsletters updating on organisation activity and satisfaction surveys are all a positive source of improving business communication. Getting feedback from and giving feedback to partners
is useful, both formally through the surveys but also during social
gatherings with off-the-record informal feedback. Acting on the
feedback then is essential so be careful what you wish for!

PROPOSITION ATTRACTIVENESS

In October 2005 Unisys, the large IT services provider, declared
third quarter losses of $54 m[99]. Implicit in this loss was the increased
costs of outsourcing contracts the company was managing as a
result of not closely scrutinising the attractiveness and risks in
propositions under $100 m. In announcing the results the company
stated it would increase bid qualification for outsourcing deals of
$30 m or greater and also assess opportunities with financial or risk
characteristics considered to be above the norm. In addition it
would take into account the existing relationship with the client

and the way business was conducted. Unisys' global bid review board would provide legal, financial and operational oversight.

Unisys is not unlike another services provider who lost significant value from its outsourcing alliance activity. In its haste to close deals and move on to the next opportunity, sales and alliance teams would 'spin' the attractiveness of propositions to internal 'review boards' which in practice could mean a quick phone call to a budget holder as opposed to a formal governance board. Problems would be metaphorically 'thrown' over to delivery teams to solve once agreements were concluded and efforts then made to recover losses post-transition with customer agreement small print, and arguments over responsibility with alliance delivery partners. This situation did little to encourage collaboration and mutual benefit internally, with the partners and with the customer. It is surprising how many organisations do not have formal controls around setting up all types of alliances, not just customer facing outsourcing alliances, and suffer afterwards. Deloitte research found that 'hurdle rates', being the level of authority and financial returns modelling, were too low, meaning many alliances were not closely scrutinised[100]. M&A and internal development activity in comparison usually has clear processes around return on investment, risk acceptance and high authority levels for investment decisions. How effective is your organisation at ensuring propositions are attractive? Consider the statements in Table 13.7.

Leading alliance brands answer Yes to each question and also manage their exposure to unnecessary resource cost and risk in assessing propositions using filters or gateway mechanisms. Just like three legs of a stool are needed for it to work, alliance propositions also need to be considered for their attractiveness from three dimensions: WIFC, WIFT and WIFU. This means 'what's in it for clients', what's in it for them (partner) and what's in it for us, being the organisation. Failure to consider these dimensions will result in value destruction and alliance failure.

Table 13.7 Proposition attractiveness checklist.

Statement	Yes/No	Evidence/comments
Before embarking on an alliance, propositions are subject to make, buy, ally tests to ensure the correct strategic choice is being made.		
When pursuing an alliance idea propositions are subject to financial and nonfinancial return on investment and risk assessment that is at least equal to equivalent M&A and internal development investment decisions.		
Consideration is also given to the attractiveness and risks of the proposition for clients.		
Consideration is also given to the attractiveness and risks of the proposition for the partner.		
Alliance propositions which are turned down are kept on file for future reference and learning.		

Make, buy, ally tests similar to those shown in Chapter 9 on strategic choice will help clarify if the most attractive practical proposition will be achieved through alliances as opposed to M&A or internal development. Alliance proposition attractiveness tests can then be made with a simple screening mechanism or checklist to ensure they pass a certain hurdle rate before moving into more detailed alliance planning processes. One organisation simply would not entertain any investigation on alliance proposals that did not exceed revenue growth by at least £10m per annum, citing that as a minimum threshold where their primary goal was revenue growth. Another large firm introduced a quick test and alliance proposal form that meant ideas needed to be screened using a simple spreadsheet tool looking at the financial and nonfinancial return assessing factors such as strategic fit, brand association and degree of integration required. This test provided an initial view to senior management of the potential attractiveness and also created a situation where alliance proposers needed to think through their ideas in more detail than before. This quick test led to 95% of all ideas going back to the drawing board or being canned early on without incurring significant risk or cost to the firm.

Detailed assessment should look at specific example scenarios to ensure they stack up as well as give consideration to the size and attractiveness of the market for total return on investment purposes. The strategic planning tools highlighted earlier will prove helpful as will tools like whole product modelling originally introduced by Kotler back in 1991[101], and explored in more detail during Part III. Alliance brands have a methodology and tools for use with partners that help screen alliance investments and ensure that the propositions are attractive for it as well as clients and partners. Siebel introduced its basic CHAMP methodology to help sell the principle of alliances to prospective partners in its early days. As expressed in Part I with the Siebel IBM alliance example, Siebel would present alliance propositions to partners citing the return it would get from its investments and how that compared with Siebel's share of the spoils. From a customer perspective, regardless of whether the customer is internal or external, the proposition needs to be attractive and compelling to them or they will not buy it. Smart buyers will look holistically over the lifecycle at the financial and nonfinancial value so the firm and its partner should consider this aspect carefully when crafting the initial alliance value proposition and whole product model. Partners also need to get value over the lifetime of the alliance as well. So often in alliances one party is left bitter because one or more promises failed to materialise. To reiterate from Part I, up to 70% of alliances fail with the three most frequent reasons for failure occurring as a result of propositions being unattractive for one or more of the parties; lack of alliance commitment, lack of shared benefits and slower results or payback. This manifests itself with any of the following points, inevitably leading to alliance termination and value destruction:

- Delays and frustration for the other partner leading to increased reputational risks from nondelivery
- Increasing financial risk of opportunistic behaviour such as stealing confidential information, other assets and poaching staff
- Removal of key staff or assets that are reassigned to more attractive and sustainable alliance propositions

Just as the content of the alliance proposition needs to be attractive, so does its presentation. Not unlike programmes such as BBC TV's *Dragon's Den* or an investor pitch to a business angel, alliance propositions need to get to the heart of the costs and benefits quickly to get air time with senior management. Whether it is in the form of an elevator pitch or a few presentation slides, an attractive proposition articulates clearly where the value is for each party and what commitments it will take to access it. Those firms that are able to place values on their assets as described in the chapter on attractiveness of assets will be better placed to communicate the benefits of working with them and achieve better returns on their alliance investments and propositions. ALLIANTIST ICE Map is addressed in detail during Part III, and Chapter 15, Phase 2: Pre-Partner in particular, offers a deeper insight into developing attractive and sustainable propositions.

ABILITY TO SELECT THE RIGHT PARTNERS AND RELATIONSHIPS

Having determined the attractiveness of an alliance proposition and a requirement for a partner, the firm needs to consider who is best placed to help them meet their need. Fundamentally alliances are about people and the relationships they form, with many alliances and partnerships crafted on the back of existing personal relationships in a relatively informal fashion. This might be a good starting point for selecting alliance partners but it is not enough to guarantee success. Balancing these 'softer' factors needs to be 'harder' factors such as structure, process and appropriate safeguards brought about by effective due diligence and enquiry. As shareholder and legislative pressures continually force greater improvements in performance and transparency of operation there will be even greater need for demonstrating the balance exists and that alliances are developed and managed in a professional, sustainable manner. Consider the statements in Table 13.8 where alliance brands can answer Yes to each one.

Positive partner relationships are crucial for success yet creating alliances with pals from the golf club, based on the strength of their golf swing, may not be a satisfactory answer for the audit committee! At the other extreme, supplier selection has also become a more scientific, faceless discipline in recent years with many firms offering online tools and complex software algorithms to help determine the cheapest supplier or the vendor who is the best match for a tender over an e-auction. While these tools have an important role to play they have not yet added meaningful value to the collaborative alliance arena and remain more suitable for arm's length activity and commodity type buyer/supplier transactions. Using these tools as part of a competitive tender approach under the wrong circumstances can be a positive turn–off for true alliance partner prospects. Imagine being 'invited' to construct an alliance that will enable effective partnering and innovation with

Table 13.8   Partner selection controls checklist.

Statement	Yes/No	Evidence/ comments
The organisation can demonstrate objectivity in its partner selection processes and systems.		
The organisation uses criteria for selection of partners based on their value and importance, considering factors such as strategic fit, operational capability, relationship compatibility and commercial implications.		
Partner selection tools and processes are used consistently across the organisation and transcend behaviours of any one individual.		
Specialist alliance creation support teams and ongoing execution resources are engaged at the earliest opportunity.		
The firm can demonstrate an effective audit trail in the process of information gathering and partner decision-making to satisfy audit and compliance guidelines.		
Unsuccessful partner prospects are debriefed professionally and told exactly why they were not chosen with details logged for future reference.		

shared benefits for both partners and then be expected to compete aggressively on price or other dimensions over an e-auction; it happens. That is not collaborative behaviour and it sends the wrong signals for alliances, creating barriers early in the process which will be difficult to recover from. This is also one of the challenges in public sector alliance activity where EU legislation and a widespread noncollaborative culture affect how much firms can openly collaborate and innovate during the partner selection process.

Partner selection is a two-way process and each partner needs to demonstrate its ability to add value to the other over the duration of the alliance. Selection needs to be about many different factors outside of pure financial issues as well. Factors that alliance brands look at include strategic fit, operational fit, relationship compatibility as well as commercial implications as will be seen in more depth during Part III when ALLIANTIST TOPSCORER Map is introduced.

Getting the balance right between art and science, and ethical or unethical collaborative partner selection is tough but it can be done. The way to do it is by adopting an enabling (not disabling) methodology with explicit criteria and transparent processes, with supporting workflow, tools and systems managed by the effective alliance resources described earlier. ALLIANTIST ICE Map alluded to earlier and detailed in Part III is one such approach that covers the whole lifecycle, not just partner selection per se. This, along with ALLIANTIST TOPSCORER Map, helps satisfy CSF 2; having the right partners. Partner selection is such an important topic and implicit in CSF 2; having the best partners, so is covered in much more detail in Part III.

ABILITY TO DELIVER ON ALLIANCE COMMITMENTS

Leading alliance brands do have their alliance failures but these usually come about because of events beyond their control such as a change in control of their partner, or because the alliance was a hedge on the future, for example an early stage innovation alliance that did not bear fruit. Their alliances rarely fail through not delivering on their commitments or because of the way the alliance was structured and governed. Sadly, many alliances do fail to deliver, even shortly after the press release. Selecting a partner for an alliance is not the end; it is just the beginning, yet so often those who drove the selection process fall away chasing the next hot alliance or big idea. As expressed in the resources section earlier it is imperative that any alliance selection activity includes the resources that are expected to manage and deliver the alliance afterwards. Having identified who they think is the right partner, both parties should give considerable investment to the key outputs described below during the creation period which will affect delivery of the commitments:

- **What** the alliance is aiming to achieve and **why**
- **How** the partners will achieve it together with clarity on **who** does **what** in the alliance and **why**
- **How** the parties will know success is being achieved
- **What** happens when it is all over

As seen in the section above, in constructing the alliance proposition, both parties should know what the alliance is trying to achieve and why. Less emphasis is generally put on how the alliance will achieve it, leaving that to an afterthought once the alliance has been announced. However, one of the reasons for alliance failure is misunderstood operating principles, where for whatever reason there is disagreement over who should do what or how something should be done. By working together in the alliance planning stages both parties can determine which partner does certain tasks, how it will affect the other and what implications need to be addressed at any handover stages. Simple task lists and high-level process charts can help get clarity at an early stage on who should do what and why, with problems addressed early on. For example, successful alliances have workflow and process maps put together to identify how joint teams work together in practice. Both parties' respective methods and practices are mapped along with key touchpoints, so hand-offs, gaps or overlaps are addressed and ensure complementarity without driving in extra process for each team but also making sure that effective controls are in place.

It is also important to give consideration to the implications of making public announcements too early without firm agreement on the alliance tasks and exit strategy. One organisation was leading up to its annual results with a need for good news. It was in early stage alliance discussions with an attractive partner over a new technology solution. The alliance idea was good; however, the actual tasks and share of rewards were not nailed down nor was the exit strategy. It required serious negotiation because of a small but important overlap in capability and the creation of attractive new intellectual property rights (IPR). Sure enough the CEO wanted to make the alliance announcement at the same time as the annual results, giving little thought to the implications of alliance negotiations. The partner could sense an opportunity to improve its share of the spoils and delayed negotiating until after the public announcement, which could only enhance its position. As a result, there was no way the CEO could back out of the alliance meaning the partner's negotiation position had improved as forecast. As part of exit strategy negotiations, undertaken during the alliance creation, the partner secured ownership of the jointly created IPR, giving it most of the benefits once the alliance was over. In addition it harvested a greater share of the rewards during alliance delivery, although was careful enough to leave some value on the table for the organisation. Had the CEO kept quiet his organisation would have enjoyed a greater share of the alliance rewards and been in a better position to retain ownership of the jointly created IPR.

Having crafted a mutually acceptable set of delivery tasks and identified who will do what when, consideration needs to be given to the safeguards needed for success and the governance of the alliance, monitoring how it will be kept on track. Results are clearly important; however, another important facet to measure and monitor during the alliance is relationship health. It is an early indicator and barometer for likely future performance and a key task for the alliance manager to keep in a positive position. One size does not fit all with governance and reinforcing safeguards yet in this instance many companies do one of two extremes:

1. The more powerful partner will put forward a standard non-negotiable agreement with many unnecessary clauses, usually led by the legal team. This may be a suitable solution depending on past performance although it is likely to stifle collaboration and compromise the relationship development between the parties and could affect innovation.
2. Leave the agreement at a verbal level or at best document the aims of the alliance on a one pager. This too may be appropriate for partners that know each other well and have absolutely complementary capabilities. However, if trust breaks down or resources change, then it can leave one or both of the parties in a vulnerable position when the alliance ends or dispute occurs as demonstrated with the Mark & Spencer and William Baird case discussed in Part I.

Leading alliance brands have the infrastructure in place to deliver on their alliance commitments and while they use a framework and a set of principles to architect alliances for success, a one size approach does not fit all circumstances. Reflect on your company's alliance delivery activity and consider the statements in Table 13.9.

Those firms that cannot even measure their alliance success rate have far to travel. While leading alliance brands consistently answer Yes to the statements above for each alliance, most firms will struggle to point to many alliances in their portfolio where those practices exist and can be replicated easily in other alliances. Having the right partners is a CSF 2 and addressed with

Table 13.9   Delivering on alliance commitments.

Statement	Yes/No	Evidence/ comments
The organisation can easily measure its alliance success rate and has clarity on the value created and destroyed.		
A consistent framework and set of governance principles are used to help architect alliance agreements.		
Legal safeguards are built according to the alliance objectives and past experience between the parties rather than an off-the-shelf contract that might stifle collaboration or verbal agreements that might unravel when players change.		
Alliance managers and delivery resources execute to agreed tasks driven by a joint alliance business plan.		
Information is shared effectively between the partners in good time for the creation of mutual benefits.		
The alliance inputs and outputs in terms of results and relationships health are regularly measured and reported on to aid course corrections and address new opportunities or threats.		
Governing bodies facilitate alliance success and regularly review both the operational activities as well as the strategic environment.		
Disputes and disagreements are handled according to an agreed resolution process that aims to avoid litigation and further conflict.		
Exit implications are planned at the creation stage and appropriate mechanisms agreed within the legal safeguards.		

ALLIANTIST ICE Map in Part II. However, without the right platform on which to build and deliver the alliance it will still fail. Therefore in Part III the ERA Map also outlines how firms can get CSF 3 which is effective relationship architectures (ERA). ERA underpins the alliance to help facilitate alliance success and mitigate against surprise or failure.

ABILITY TO DEVELOP, PROTECT AND SHARE KNOWLEDGE

Successful alliances are about teams, collaboration and sharing. Throughout the alliance lifecycle, ideas, information and people come together to form better solutions than they could achieve alone. Yet rarely is the technology infrastructure in place to enable sharing within organisations let alone across external boundaries. Aspects that need to be considered include the management of information and knowledge assets as they affect productivity, alliance performance and competitive advantage. As more firms turn to remote home working and increasing specialisation of work tasks, it means more people get involved, but operating from different locations. The risks of communication breakdown and task failure increase exponentially. As such technology will play an increasing part in aiding collaboration, helping navigate complex partnering activity within the organisation as well as with external partners based in different locations. Technology can also help listed organisations produce more effective compliance and audit trails along with accurate performance reporting.

Some organisations trust one alliance practitioner to hold all the relevant alliance information on their laptop and wonder why performance suffers when that individual leaves. Other organisations share files by email which leads to important information being held in multiple copies on different hard drives inaccessible to other interested parties and many unsure of the master versions. Shared file systems go someway but the structure of large filing systems can be hard to navigate and may mean duplication and wasted time. There are many content management solutions that aid performance from a generic perspective and a growing array of complementary technology products such as contact relationship and contract management systems which can help protect and share information but these do not have an alliance or partner centric perspective, so it can be like pushing a square peg in a round hole. Many organisations now have internal intranets that can be used to communicate and publish information to interested parties internally. Leading technology users like Cisco, IBM, Siebel and others have secure partner extranets to share product information, sales and marketing material, alliance information and performance reports. Products such as Microsoft Sharepoint offer an integrated portfolio of collaboration and communication services to connect people, information, processes and systems both within the company and beyond to its partners and other stakeholders.

Some organisations mandate the use of unwieldy expensive relationship management solutions or attempt to shoehorn alliance workflow into inappropriate enterprise management systems. In these instances the technology hinders collaboration and actively stifles performance. Whatever technology is used it needs to complement physical working and be easy to use, serving the individual and team, not the other way around. Technology solutions are not necessarily cheap to purchase and operate; however, what really needs to be considered is the return on investment that they offer, and the potential opportunity costs and risks incurred by not having them. Consider what extra value your organisation might create if it had effective technology in place, both internally and with partners or other stakeholders. Then, consider what the potential losses and risks might be by not having that support infrastructure and compare the two scenarios. It is likely that the right technology solution will deliver a compelling return on investment and make doing business far more effective and efficient for the organisation and its partners.

PART II SUMMARY

P art II has addressed how organisations can achieve CSF 1
and get a capability to partner. By following ALLIANTIST VIP
Map the organisation will have a capability to partner and
achieve:

- **Clarity on its strategy and direction** offering a path towards
  competitive advantage that both the organisation and its partners find compelling to follow.
- **Clarity on its core competences** optimising the organisation's internal resources to focus on the things that create
  value and advantage, working with partners and others for
  everything else.
- **An ability to make effective strategic choices** meaning
  it knows when to make, buy or ally for optimal value creation
  and prevention of unnecessary business risks and costs.
- **Clarity on the attractiveness of its assets** enabling both
  protection and optimisation of the returns from its alliance

investments while raising the profile of the organisation as a partner.

- **An ability to collaborate internally and externally** meaning that it can deliver on its promises and work efficiently and effectively with partners both internally and externally.
- **Effective governance and be able to manage complex relationships** offering confidence in the organisation's controls, as well as addressing opportunities and threats that cross multiple relationship dimensions.
- **An alliance infrastructure** suitable to meet the organisation's partnering aspirations and provide a compelling return on its alliance investments.

Achievement of CSF 1 will position the organisation well for obtaining the maximum future rewards from its alliance activity, as well as no doubt improving broader organisational effectiveness and efficiency in the process. The organisation is then ready to have the right partners (CSF 2) in its portfolio and build effective relationship architectures to underpin the alliances (CSF 3). These two CSF are the core subject of Part III as it introduces how to go about building winning alliances and leveraging from the capability built in CSF 1.

## PART III

WINNING WITH ALLIANCES

*C*hapter 13 stated that attractiveness of alliance propositions, ability to select the right partners and an ability to deliver on alliance commitments are an integral part of achieving CSF 1. Leading alliance brands therefore have processes, tools and systems in place to enable alliance resources to investigate, create and execute winning alliances. Having the right partners is also CSF 2 and building effective relationship architectures is CSF 3. Only once these three CSF are achieved can the organisation achieve its desired results and reputation.

ALLIANTIST ICE Map addresses the two remaining CSF in a holistic fashion while working across the alliance lifecycle as shown in Figure III.1. This map guides organisations through the investigation, creation and execution phases on the journey to success. To draw from CSF 1 it tests whether an alliance is really necessary, then ensures there is an attractive proposition for participants and that the organisation is ready for the alliance. It then

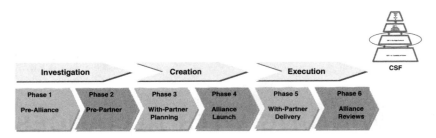

Figure III.1   ALLIANTIST ICE Map.

helps selection of partners, aided by ALLIANTIST TOPSCORER Map, to ensure the organisation has the right partners (CSF 2) before turning to help achieve CSF 3. In Phase 3 the organisation works with the partner using ALLIANTIST ERA Map to create its effective relationship architecture and attain CSF 3. During the journey there are also numerous tools and techniques presented to increase the probability of sustainable success as well as speed time to value and mutual benefit.

To reiterate the comments in Part II, the maps are not the territory and so what the organisation might encounter on the ground may mean tailoring the maps and tools for optimal performance. While there are many similarities in each type of alliance, elements do differ and careful consideration is needed, for example when forming technical criteria against which to assess prospective partners.

The maps are a guide, not a strait-jacket. Real life suggests that many of the tasks and outputs prescribed in this part may be conducted in parallel whereas they are presented in series in the subsequent chapters more for the ease of explanation. The depth of analysis and effort at each phase should also reflect the value and importance as well as the risks and rewards associated with the alliance activity. Some organisations may choose to use each map simply as a checklist and gain benefit from it that way. This will surely help alliance success, but for optimal value creation, committed organisations will licence and adapt the maps and tools as a more comprehensive integrated solution and speed down the path to become a leading alliance brand.

## CHAPTER 14

PHASE 1: PRE-ALLIANCE

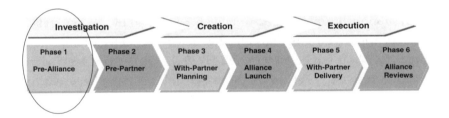

CONTEXT

Someone will have initiated the idea that an alliance is a good thing to do for the organisation. It might have been the sales director reading the business press and concluding that an adjacent industry is experiencing growth and she wants to get in on the act but needs a route in. The procurement director may have met a peer at a networking event that highlighted how a similar organisation stripped massive costs out of its business through an alliance. It could be the CEO was playing golf with a customer and had his ear bent about how his software products could be so much better if they could fit more easily with another application used in the customer organisation. Whatever the catalyst, what usually happens is that someone then kicks off an external facing exercise that seeks to find a partner to exploit the opportunity or solve the problem. That could be mistake number one. Going externally before clarifying internally could lead to sharing information and intelligence which costs future advantage and wastes precious resources. It might also negatively distract customers, suppliers, partners or other complementors and affect the organisation's partnering reputation for the future.

PHASE 1 AIMS

Starting with the end in mind, the key outputs of Phase 1 are outlined in Table 14.1. A typical deliverable would include the outputs of Table 14.1 articulated in a one or two page proposal, with supporting appendices, suitable for approval by the key stakeholders prior to moving into Phase 2. The importance of this phase and Phase 2 cannot be understated given they will shape any future creation activity. That said, this phase could be completed within hours depending on the organisation's stage of maturity and desire for detail.

OUTPUT A: FORCES PUSHING FOR THE ALLIANCE

In Part I many of the forces pushing for alliances were discussed. It is essential that the organisation identifies the key drivers behind the initiative and considers the implications from both taking action and taking no action. These forces will drive the whole alliance and underpin the alliance value proposition crafted in Phase 2. After identifying and confirming the forces, doing

Table 14.1 Phase 1 output checklist.

No.	Phase 1 output	Tick when completed	Comments
A	The forces for the proposed alliance are understood and confirmed as material reasons for further investigation.		
B	The organisation has clarity on its strategy and direction, core competences and ability to make effective strategic choices, meaning that an alliance is confirmed as being the right choice to address the forces.		
C	A headline financial number on anticipated cost/benefit for the organisation from the alliance is put forward as a 'stake in the ground' with commentary on nonfinancial rewards.		
D	Headline risks and issues are understood.		
E	The sponsor is identified, stakeholders aligned and supportive, ready for approval to move into Phase 2.		
F	Necessary resources to undertake Phase 2 onwards are identified with approximate times and other costs of investment.		

nothing is not usually an option. When Reuters outsourced to Fujitsu as described in Part II it was clear about its motives and the rationale for the alliance was well considered. Reuters needed to focus on what it did well given growing internal pressures;

competitors like Bloomberg were offering more attractive hardware and service solutions to customers; and by allying it solved
a number of increasing challenges and repositioned Reuters well
for the future. Fujitsu had complementary forces and drivers so
the subsequent value proposition made sense for both parties and
their customers. Similarly BT and HP had a good understanding
of the respective forces pushing them together and had both inde-
pendently arrived at similar conclusions before coming together.
These forces included increasing customer demands for joined-up
ICT solutions, and common competitors in the shape of firms like
IBM.

OUTPUT B: ALLIANCE AS THE RIGHT CHOICE

Phase 1 (and 2) of the Investigation stage acts as a sanity check on
many of the organisational elements in ALLIANTIST VIP Map
and confirms that an alliance is the right strategic choice. What
will the organisation achieve towards its stated goals by undertaking the alliance instead of another form of strategic choice? This
question enables the organisation to consider these aspects in more
depth:

- The stated business goals for the organisation
- How the alliance helps the organisation achieve its stated business goals (over the duration of the alliance relationship, e.g.
  as a three-year vision)
- Why an alliance will be more effective than other make or
  buy choices

The tools and frameworks presented in Part II should be used to
aid confirmation of the strategy and direction (Chapter 7) and core

competences (Chapter 8) as well as confirmation of an alliance being the correct strategic choice (Chapter 9).

OUTPUT C: HEADLINE BENEFITS

A very basic cost/benefit analysis will send the right signals to stakeholders about the potential value and importance of the alliance. This is the first real 'hurdle' assessing the relative importance of the alliance idea, for example in comparison with other initiatives the organisation may wish to invest its resources in. At this stage it may be as simple as looking at existing budgets and overheads, making high-level assumptions on fixed cost removal or changes in variable costs by (say) outsourcing, along with commentary on how (say) existing poor service levels might quickly improve. Or it could be making simple assumptions around innovation wins, sharing of risks, product volume or market share increases and growth in sales revenues by adding a reselling or co-selling partner into the mix.

OUTPUT D: HEADLINE RISKS

A primary risk assessment should be carried out highlighting any immediately obvious risks or issues that might arise from the alliance initiative. This can follow similar principles to that highlighted in Chapter 10 when looking at asset risks, assessing probability and impact and prioritising risks as shown in Figure 14.1. The completed template then forms the basis of a risk register which the alliance team builds on in Phase 2 and considers how it might remove, transfer, mitigate or accept the risks going forward.

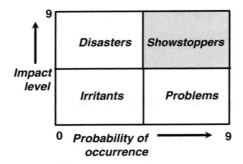

Figure 14.1   Risk assessment matrix.

OUTPUT E: SPONSOR IDENTIFIED AND STAKEHOLDERS ON BOARD

The section within alliance infrastructure in Part II addressing alliance resources confirmed the role and importance of a sponsor. Having completed outputs A–D there should be a clear idea about what level of sponsor would be appropriate and who might fill the role, if one is not already identified. The sponsor should be someone who can help identify and manage other important stakeholders as well as push the initiative forward and overcome any political or emotional challenges. Not all stakeholders are equal and unless their power and interest is well understood, the alliance may not get off the ground, or could be stifled by well-meaning but ineffective players. A useful tool for positioning stakeholders and understanding their power and interest is shown in Figure 14.2. Power relates to the individual's ability to affect outcomes, and interest considers the relative importance or impact the initiative has on the individual's day-to-day activity.

In the simple example in Figure 14.2 it can be seen that Paula Jones (the names have been changed) is keen to build a new go-to-market global alliance that will support delivery of the strategic goals around revenue growth. There are some risks that need

Stakeholder name	Power (H,M,L)	Interest (H,M,L)	Decision-making/ shaping role	Current support level	Advocate relationships	Positive messages	Barriers to address
Stan Smith CEO	H	L	Accountable	Neutral		New revenues	UKI Manager
Paula Jones Global Sales Director	H	H	Responsible	High	Jane Pullen	Gains % of sales towards target	Potential channel conflict on direct sales team
Jane Pullen UKI Mgr	M	H	Consulted	Low	Paula Jones	New revenues	Impact on current alliance relationships. No benefit from global sales

Figure 14.2 Stakeholder template.

addressing around potential conflict she has noted in the risk register but otherwise she is satisfied at this stage. Her other stakeholders may be less keen, however. Before Stan Smith, the CEO, will feel comfortable with progress he wants to see Jane Pullen brought onside by Paula. He sees this as important but it is not a day-to-day activity for him so he is registered as low interest, although with his high power he can veto proposals and needs to be kept satisfied. Fortunately Paula and Jane have a positive relationship, although challenges that need to be addressed are Jane's existing in-country alliance and the fact she gets no revenue recognition for global sales.

The simple little template along with the risk register demonstrates how complex stakeholder mapping is undertaken. It shows a way to organise the multiple stakeholders and outlines how to use other advocates to help address barriers at this early stage of alliance discussions. RACI analysis is useful to help identify those resources that are Responsible, Accountable, Consulted and Informed. RACI goes a long way to help resolve potential misunderstandings over who should do what and why, both internally and with partners, and has a key role to play later in the alliance creation phases.

Figure 14.3 offers a graphical representation of the stakeholders, where in ideal circumstances the keep satisfied and key players in the top boxes will have blacked out circles, representing their full support for the alliance. If this is not the case, strategies and actions need to be presented as part of the output for this phase to bring them onside as the alliance discussion evolves. Stakeholders in the bottom boxes can be addressed as and when the time is right.

Bear in mind that stakeholders may come in and out of the alliance scope depending on its position in the lifecycle and those stakeholders' positions in terms of support for or against alliance activity may change so constant monitoring is required. This stakeholder framework is therefore used across the whole ICE Map lifecycle and is constantly evolving as the alliance progresses.

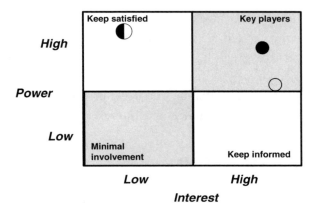

Figure 14.3   Stakeholder map.

OUTPUT F: SUPPORT RESOURCES AND COSTS

Alliance investigation and specialist support resources needed to help construct the case and build the alliance should also be identified and their availability considered. A ballpark estimate on the approximate time and involvement should be factored in at this stage as organisations frequently underestimate the cost of the set-up which can affect the attractiveness of the returns or expose opportunity costs. Other costs such as external specialists, business developments funds, contract termination costs, training and equipment should also be considered, although detailed analysis will wait until Phases 2 and 3.

PROGRESS TO PHASE 2

Having completed outputs A–F above, a one or two page proposal should be presented to the appropriate stakeholders with the stakeholder map and risk matrix as appendices. The decision-makers will then have a clear idea on whether the idea should progress to the next stage, and if so under what conditions. Assuming the initiative gets the green light the alliance project could be given a special project name, as usually happens with large projects and M&A activity. Giving alliance initiatives project names helps raise their psychological importance and interest to other stakeholders.

PITFALLS TO AVOID

This phase should be a lightweight taster for both alliance proposer and organisation to test the appetite for investing further in the initiative. It should not be a theoretical exercise with a 300 page business case. Existing organisation policies may mean that other factors need to be considered, either before or during this phase, but if the organisation has clarity on the key organisational elements expressed in the VIP Map during Part II this phase should be a relatively simple exercise.

Other pitfalls include:

- Failing to engage and get buy-in from the key and keep satisfied stakeholders early enough, so they decide not to support the initiative, or take longer to get on board
- Disclosing information too early to prospects when the organisation is not capable of executing its part. This could either leave the organisation trailing so the prospects go elsewhere, or the delays frustrate the prospects and their interest goes off the boil

SUMMARY OF TOOLS NEEDED FOR PHASE 1

- Phase 1 output checklist and summary proposal document
- Clarity on strategy (Chapter 7), clarity on core competences (Chapter 8), effective strategic choices (Chapter 9)

- Quick test on value and importance of alliance opportunity and/or headline cost/benefit statement (Chapter 13)
- Risk register and risk assessment matrix
- Stakeholder management template with RACI, and power/ importance positioning map
- Project plan to map and monitor Phase 1–6 outputs, allocate tasks and agree milestone dates

PHASE 2: PRE-PARTNER

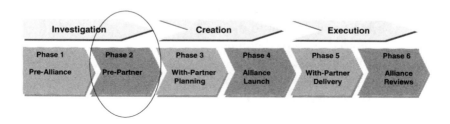

CONTEXT

Having received approval to progress to the next stage, the sponsor will need to build a team capable of executing Phase 2. This phase drills into more detail around the alliance opportunity and is carried out before getting into too much detail with one preferred partner.

PHASE 2 AIMS

Table 15.1 highlights the proposed outputs for this phase. The main goals are to ensure there is a value proposition that is attractive and sustainable for the key participants, and that the organisation is ready to partner. In addition the characteristics of the ideal partner are identified and the preferred partner selected.

OUTPUT A: ALLIANCE TEAM ALIGNMENT

Part II expressed the importance of the organisation having a collaborative culture and demonstrated how it could go about

Table 15.1 Phase 2 output checklist.

No.	Phase 2 output	Tick when completed	Comments
A	Internal alliance team assembled with commitment to the project and agreed ground rules in place.		
B	Clearly articulated and compelling value proposition for the organisation, target customers and partners.		
C	Organisation readiness statement with actions on areas to address before formal engagement.		
D	Ideal partner characteristics identified.		
E	Preferred partner selected to move into Phase 3.		
F	Ongoing stakeholder management and risk assessment.		

aligning and motivating the resources focused on alliances. Those principles also apply at this stage for the team responsible for investigating and delivering on Phase 2. Whether the team are co-located in a special project environment full time or work occasionally on the alliance, their commitment and attention will determine the success of the subsequent outputs. It is for the sponsor and other key stakeholders to ensure that any potential demotivators (e.g. too much other work, no rewards for success) are addressed. In one organisation the sponsor acknowledged that the success of a high value and important alliance initiative was dependent on bringing the team together as well as addressing barriers around existing workload and incongruent rewards. As such he set up a 'war room' specifically for the alliance team to work closely together, and took responsibility for helping delegate other work or putting it on hold. In addition he gained support for a one-off reward pot to be shared among team members depending on the team hitting key milestones and launching the alliance successfully.

Alongside the factors that affect collaboration, other key aspects to address at this juncture of formal alliance project kick-off include:

- Explicit team purpose: this outlines what the team has been brought together to achieve and why. It will include a sharing of the information produced in Phase 1 as well as directions around deadlines and expectation on delivery of Phase 2 outputs.
- Clear roles and responsibilities: help ensure team members know who is responsible for specific tasks and activities. Using RACI may be over the top for collaborative team members; however, if the organisation has a history of not meeting tasks on time this will help demonstrate where responsibility lies. Examples of team roles were noted in Chapter 13 about the resources focused on alliances. Large alliance projects will also

probably include an overarching project management work-stream, ensuring delivery of all the outputs noted in Phases 2, 3 and 4 of the ICE Map. Some organisations will also want to set up a steering committee or review board with high power stakeholders on it who can help govern the initiative and guide progress.

■ Ground rules and processes help ensure the team remain aligned and incur no risks from the way they operate. Examples include:

(a) Confidentiality: 'loose lips sink ships' so members need to know what, if anything, is confidential about the project and who is party to the knowledge (this can be managed via the stakeholder template).

(b) Teamworking and communication: such as setting expectations on how members work together in terms of respecting differences, responding to deadlines and dealing with disputes. For long-term alliance investigation projects involving team members who don't know each other well, consideration should be given to relationship building activities alongside the formal kick-off. This could be as simple as an informal team meal (during working hours), or may involve aspects such as team building away days.

(c) 'Party line': for external communications (i.e. outside of the project team) party line is a useful concept for managing potential ambiguity in communications. At certain stages of projects there can be more than one 'right' answer and unless appropriate signals are sent to external parties' team members may make their own interpretation and cause future problems. Poor or inappropriate communication could affect each partner's share of alliance rewards or even compromise the whole alliance initiative.

(d) 'Voice of authority': with clear roles and responsibilities among the team, there should be clarity on which team members are the point of authority for certain questions and issues. Building on the party line, this helps clarify who sets the party line and manages communication. In most instances it could be the alliance negotiator or sponsor as the face of authority; however, they will undoubtedly refer back to a voice of authority such as a lawyer, accountant or technical specialist.

(e) 'Negotiation brief': this is an internal document not to be shared outside the team. An effective negotiation brief does what it says on the tin; it is used as a brief for effective negotiations with partner prospects and if appropriate other stakeholders. The contents of the brief will evolve significantly during Phases 2 and 3 and include:

(i) Confirmation of the organisation's wants and needs including 'must have' and 'nice to have' assets and other partner capabilities it should bring into the alliance along with the typical value of those assets.

(ii) Confirmation of the organisation's own assets and activities that it is prepared to share in the alliance and what value is placed on those assets, valued from the partner's perspective. This and the point above forms part of the 'value exchange' and helps identify what 'trades' may be made in exchange for commitments from the partner.

(iii) What risks and issues it wants to share with the prospect and how they can work together on reducing or mitigating them, e.g. by transferring risk or sharing it.

(iv) What is the organisation's best alternative to negotiated agreement (BATNA)[102]. By understanding each party's BATNA the organisation will have a good idea of how far it should go in negotiations as well as understand its own bottom line.

Figure 15.1   Output B breakdown and linkage with other outputs.

OUTPUT B: ATTRACTIVE VALUE PROPOSITION FOR THE PARTICIPANTS

In Phase 1 the organisation got a glimpse of what its rewards might be from the alliance. In this output there is a need to get more specific for all of the participants; the organisation, its customers and the partners to the alliance. Crafting the value proposition correctly sets the scene for the subsequent outputs in C, D and E as shown in Figure 15.1 which highlights the interdependence of these key outputs. Failure to address this aspect of the phase may well affect the type of partner prospects engaged and risk the creation of optimal value in the future. In Phase 2 negotiations, and Phase 3, this area is discussed and critiqued with partner prospects to include their contributions.

Understanding the arena

This aspect serves to reinforce the understanding of how things are today and what might change as a result of the alliance. Looking at a client facing alliance, specific consideration is needed around the following customer and market-oriented environment:

■ Sanity check and critique on the forces driving change highlighted in Phase 1.

- What the specific market segment is, its overall size and make-up, along with profile of target customers (companies and target role profiles) for the existing and proposed activity.
- The maturity and volatility of the market and what the life-cycle position is of the products and services already available.
- Understanding what the customers' drivers are for making a purchase, and mapping out their reasons to buy the proposed alliance offering.
- Understanding how customers choose to source their solution, for example in the typical channels used and the process of acquisition, e.g. by tender or other means and the typical sales cycle time.
- Understanding who else plays in that arena today, including competitors, substitutes and their partners, and how they get their solutions to market. Consideration should also be given to their likely response when hearing of the proposed alliance.
- Who the key influencers, market commentators and other interested parties are and what their motivations might be to support or sabotage proposed activity.

From an organisation perspective:

- What assets, including its products and services the organisation is considering using in the alliance. Reference back to the chapter in Part II on asset attractiveness will help clarify the type of assets to include and how to value them.
- What the organisation's broader strategic goals and objectives are in this field, for example around revenue growth, brand awareness, market share and so on, built on from Phase 1.
- Clarification of the key stakeholders and their interests as described in Phase 1.
- Effective analysis and addressing of key risks and issues as described in Phase 1.

Customer and market attractiveness

Having compiled a good understanding of the arena consideration can now be given to constructing the alliance pie, i.e. considering the customer value proposition and overall market opportunity, then architecting the appropriate combination of products and services required for success. In building the alliance pie, adopt principles similar to those proposed by using value chain analysis as alluded to briefly in Part II and whole product modelling which is discussed in more depth below. When customers make a decision to source a product or service similar to what your organisation offers, ask:

■ What other complementary products/services **must** the customer have in order to complete their solution and realise the desired benefits? This could be other products your organisation provides, or those from other external complementors, or services it carries out itself internally. Using a simple example with Brightwell, end users need to purchase chemical consumables (from Brightwell partners) to use with the equipment manufactured by Brightwell or the client will not get its desired benefit.

■ What other complementary products/services **might** the customer choose to use in order to complete their solution and realise even greater benefits? Following the example above, the end user might choose to take out a service contract for equipment maintenance rather than do it in-house or not have it at all. The client will still obtain its desired benefit if it does nothing, at least until such time as the equipment fails or needs recalibrating.

■ Where would the client probably source this solution? Is it likely to be the channels reflected above or are they likely to value an alternative route? For example, it might mean an opportunity for consolidation with other products and simplify their purchasing processes into a one stop shop as well as deliver integrated solution benefits, as evidenced with convergence in the ICT marketplace.

■ Who pulls who in the solution sale? Where does the initial business pull come from and where does your product or service get specified from? This is a key point to consider in terms of mindshare and positioning with customers and alliance partners. The more attractive the organisation's assets, the more likely it is to be closer to the top of the chain influencing what other products and services get pulled through. Pulling is better than being pulled as leading alliance brands like Cisco will testify even though they are not necessarily the primary route to market.

Having carried out the analysis, a suitable whole product model or solution stack can be architected at two levels:

1. A typical customer solution as demonstrated with the example in Figure 15.2. Various assumptions on client size, purchase volumes, lead to close ratios, cost of business and so on need to be documented for discussion and testing with partner prospects later in this phase and Phase 3.
2. The total market size and overall alliance opportunity, i.e. aggregation of the total amount of customer solutions likely to be required within a particular geography, timescale, industry or sector.

As well as focusing on the benefits, costs also need to be considered to offer return on investment (ROI) measures to ensure that returns will be positive over the period. High value and important alliances may need to have discounted cashflows and detailed sensitivity scenarios undertaken as well, ideally with an objective review and critique by the finance office. This is an area where too many organisations sweep over the downside risks,

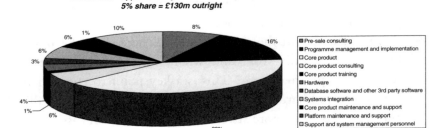

Figure 15.2 Example whole product model for technology solution.

forget the real costs involved and focus optimistically on large returns. By having more stringent controls and performance thresholds akin to similar M&A investments it will bring more clarity to the actual returns, and mitigate failure risks through poor results or slow payback.

Consideration also needs to be given to how attractive the proposition really is from the customer's perspective. The knowledge gained in understanding the arena will have helped determine existing activity but what is it about this proposed alliance that will compel customers to purchase this solution over others? Completing the following statement honestly and objectively will help, as will testing it with potential customer and partner's prospects at the right time and comparing it to current competitors and substitutes:

> For [target customer or market] who have a [compelling reason to buy] this alliance offers [sum of parts] that provides [the key benefit that addresses the compelling reason to buy].

Here is an example from an alliance at Reuters when it first brought out its leading Reuters 3000Xtra hosted solution. The technology-based sales and marketing alliance was important for Reuters and it soon led to the Reuters 3000Xtra hosted solution becoming one of its best selling products serving over 10 000 users. Its partner, Citrix, also got real value by seeing its hitherto back office thin client technology visibly supporting a business critical application used for supporting trading worth many billions of pounds. This meant Citrix could leverage the alliance as a case study for winning many other opportunities[103]. The customer also got great benefits too as described in an early draft of the alliance value proposition:

> The benefits of this alliance are targeted at a) the Finance Industry CTO who are under pressure to drive out cost whilst increasing end user mobility and functionality, and b) new users in smaller organisations. The alliance offers all the core functionality of 3000Xtra with greater business agility to satisfy end users. It also has a lower total cost of ownership with confidence that Reuters and Citrix are working closely together to deliver the service.

It is worth touching on supply side alliances at this stage as well. The principles are very similar to that above for the internal and supply market although questions on business pull and complementary activities are focused internally and upstream, and the customer is an internal one as opposed to external. This should not mean any less effort is applied to satisfying the customer though; indeed one of the strengths of external alliance partners is the opportunity to bring out far more effective and objective performance than an internally provided service. Using whole product analysis derived from value chain analysis, Figure 15.3 highlights an approach for transforming the way that products and services are procured in the NHS, using hips as an example.

Improving traditional procurement of hips through Collaborative Procurement Hubs (CPH) is a positive step forward for the NHS and should release valuable cash savings. However, it may not go far enough to make a long-term difference and the metrics used for success by procurement, i.e. lower hip prices may compromise greater savings opportunities in the whole product. Instead

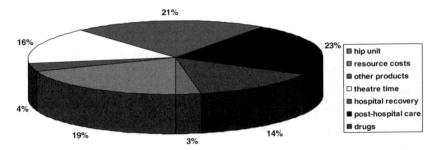

21%

16%   23%

■	hip unit
■	resource costs
■	other products
□	theatre time
■	hospital recovery
■	post-hospital care
■	drugs

4%

19%   3%   14%

Figure 15.3   Whole product model for hip procedure (conceptual).

of just seeking lower unit prices from suppliers in arm's length transactions, by constructing deeper alliances with relevant suppliers and clinical professionals addressing the whole life cost and quality around (say) a hip replacement operation it may yield significant results directly attributable back to patient well-being and Trust KPIs. In practice this might actually mean that the hip product goes up in price, but the overall pie (i.e. the average cost of procedure for the NHS) gets smaller, and the probability of procedure success and patient recovery time improves as well.

Staff motivations would need to reflect the holistic alignment back to Trust KPIs and whole life costing, and not encourage low hip unit price negotiation that could leave big opportunity costs and risks. However, therein lies one of the many big stumbling blocks for success, because some parts of the NHS and its supplier base are not yet ready for that sort of collaborative culture and practice internally or externally. There are pockets of such positive practice, for example in leading Trusts like Oldham Primary Care Trust and Christie's, the leading cancer hospital in Manchester. Other barriers to success include EU procurement legislation and a lack of alliance practitioner skills and capabilities required for such transformational success. It is not just hips either; consider many other clinical opportunities such as pharmacy, pathology, sterile services, single use agenda and other national tariff procedures. Nonclinical opportunities include printing and document management, catering, cleaning, laundry, portering and security as well as large capital projects.

Organisation and partner attractiveness

The modelling above has identified the complete alliance pie. One of the reasons for the organisation making the first cut of the total pie is to consider what share it wants to take. The fun in alliance negotiations can start when both partners have a view that they want to take a similar piece of the pie, especially if the alliance has co-opetition elements to it where the partner's competences overlap to some degree. Having undertaken the core competence analysis and gained a good understanding of where value is created, the organisation will be well placed to identify what aspects of the pie it can take on. A key point to ensure is that the elements offered to a partner prospect are both attractive and sustainable, and are relative to any inputs they are expected to commit to during negotiations. Alliance failure is highly likely when benefits are not shared or payback is slower than expected for one or both partners.

A sensible way of drawing up who does what and why in the alliance is through the use of a task list as shown with a simple example in Table 15.2. This one is a high-level task list for alliance and sales related tasks. Similar task lists need to be drawn up for operational activities and supply of products and services from the whole product model completed above, and measures can be added if appropriate as well as RACI. In high value important co-selling alliances such as the BT and HP example expressed earlier, detailed sales process mapping took place to ensure the two organisations' differing sales methodologies were aligned.

Completing the task list also enables the organisation to consider the cost of doing business and what capabilities are required

Table 15.2 Basic task list.

Task (derived from sales method)	Who does it (organisation, partner, both, or n/a – RACI)	Resources/investments required (list all inputs as this helps determine share of benefits/costs of doing business later)
Market intelligence/research		
Demand creation – general marketing		
Marketing internally and general education		
Pipeline management		
Lead/prospecting/targeted clients		
Initial contact		
Qualification		
Demonstration/reference site visits		
Formal customer proposal		
Customer negotiation		
Contracting		
Billing		
Customer account management		

to execute each task as well as where potential overlaps might be removed or managed coherently in front of the customer. This then helps in apportioning costs and agreeing ground rules during detailed alliance negotiations later in this phase and Phase 3.

Making first attempts at this stage to carve up the pie and identify key tasks also enables two other outputs to be considered:

- Is the organisation ready to execute on its proposed part of the alliance (output C)?
- Given the list of proposed tasks and activities for the partner, an ideal partner profile can be established (output D).

OUTPUT C: ORGANISATION READINESS

Having identified what aspects of the alliance it wants to take on, the organisation needs to consider two readiness questions in depth before it is subjected to due diligence by the selected partner prospect in Phase 3:

1. Are its in-scope assets, such as products and services, ready for partnering?
2. Is the organisation capable of delivering on its prospective commitments?

1. Are its in-scope assets, such as products and services, ready for partnering?

Organisations often seek to outsource problems or ally away issues they cannot easily address internally. Sometimes they are also unaware that their products and services are not yet optimised for partnering. This can mean huge value is left on the table for the smart partner as can be seen in Figure 15.4.

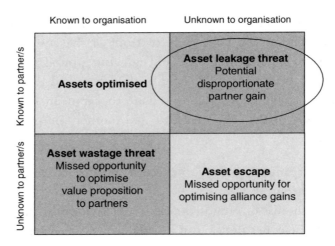

Figure 15.4　Asset attractiveness leakage threat.

One large organisation got itself in a bit of a mess with a back office service to the extent that key stakeholders considered outsourcing would make sense as it was a noncore area and better delivered by others. It was not short of suitors who were attracted to the alliance opportunity. As a result of the way it approached the potential outsource it failed to consider what the future could look like first and what it could do to improve service or drive out cost before partnering. It would not actually have to do the work, but could factor that into its starting point for negotiation, knowing the partner could get there quickly at little or no cost. Instead, it initially left prospects to shape solutions and make proposals which would potentially leave them disproportionate gains. Fortunately the approach was rearchitected in time and the organisation was able to re-establish more attractive gains from its assets and prevent the unnecessary loss of many millions of pounds.

On the sales and marketing side, many direct selling firms turn to reseller and value added reseller alliances to help expand

sales and penetrate new markets. This is great in theory but one
of the problems of a hitherto direct product supply is that sometimes far more investment needs to go into making products
channel partner ready. Examples include training programmes,
marketing materials, and changes to the product itself, as well as
alliance management costs and processes to manage indirect
channel activity. One firm could not keep its in-house consulting
and integration costs down for its software product, and while the
market was expanding, new entrants were also competing on
price squeezing the organisation profits and share. It decided to
find system integration (SI) alliance partners. There was an attractive proposition for all parties, and assuming the SI partner could
get smarter about integration, everyone would win. During due
diligence it was found that the product had so many bugs, and
there was no training programme; it was just not channel ready.
This was actually the main reason why the organisation's own
consulting and integration costs were so high. Its engineers were
bug fixing on site in order to try to do a good job that the time
to integrate took so much longer. As training was passed on
informally without effective material or checking, it was also
unable to manage quality issues in a consistent fashion. The costs
for investing in building the channel partner programme grew to
make it a sizeable initial investment which put off the senior
management from taking the risk, despite potentially attractive
returns.

David Johnson, Global Marketing Director for Reuters and
the original driver for Reuters' global alliance programme, had a
point of view around outsourcing and alliances where he said: 'we
need to get inside the area first before we can effectively partner
for it'. By that he made it clear that the organisation should not
just hand something over or abdicate responsibility for delivery
without first understanding more about the opportunities and
threats from the alliance activity.

2. Is the organisation capable of delivering on its prospective commitments?

Having architected the next layer of detail for the alliance, the organisation will start getting clearer about the resources it needs to invest and how the alliance may integrate with the wider business activities. As such it needs to reflect on the factors that affect collaboration in Chapter 11, making sure that the alliance stands the best chance of success on the ground. This could include looking to how alliance delivery resources are organised, skilled, rewarded and targeted, and what other priorities they might have conflicting with this alliance, as well as what systems and technology might aid or hinder performance and so on. As seen in the NHS example, this can be very challenging to address.

Proposals for changes in both (1) and (2) above should be made as part of a Phase 2 deliverable and if necessary noted on the risk register for future reference. Any 'showstoppers', i.e. factors that will compromise or prevent alliance success, should be raised immediately and addressed before proceeding further.

OUTPUT D: IDEAL PARTNER CHARACTERISTICS

A strength of going through the process noted above and carving up the pie in the manner described is that the opportunity is well specified and the remaining tasks are clear. As such, organisations can put together a profile of what their ideal partner would look like.

It may be that more than one partner is required or a partner prospect is already in mind or indeed close to the initiative already. If so, the recommendation is to suspend judgement, albeit briefly and consider architecting the ideal partner profile as there might be some surprises. At the very least it might increase awareness of some important aspects that may not have otherwise been considered in negotiations, thus improving the alliance agreement. A useful way to profile partners is by following ALLIANTIST TOPSCORER Map shown in Figure 15.5. TOPSCORER Map is a useful mnemonic to help remember the critical characteristics around selecting the right partner. Organisations might also consider the value from doing a TOPSCORER Map review on their own organisation (derived from the earlier VIP Map analysis in Part I) and do a compare/contrast of the possible fit between the parties for the specific alliance.

Looking at the characteristics in more detail and considering what should fall under each heading in practice, each one is discussed below:

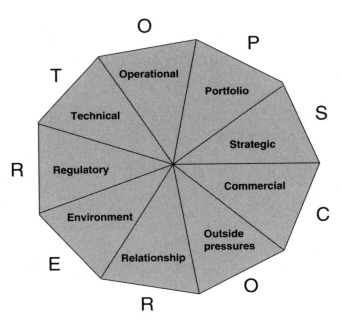

Figure 15.5 ALLIANTIST TOPSCORER Map.

Technical: this is what the alliance partner prospect brings in terms of core competences and other assets the firm wishes to access. It could include its products, services, key resources, IPR, equipment, customers, brand, distribution channel, in-country/ local knowledge, capital or other assets. This characteristic will also include assessing its asset readiness, strength and depth, i.e. in terms of size, experience and capacity as well as ability to hit the ground running.

Operational: this takes into account the prospect's ability to execute in terms of how it works in practice on the ground with its delivery resources, including its systems, technology and business processes which might need to integrate with the organisation. It also includes its approach to governance, risk management and controls, a key issue for listed organisations as expressed in Chapter 12. Great emphasis has been made on having a capability to partner and so it is with partner prospects as well. Other characteristics in TOPSCORER Map cover many elements of the VIP Map but this characteristic also looks at the elements surrounding operational alliance infrastructure and its past experience regarding successful delivery of alliance activity.

Portfolio: there are two aspects to this characteristic: one is the fit of the prospect within the organisation's portfolio and how it complements or competes with the organisation and its current partner's capabilities. The second is the prospect's portfolio and how the organisation will complement or compete with the partner prospect's capabilities and those of its partners.

Strategic: as seen from the VIP Map, clarity on strategy and direction and core competences is important, so strong strategic fit and complementary objectives during the life of the alliance are essential. Other factors to consider under this characteristic include assessing the complementarity of alliance drivers such as common competitors, similar customer demands as well as a compelling mutual need. Factors that might destroy value should also be considered here such as frequency of changes in direction in the prospect which might signal future competitive threat. An additional consideration is the value and importance that the organisation has in terms of contribution to each other's strategic goals. A good question to consider is what impact the alliance would have on the prospects business if it were terminated suddenly at some future point.

Commercial: financial attractiveness of any prospect contribution and overall alliance proposition should be considered under this aspect as will the upfront 'skin in the game' which helps signal commitment. These commitments could be derived from any of the assets discussed in Chapter 10. Depending on alliance value and importance this aspect might also call for detailed financial modelling and ROI calculations as described earlier, all of which will be fine-tuned with the selected partner during Phase 3. The relative sharing of benefits and time to benefit for each party should also be taken into account. The financial health and commercial well-being of the prospect should also be considered.

Outside pressures: Part I discussed how alliances face big challenges due to organisations having other priorities or outside pressures competing for management time. When questioned, if the proposed alliance resources from the prospect see the organisation as anything less than its number one priority, it should raise serious questions. Consider potential external distractions such as M&A activity, leadership challenges, other important partners or customers, poor overall partner commercial performance as well as frequently changing staff which might indicate deeper problems inside the prospect.

Relationship: this aspect looks at how the prospect's ability to collaborate both organisationally and individually fits with that of the organisation and its proposed alliance team. By referring back to Chapter 4, with the trust framework, and in particular Chapter 11 with the collaboration checklists and commentary, there are many examples of relationship fit criteria to consider assessing. In terms of ability to collaborate, the cultures and practices do not necessarily have to be the same, but a strong relationship fit is essential for success. Indeed, sometimes a markedly different performance culture is required for success, for example in shaking up a poor performing business unit an assertive outsourcing partner might positively improve productivity. Other aspects to consider include comparing leadership styles, values and beliefs, organisational structure and decision-making, the way people are managed and motivated, attitude to risk as well as approach to policy and practice from a legal and compliance perspective. Partner prospects also need to demonstrate that their stakeholder map has all the relevant high power stakeholders supporting the initiative and a suitable sponsor in place.

Environment: means understanding the impact of the alliance with this prospect on the specific marketplace in terms of how customers and competitors are likely to react as well as other interested parties, for example market commentators and shareholders. It also encapsulates any relevant aspects around corporate social responsibility and sustainable business impact.

Regulatory: includes broader assessment of macro factors in the regulatory environment facing the prospect and the alliance as well as any legal compliance for example, around industry regulations, anticompetitive practices, TUPE and other factors that might need to be addressed with legal safeguards in Phase 3.

Brainstorming as a team, or looking individually at each of the TOPSCORER characteristics then discussing them as a group, will help produce the right partner profile. If appropriate the criteria can also be built into a database and weighted according to the organisation's needs and areas it considers more important than others. This is especially useful if a choice of partners exists or the organisation is going to hold a 'beauty parade' (see output E). Arriving at a set of scores where one prospect's result is higher than another is useful, but the key is to go through the process and get more awareness of prospects' capabilities vis-à-vis others against the ideal profile. Definitive criteria also help:

- Clarify ambiguity and remove subjectivity of decision-makers
- Enable more effective analysis of prospect strengths and weaknesses against the ideal profile
- Baselining partner performance before alliance launch and setting performance improvements
- Deal with potential future audit enquiries on selection decisions
- Give unsuccessful partners valuable feedback on where they can improve for next time

OUTPUT E: ENGAGEMENT PLAN AND PARTNER SELECTION

Having crafted the ideal partner profile steps can be taken to engage and select the right partner. There are various different methods including informal activity (say) on the golf course through to quite comprehensive partner selection processes and beauty parades. Internal policies and legislation may also affect how the organisation approaches the marketplace. One thing is clear: do not treat this as an adversarial tender with restrictive

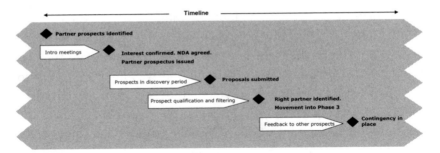

Figure 15.6 Example engagement plan for partner selection.

practices around sharing relevant information and making the exercise onerous for prospects. Other poor practices include giving prospects little time to respond, unnecessary work to perform and not allowing them to come onsite to meet key stakeholders during the beauty parade period. Prospects should not be able to roam free unsupervised or delay progress unnecessarily, but so many procurement-oriented tenders stifle collaboration and innovation during the discovery period it is no wonder that many supply-based alliances fail to work in practice.

Lets assume the organisation chooses to go down an auditable route and issues a partnering prospectus to interested parties, then subsequently works through a comprehensive selection process. A high-level example of the approach is shown in Figure 15.6 and discussed below.

Partner prospects identified

This will be from various sources including existing partners, customers, suppliers and competitors as well as the environment analysis undertaken earlier. Imagine a funnel process where an initial screening using a high-level form of TOPSCORER Map will enable prospects to be filtered to a reasonable number; probably no more than five or six depending on the alliance, assuming one or two will fall away following the introductory meeting.

Interest confirmed; NDA agreed and prospectus issued

Without unnecessarily giving away confidential information or risking loss of future advantage, in the introductory meetings the organisation should seek to establish the appetite and capability of the prospect to enter an alliance. Assuming the prospect signals the right desire and demonstrates an initial capacity to execute within the required timescales then a mutual nondisclosure agreement (NDA) should be put in place and the alliance partner prospectus issued. The mutual NDA will enable two-way sharing of information during the discovery period. It is important to note that negotiation commences immediately the parties engage, not at some future point. As such firm 'party lines' to shape direction and a well set out 'negotiation brief' should be used as early as possible to keep team members aligned and focused as described in Phase 1.

The prospectus should include the following information:

■ Alliance objectives and background to the opportunity with timescales for making decisions and the proposed process for doing so, along with key sponsors and alliance team contacts.
■ Content that enables prospects to effectively reach their own conclusions about the opportunity. For example, using the whole product model demonstrating the size of the market as well as the opportunities and issues around a typical customer scenario or current operating practice.
■ What the organisation sees as the most important assets and characteristics for its successful alliance partner to offer, with

their ranking of importance, taken from the TOPSCORER analysis and the draft task lists.

- Operating ground rules such as minimum 'skin in the game commitments', legal issues and conditions on alliance exit, for example handover of specific assets and transfer of IPR ownership.

- Any beauty parade ground rules concerning how the process is managed such as confirmation that the organisation is not obliged to accept any proposals, and that it will not fund prospects' discovery activity.

The prospects should be encouraged to meet with the key stakeholders for individual sessions and workshops to help the discovery process as well as aid relationship building. This should be structured in a fashion to ensure fairness between the prospects and enable optimal learning for the organisation. It may also include informal activity as well, for example after a workshop there could be a meal and drinks to see how prospects behave in different circumstances. In one alliance project the proposed alliance manager of the partner prospect turned out to be a less attractive character after having drunk alcohol and his true colours shone through. As a result he was replaced. This face-to-face activity enables ongoing qualification, and feedback should be captured within the TOPSCORER Map database if one has been built to aid the selection decision-making.

Proposals submitted

Having been given an appropriate amount of time to complete discovery and submit its proposal in the requested format, backed up with a summary verbal presentation, the organisation can commence its detailed analysis. This may lead to further workshops or

clarification activity with the prospects as opposed to isolated proposal screening and silence. While deep and expensive due diligence may be inappropriate at this stage, some investigation into
proposal statements and representations should be made.

If using a scoring-based approach to 'mark' the proposals
against the ideal partner profile a useful way to achieve this is by
first having independent reviews from each of the relevant alliance
team members. They score their results subjectively and add them
into the database. Then, coming together as a team, the independent reviews are compared and contrasted with debate and learning taking place, with individual scores adjusted as they deem
necessary to then arrive at a consolidated group score.

Learning from this process informs the negotiation brief and
subsequent prospect negotiations, leading to filtering of the prospects and identification of the right partner to go into Phase 3.
The organisation may need to present its proposals to a steering
committee or executive board at this stage, before commencing
final negotiations. Depending on the level of risk in the alliance
and trust exhibited to date with the preferred partner, selection
may need to be formalised with a legal memorandum of understanding, or nonbinding heads of agreement, or term sheet outlining the key areas of agreement to date.

Contingency in place

Having identified the right partner to take into Phase 3, the
organisation should formally close down discussions with the other
prospects debriefing them on areas of strength and weakness and
the rationale for the decisions. This is not only a professional cour-
tesy given the investment they made to date, but also enables one
or more prospects to be kept warm in the event Phase 3 does not
work out as planned with the first selected partner.

OUTPUT F: STAKEHOLDER AND RISK MANAGEMENT

Building from Phase 1 the stakeholder template should be updated and where appropriate partner prospect stakeholders added as well. The risk register should continue to be managed and updated as necessary, highlighting actions agreed with the selected partner that would change the risk assessment for the organisation. These actions may then need to be included in the legal safeguards or ground rules agreed in Phase 3.

PROGRESS TO PHASE 3

Phase 2 is a much deeper piece of work than Phase 1. There are also key decisions to be made during this phase that will likely mean regular checkpoints with sponsors and other stakeholders, perhaps using a steering committee or review board, for example clarifying the alliance opportunity and the partner selection. Past experience suggests that sponsors and review boards should make their mark on the selection of the partner and contribute to the final negotiation. This is important for their buy-in as well. Leaving a small but important piece of value on the table for these stake-holders to 'negotiate' together can also help cement the selection decision and make the path into Phase 3 far more collaborative at all alliance touchpoints.

PITFALLS TO AVOID

Be careful about accepting prospect statements based purely on their proposal alone, hence why relationship building and character assessment are important at this early stage. Trust may still be being built and the possibility of 'spin' should not be misread as 'sub-stance'. For example, if seeking a global alliance partner and a

prospect suggests it can really execute a global alliance in a consistent fashion then look carefully at its ability to collaborate and
get under the covers of the factors that affect collaboration as
described in Chapter 11. Also look at past examples and talk with
current partners of the prospect. Few global alliances really work
as hoped in practice. Whether it is structure, culture, internal
accounting rules, leadership or politics, the successful alliance will
have covered its bases in all those areas.

One organisation thought it was negotiating a global alliance.
In moving into due diligence it turned out the leading global alliance representative, a senior country figure, had no operational
mandate globally and could not enforce or really influence other
country activity. To ensure success the alliance needed to be 'negotiated' and operated at a country level with the country leaders
who were responsible for in-country resources and financial performance. Other factors to consider are that despite having global
marketing presence, some prospects will have little more than 'one
man and a dog' in certain territories so capacity and coverage needs
to be investigated. This is an important point for aspiring global
alliances and a good reason to avoid exclusive commitments.
Ensure that the negotiation representatives are able to make the
decisions and see them executed in practice; ideally they or the
sponsor will have P&L accountability for the success. Otherwise,
existing local alliances that already do a good job may feel threatened by a 'global alliance' and see it as a signal to go elsewhere.
Then, under a worst case scenario when the global alliance fails
to deliver, the organisation has lost out completely. A better solution may have been to build alliances on a country by country
basis in the beginning.

Other pitfalls to avoid include:

■ Taking two or more partners into Phase 3 unless the solution calls
for multiple partners. There may be on occasion good reasons for
taking more than one partner into deeper negotiation and due

diligence. Consider carefully the extra costs, resources and time needed as well as the opportunity costs of letting one down right at the end. Rather than take two parties into Phase 3, use it as a formal filter to help raise the stakes and set deadlines with the prospects. If necessary, conduct some of the Phase 3 work in Phase 2 to help arrive at the right selection.

- Overengineering selection models and looking for fractions or decimal point differences in scoring. Too much focus on the 'how', rather than 'what', will lead to paralysis by analysis and upset results-oriented practitioners who just want to get on with delivery, even if it is with the wrong partner!

- Creating a market opportunity (pie) that doesn't really exist and can't be substantiated in negotiations. Also carving up the pie in an unreasonable manner or not being open to moving around slices in negotiation will likely lead to stand-offs and adversarial or opportunistic behaviours.

- Failing to expressly agree roles for each team member and use inexperienced staff, especially when it comes to the negotiation team and dealing with the partner prospects. Consider 'divide and conquer', 'loose lips sink ships' and 'a little knowledge is a dangerous thing' . . . these all are experienced by poor collaborative negotiators and exploited by smart partner prospects.

SUMMARY OF TOOLS NEEDED FOR PHASE 2

- Phase 2 output checklist and proposal document to move into Phase 3
- Team kick-off pack and ground rules
- Risk register and risk assessment matrix
- Stakeholder coordination template with RACI, and power/ importance positioning map

- Attractiveness of assets, identification, valuing and optimising including menu of benefits to offer prospects (Chapter 10)
- Market and customer arena profiling
- Whole product model, value chain and customer value proposition statement
- Alliance task lists
- Organisation and alliance readiness assessment including factors affecting collaboration internally and externally (Chapter 11)
- TOPSCORER Map and selection model
- Beauty parade alliance partner prospectus and engagement plan
- Negotiation brief including party line messages and voice of authority statements
- Alliance term sheet or similars
- Stakeholder map and risk register

## CHAPTER 16

PHASE 3: WITH-PARTNER PLANNING

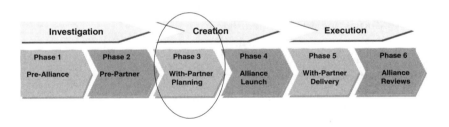

CONTEXT

With a mandate from the review board to get close to the selected partner much deeper focus and investment is made in this phase on bringing the alliance to life together. The alliance idea now needs to move from being the idea of one firm into the shared passion of both parties.

PHASE 3 AIMS

This phase has three outputs with each one a major test for the future success of the alliance. Outputs A and B will generally be completed in parallel, with output C being the architecture and glue that pull together all the relevant findings from this and earlier phases, as well as past experiences with the selected partner. In achieving output C the parties will have constructed an effective relationship architecture which attains CSF 3 and positions the organisation (and its partner) well for winning with this alliance.

Table 16.1 Phase 3 output checklist.

No.	Phase 3 output	Tick when completed	Comments
A	Compelling value proposition agreed between the parties and roadmap of targets aligned.		
B	Mutual operational due diligence completed to each partner's satisfaction.		
C	An effective relationship architecture designed that will facilitate alliance success and mitigate against surprise or failure, thus addressing CSF 3.		

OUTPUT A: COMPELLING VALUE PROPOSITION AND TARGETS ALIGNED

Phase 2 introduced the need for the value proposition to make sense for all participants. Some or all of this information will have been shared with the partner prospects in Phase 2, but may not have been subject to detailed review and critique. At this stage, therefore, both parties need to get inside the assumptions and ensure the value proposition stacks up to the degree that makes them both comfortable in making the necessary investments. The degree of openness and sharing exhibited is a good test of the collaborative nature of the relationship. The output will be clarity in the whole product, with assumptions and projections explicitly agreed between the parties and the tasks required for success allocated and documented in the task lists. Ideally, actual beach head clients and prospective pilots will have been identified to help craft the scenarios around something plausible and may even be subtly tested with the target audience for appetite.

Having constructed and agreed the value proposition it will enable sanity check and alignment of the alliance roadmap in terms of targets and execution over the lifecycle. A good exercise for ensuring alignment between the partners is the Alliance Timeline Exercise which can also be great fun and help develop relationships. It forms a one day workshop and an independent facilitator may be helpful given the need for objectivity between the partners. Figure 16.1 highlights the exercise process which is described in further detail below.

Figure 16.1   Alliance Timeline Exercises.

Exercise 1 Alliance birth

Using flip charts and working as separate partners for up to 30 minutes, then coming together to compare and contrast proposals, the partners produce a maximum one page flip chart spoof 'press release' announcing the alliance to the marketplace. It needs to draw from the value proposition work and include key information about the alliance goals, rationale for the alliance, target audience and objectives over the course of the alliance. It should also outline the initial key tasks the partners will perform prior to launch and over the first 30 and 60 days. Statements from both sponsors would also be included. To introduce the element of fun, this could be delivered in any genre; examples could include *News at Ten*, cartoon figures, characters from *Coronation Street* or whatever. Spend no more than one hour on the compare and contrast activity. If the spoof releases differ markedly and disputes arise that are not easily addressed, put it on hold and go onto the next exercise, returning to the issues at the end as part of the wrap-up and next steps.

This exercise will ensure the alliance course is set and aligned in terms of objectives and initial tasks, providing insight into the Phase 4 alliance launch and help identify what needs to be addressed before any formal press release. Clearly the content is most important but the presentation medium of a light-hearted genre can be fun and help improve relations.

Exercise 2 Mid-term best case

Agree on a time period mid way in the alliance lifecycle, perhaps one or two years out. Imagine that the alliance is receiving an award for the best alliance in the world. Consider two key aspects and within 30 minutes note:

- What the alliance has achieved at this period in terms of its key results and deliverables
- How it achieved them and what were the top five reasons for success from both parties

These factors should not be generic or vague; they should be specifically targeted at the alliance. For example, it could be the close working of the team in the shared R&D location, which might indicate a need to look closely at that area to see how best to architect it for success. Again, the exercise should be done as individual organisations then discussed together as partners to compare and contrast, spending no more than one hour on the task. Whoever presented first last time gets to go second on this occasion. Continue with the genre theme if it worked well in the first instance.

This exercise will test alignment over the course of the alliance and help set stage goals, explicitly drawing out factors that both parties see as crucial for the success and may be investigated in due diligence or during the construction of the effective relationship architecture.

Exercise 3 Mid-term worst case

Adopt a similar process as with exercise 2, but this time imagine the alliance is being slated in the press as a terrible example of alliance practice.

- What are the results and why are they so bad?
- How has it achieved them and what are the top five reasons for the poor performance?

This exercise also looks at the factors both parties will need to address for success and asks questions from a different frame which may bring out new information to address in due diligence or in building the effective relationship architecture.

Exercise 4 Alliance obituary

Having had a wonderful alliance life, it has now drawn to an end and everyone should celebrate its contribution. Imagine fast forwarding to that point in time, and by looking back at a great life, consider what results the alliance achieved. (If not clear from the alliance discussions to date agree on an end of life time period.)

Again with the partners working alone, for up to one hour, each should consider what the alliance results were over the life, looking back at each year and seeing what was achieved in each key period. Note the results and assess how the relationship health evolved between the parties as well. Then consider other key milestones, such as new products, new markets and major successes. Having then articulated the results, consider how they were arrived at. What were the essential points from how the parties worked together that brought about success? Consider what happened next for both organisations and how the exit came about and who got what from it. For example, did it end in a new alliance, a takeover by one partner or the fair division of alliance created assets or something else?

This exercise builds on the previous ones and sets out the overall alliance goals, major milestones and roadmap of targets and objectives. In addition it helps determine the exit strategy and what obligations to commit each other to when the alliance comes to an end, for whatever reason.

At the end of the one day workshop both parties will have a good idea of how aligned they are in practice. They should have the ability to formalise the alliance proposition and roadmap of targets and objectives to be achieved over the alliance life in a joint relationship and alliance plan. Any remaining issues can be identified and actions agreed as to how they will be overcome, for example in the due diligence work noted in output B below. This set of exercises can also be completed in reverse, i.e. start with alliance obituary and then work back to what needs to happen before press release.

OUTPUT B: COMPLETE MUTUAL DUE DILIGENCE

Both parties will have worked closely on the customer focused due diligence in output A and felt comfortable the proposition is worthwhile pursuing. This next level of due diligence should be mutual and seek validation of the TOPSCORER Map assumptions that were behind the selection. While the organisation will dig deeper into the TOPSCORER Map characteristics and check out areas of concern or validation, so will the partner. It will look to the organisation's readiness and therefore any risks or issues highlighted during Phase 2 output C will need to have been addressed successfully, else it may threaten the alliance or result in less attractive agreement terms for the organisation.

In commencing the TOPSCORER Map due diligence, there are risks of partner fallout and disagreement. To mitigate these risks both partners should first agree the process of due diligence, its scope and timescales for completion. Use of external advisors, if appropriate, should also be agreed early on. The partners obviously need to be assertive on the content of due diligence, but remain fair on the relationship itself and agree what happens during due diligence. For example, how will sensitivities be managed over distracting staff or business operations if they need to be investigated? Will the relevant information be kept in a clean room with limited access for certain staff or will the partner be able to roam across the organisation at its leisure?

Before undertaking due diligence the partners should also agree what will happen with the findings. Areas of issue or risk and any new information that affects the previous discussions should be noted and considered in the context of the subsequent negotiations and added to the negotiation brief. The partners should also agree how they will deal with new information and issues, especially showstoppers. Should they be negotiated one at a time, or held over to a specific final negotiation? Each circumstance differs, but those organisations that drip feed concessions from partners and creep up their share of the benefits may affect trust as the process continues. One of the most successful collaborative negotiations for two large alliance partners came about following due diligence. There were many areas to resolve. Both parties agreed to a full and frank disclosure and put all the issues up on a whiteboard at once with a commitment not to leave the room until they had thrashed out a mutually beneficial solution. It came after some ten hours, in the early hours of the next morning!

Having completed the due diligence and negotiated around the implications, both parties will be ready to move into the process of building the effective relationship architecture.

OUTPUT C: EFFECTIVE RELATIONSHIP ARCHITECTURE DESIGNED

To summarise, the organisation has demonstrated that it has developed a capability to partner (CSF 1) by building from Part II using the VIP Map. By adopting the practices proposed throughout the ICE Map in these first three phases, in particular using the TOP-SCORER Map and completing mutual due diligence, it can be sure it has at least selected the right partner (CSF 2). In order to successfully achieve the alliance objectives and deliver effectively, it remains to build a construct that supports the alliance goals and enables subsequent phases to be executed as envisaged. This then is CSF 3; the need for an effective relationship architecture to glue the organisations together in the manner necessary for both parties to win.

ALLIANTIST ERA Map addresses CSF 3 and helps pinpoint what relationship architecture is required for success. The ERA Map facilitates achievement of the alliance objectives and mitigates the risk of failure or surprise while optimising costs of governance. In simple terms the ERA Map helps the partners structure the alliance while taking into account the following points gathered so far:

- **The alliance and relationship goals and objectives:** this symbolises the importance of the alliance to both parties and the depth of investment that might be appropriate for the ERA given the desired rewards.
- **The strength and maturity of the relationship between the parties concerned:** this aspect looks at the relationship between the parties, not just from this alliance initiative but also other experiences between the organisations.
- **Each partner's ability to execute their commitments:** this aspect takes into account the existing alliance brand of the partners and looks at the infrastructure surrounding the alliance. Poor capability in this area will increase the performance related risks in the alliance.

Answering a series of simple questions based on the engagement activity to date enables the organisation to plot on the ERA Map what the most effective relationship architecture might be. The ERA Map is shown in Figure 16.2.

To illustrate how this works in practice consider two simple examples:

1. Two organisations had a history of good relations and wanted to build a new alliance. They trusted each other and had credible past alliance performance working together. The alliance goals were complementary, and they had a mutual dependence on each other for success, making early stage commitments of people and funding of equipment. They scored 110 for relationship and 90 for infrastructure on the ERA Map meaning this relationship was in the top right box. Therefore the

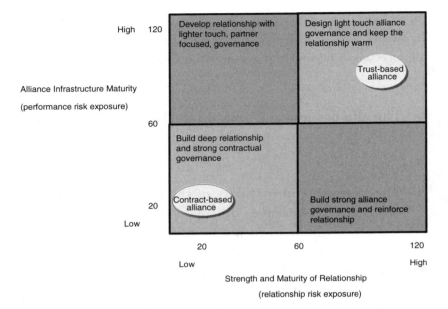

Figure 16.2 ALLIANTIST ERA Map.

effective relationship architecture only needed a lightweight alliance governance model. It included reporting of shared activity where the sponsors met formally six monthly at a strategic governance board and informally from time to time. The alliance teams, despite being in different countries, shared information daily, communicated regularly and honestly about performance, good and bad, and made time for social activities after each bi-monthly operational governance face-to-face meeting, which helped to keep their relationship warm. The safeguards were limited contractual documentation to mainly cover what happened during exit as IPR was created in the alliance that proved valuable to both parties.

2. Two past competitors saw a need to collaborate in order to exploit emerging opportunities and also defend their existing business against a common foe. The partners were still going

to compete against each other as well, although in a more limited capacity. The sponsors knew one another well and wanted a simple one page MoU (memorandum of understanding). However, the trust and positive experiences of the sponsors were not replicated across the delivery resources on the ground, who were usually rewarded for knocking out their new partner from competing sales opportunities. One partner also had a reputation for alliance failure and constant change of strategy. The scores were 60 for relationship and 50 for infrastructure pushing the alliance in the upper corner of the bottom left box. This relationship architecture needed underpinning with strong governance from three governing bodies (operations, management and strategic leadership), reinforced with clear rules of engagement and extensive contractual obligations to help deal with potential future issues. For the alliance to stand any chance of success, investment was also required in initiatives that demonstrated commitment to each other such as joint development, placing significant business with each other, and investing in activities to help change behaviours and perceptions. These activities included changing reward structures, creating joint training programmes, joint marketing activities and social programmes to help build trust and develop relationships across all alliance touch points.

Figure 16.3 highlights questions that help determine the strength and maturity of the relationship between the organisations and assess what risks may be present from a relationship risk perspective. In completing this questionnaire the organisation should draw on its learning from working with the partner and circle the most appropriate number, offering evidence or commentary where appropriate. The total score should be summed at the bottom and positioned on the ERA Map X axis.

In a similar vein, Figure 16.4 helps inform about the alliance performance dimension and considers the perspective around

Strength and maturity of relationship	Absolutely no --------- Absolutely yes 0 1 2 3 4 5 6 7 8 9 10	Comments/evidence
There is a mutual dependency on each other for business success from this alliance	0 1 2 3 4 5 6 7 8 9 10	
There is a fair sharing of organisation rewards forecast given the relative inputs (assets) provided by each party	0 1 2 3 4 5 6 7 8 9 10	
The alliance will have early 'skin in the game' and meaningful commitment of valuable assets by both parties	0 1 2 3 4 5 6 7 8 9 10	
The factors affecting collaboration in each organisation are aligned and complementary for both parties, offering strong relationship fit	0 1 2 3 4 5 6 7 8 9 10	
There are good relations at each of the proposed alliance touchpoints from sponsor down through to delivery resources	0 1 2 3 4 5 6 7 8 9 10	
The alliance is a long-term collaboration and/or open ended agreement with no quick exit available for either partner	0 1 2 3 4 5 6 7 8 9 10	
There has been a high degree of sharing through Phases 2 and 3 with trusting behaviours exhibited by both parties	0 1 2 3 4 5 6 7 8 9 10	
The organisations have worked well together in the past on similar initiatives	0 1 2 3 4 5 6 7 8 9 10	
Any complex relationship activity between the parties is well managed	0 1 2 3 4 5 6 7 8 9 10	
There are **no** examples of destructive past disputes or damaging behaviours between the organisations	0 1 2 3 4 5 6 7 8 9 10	
There are no competing initiatives or issues of co-opetition affecting the alliance now or envisaged during the alliance term	0 1 2 3 4 5 6 7 8 9 10	
The future exit strategy is clear and there are no indivisible assets or other challenges when it comes to end of alliance life	0 1 2 3 4 5 6 7 8 9 10	
Total score (out of maximum 120 points)	____ points	

Figure 16.3 ALLIANTIST ERA Map relationship axis questionnaire.

Alliance infrastructure maturity	Absolutely no ——— Absolutely yes	Comments/evidence
	0 1 2 3 4 5 6 7 8 9 10	
The partner has a positive reputation and identity for partnering in the past in this area	0 1 2 3 4 5 6 7 8 9 10	
The partner can demonstrate successful past results from its alliance activity in this area	0 1 2 3 4 5 6 7 8 9 10	
The partner demonstrates strong preventive and detective controls in its relevant operations	0 1 2 3 4 5 6 7 8 9 10	
There are effective training, tools, systems and processes already in place for delivery of the alliance tasks	0 1 2 3 4 5 6 7 8 9 10	
The controls and systems infrastructure is complementary for both partners' 'business as usual' practice with no overlap of business processes and little new learning	0 1 2 3 4 5 6 7 8 9 10	
There is a dedicated alliance management team in place focused full time on the alliance with the required budget and funding necessary for success	0 1 2 3 4 5 6 7 8 9 10	
The alliance management team have the appropriate SACKED characteristics for success	0 1 2 3 4 5 6 7 8 9 10	
The alliance management team have appropriate rewards, incentives and consequences for meeting the alliance objectives	0 1 2 3 4 5 6 7 8 9 10	
There are dedicated alliance delivery resources in place focused full time on the alliance with the required budget and funding necessary for success	0 1 2 3 4 5 6 7 8 9 10	
The alliance delivery resources have the appropriate SACKED characteristics for success	0 1 2 3 4 5 6 7 8 9 10	
The alliance delivery resources have appropriate rewards, incentives and consequences for meeting the alliance objectives	0 1 2 3 4 5 6 7 8 9 10	
The other assets necessary for success are available and ready to be invested in the alliance as required, e.g. equipment, products, services and other resources	0 1 2 3 4 5 6 7 8 9 10	
Total score (out of maximum 120 points)	_____ points	

Figure 16.4 ALLIANTIST ERA Map infrastructure axis questionnaire.

performance risks. It too should be scored and summed, with the total plotted on the Y axis giving a final positioning of the alliance on the ERA Map with an indication of the most appropriate effective relationship architecture required for success.

Alliance brands working together will score highly but few organisations demonstrate questionnaire results at the top of the right box. Experience suggests that most scores are around 50–70 for each axis placing the alliance on or near the bottom left box, meaning a somewhat heavier weight relationship architecture is required than first thought. If the scores are under 40/40 then serious consideration should be given about whether the alliance can go ahead without more work to address the very low scores which may include showstoppers.

So what are the components that make up an effective relationship architecture for alliances? Things to consider including in the design are shown in Figure 16.5.

Relationship business plan

This will outline the aims and objectives of each party as well as the specific alliance and broader relationship goals. Other factors to

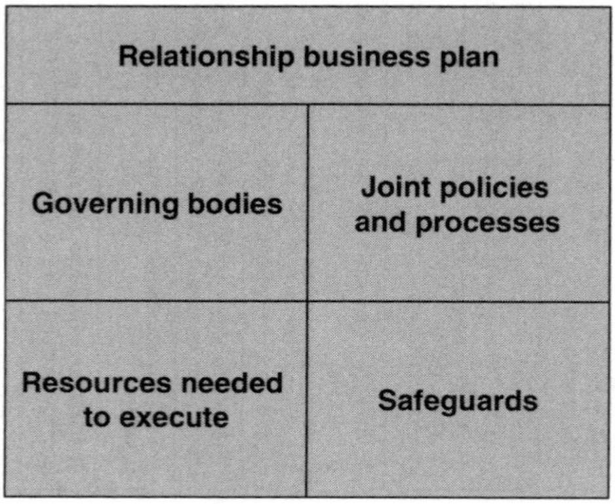

Relationship business plan	
Governing bodies	Joint policies and processes
Resources needed to execute	Safeguards

Figure 16.5 ERA components.

include are the SMART targets for each key activity on the roadmap, as derived from the alliance timeline exercise. This will also include the joint value proposition and agreed deliverables on output A above. In addition, if there are areas that are definitely out of scope, for example where the parties agree not to work together and compete, these should also be noted. If there is a complex relationship in place then the plan may also wrap all the other activities into one place. In ideal circumstances the relationship business plan should be a shared document although there may be information held by one party which affects the alliance but it does not wish to share in full with the other partner, for example internal risks and issues, competitor intelligence and competing portfolio activity. The plan should incorporate, either implicitly or explicitly, all the other components of the ERA below as well.

Effective governing bodies

These help guide the alliance and oversee progress between the partners. Heavyweight governance structures will include up to three governing bodies overseeing (1) operational reviews (e.g. weekly), (2) management activity (e.g. monthly) and (3) strategic activity (e.g. quarterly). The role of each body should be well understood with clarity on what needs to be produced for each meeting and why. Clearly specifying roles and responsibilities using RACI for key decisions made by each body and setting out a limited membership of key stakeholders is more beneficial than having unwieldy pontificating forums.

Joint policies and processes

These can take many forms depending on the nature of the alliance but common policies and processes include:

1. **Reporting and management information:** how much should be shared, who sees it, what are the metrics that should be used, where is the data pulled from, how is it presented and so on are important areas to agree, especially for those listed firms that need to have control over the end-to-end process. Consider leading and lagging indicators in a scorecard with metrics that cover value destruction and business risk as well as value creation. This is especially important if co-opetition is evident or one party has a history of failure.

2. **How joint investments are to be made by the parties:** should the investment be 50/50 or based on the relative rewards, or is it less easy to apportion a share. The process or a formula should be agreed before investments are necessary. Ideally some of the key investment decisions should be agreed at this stage to avoid future disputes. These investment decisions could include when to develop new products, enter new markets, purchase new equipment, undertake recruitment of key staff, inject business development funding, joint training programmes and so on. Harvesting of the rewards by one partner when the other wishes to continue investing for the future can lead to serious problems and early failure.

3. **How disputes will be resolved:** having disputes is healthy and positive. Resolving them constructively is also important so agreement should be reached on what happens in the event of a disagreement. Is it immediately escalated to the governing body, or should the operational teams be tasked with going away to solve it themselves first? Better practice suggests encouraging the disagreeing parties to attempt to solve it first or at least make proposals on what the resolution options might be rather than just throw it up the line. Instead of seeking litigation and threat as a means of solving problems consideration should be given to engaging impartial mediators and independent experts.

4. **Rewards and incentives:** as expressed in Part II it is imperative that the resources focused on the alliance are given some form of encouragement to do so. At the very least, factors affecting their execution, e.g. other priorities and competing rewards policies, need to be addressed. The interested parties will include the alliance management team as well as the delivery resources on the ground. Failure to agree complementary schemes between the parties will lead to poor performance and potential infighting in the alliance. Two large alliance partners had constraints from their parents about changing the rewards for the delivery sales teams on the ground. As a result the alliance stagnated until such time as that area was addressed.

5. **Relationship building:** efforts to build sustainable working relationships internally and externally should not be underestimated, especially for international alliances and cross-cultural engagement. Relationship health is crucial for alliance success and therefore a specific budget should be agreed between the parties, and initiatives identified that help cement relations and increase alliance productivity. Positioning on the ERA Map will help determine the degree of investment required, with greater funding needed if scores are on the left side. Initiatives should be focused both formally and informally with the intention of building trust and understanding. Brightwell, in building alliances with its partners in Eastern Europe, have invested heavily in understanding the local culture and practice which among other things has meant a need to learn the language and an ability to consume copious amounts of local vodka! Brighton Dive Centre (BDC), based in the Marina at Brighton, has an interesting corporate training and entertainment initiative. Designed to help build trust and enhance relationships, BDC helps team members learn to look out for each other and work together in a completely different environment which is fun, aids fitness at low cost and enables

participants to learn something new. It includes diving, water-skiing and other water-based team activities and is an exciting change from the usual cross-country hikes and raft building exercises that have been in place for some time.

6. **Technology and systems integration:** organisations collaborate and operate much more productively when the technologies and systems are aligned. Efforts to integrate and invest in seamless systems will be determined by the type, value and importance of the alliance. HP and BT, for example, have invested millions in developing joint service architecture to aid the operation and in doing so it also becomes a unique selling point of the go-to-market alliance. Partners should also agree how and where the alliance management information is going to be held and accessed, including relationship plan, contract, risk and stakeholder assessments, performance reports as well as customer facing material and information.

Safeguards

These include:

1. **Legal agreements** to cover potentially contentious issues like exclusivity, asset ownership, exit strategy and investments of assets over the alliance duration as well as sharing of the forecast rewards. Usual legal aspects such as term and termination, and legislative effects such as TUPE and data protection, if applicable, should also be addressed. There are strengths and weaknesses in agreeing exit clauses but past experience suggests the effort that goes into crafting them in advance is well worth the time. Numerous alliances have stalled at this stage because prospective partners failed to agree on what happened at exit, in particular around ownership of jointly created assets. Despite failure rates of some 70%, up to 30% of alliances do succeed!

Provisions in agreements therefore also need to consider what happens when the alliance has achieved its success as well as what happens in the event of failure. If lawyers are engaged early and have been included in the team sessions during Phase 2 they should understand the collaborative nature of the alliance and have received instructions on what areas to focus on. The significance of the legal documentation will be determined by the type of the alliance and the scores from the ERA Map, as well as both organisations' general approach in the field. The legal agreement may be a simple binding term sheet or a much deeper and more comprehensive tome. Legal safeguards are vital for protecting interests but it should be remembered that the alliance will probably not be able to specify all actions and obligations legally at an early stage, hence the need for collaboration and interdependence. Transferring risks and obligations to the partner in a legal contract just for the organisation to avoid them may not be the best solution for the long-term alliance success. Consideration should also be given to any potential risks from an anti-competition perspective if the alliance has a significant impact on the market. In reiterating comments expressed earlier, use of the term partner also carries legal obligations therefore it is worthwhile inserting a clause to confirm that terminology around 'partners' is a marketing term only.

2. **Ground rules:** there may be many areas in an alliance that don't necessarily need to be part of a formal legal agreement but need to have working practices documented to avoid ambiguity or dispute. Many of these will be already identified on the risk register and task lists. Others include things like internal and external communications and formal marketing plans. Another way of looking for areas that might need ground rules is to consider the alliance value chain itself and look for weak links or areas where hand-offs internally or touchpoints with the partner might lead to breakdown or overlap. Examples of

'sales' ground rules include which partner leads the sale, who takes the revenues in prime contractor circumstances, how discounts are agreed, and how the sales team would work together in practice across the sales cycle.

3. **Risk management and controls:** operating a shared risk register and reviewing progress on it is likely to be the minimum level of risk control required. For listed firms, demonstrating controls akin to that shown in Part II Chapter 12 may be necessary. If both parties are operating to the COSO ERM framework then it is likely that language, definitions and terminology are consistent which in itself will reduce risk further, otherwise explicit definitions and processes may need to be agreed to avoid ambiguity and satisfy auditors.

4. **Partner and alliance relationship reviews:** agreeing the extent and frequency of formal reviews early on signals a desire to remain transparent and be open to learning throughout the alliance lifecycle. Reviews by each other, on each other, are positive, although there may be occasions when an independent assessment is better, for example at an objective annual review and if the alliance is underperforming and partners are unclear about the underlying causes. Phase 6 offers up ALLIANTIST PARA Map to aid comprehensive alliance and partner reviews.

Ensuring each party is completely organised to execute

This means that not only are the right resources in place from an alliance management and alliance delivery perspective, but that both parties' touchpoints back into their organisations are in full working order as well. Imagine the complexity of governance around a joint go-to-market alliance where the alliance partners also need to build tailored governance for each customer. Figure

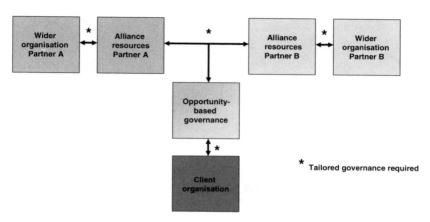

Figure 16.6 Governance complexity with alliances.

16.6 highlights the four dimensions where tailored governance and effective resource organisation is required. This is particularly important to get right in large complex alliances with multiple stakeholders. For example, architecting an environment that stifles decision-making or means that the alliance management team doesn't have P&L accountability can mean lots of extra red tape, far more stakeholders to engage and a risk of spending more time on internal bureaucracy than external alliance value creation. It can then lead to staff and partner frustration and delays in executing the alliance which affects total returns from the alliance investments.

Using the ERA Map and following the principles laid out above will facilitate alliance success and mitigate the risks of surprise or failure while optimising governance costs. In addition the ERA approach offers alliance partners a unique selling point in their alliance proposition. It was described earlier how customers are getting smarter and looking more deeply than just a logo fit between partners. ERA offers customers belief and proof that the architecture between the partners will enable success. Some large vertically integrated solution providers will actively seek to sell against alliances from a governance perspective and suggest to customers they check the partner's governance because it is high risk. This approach not only neutralises that issue but it demonstrates a positive governance and relationship architecture that, if closely checked, many vertically integrated firms don't have themselves!

PROGRESS TO PHASE 4

It might be that as with the previous phase, the final piece of negotiation will best be done, at least politically, by the sponsor or review board. Appropriate documentation such as the completed legal agreement and ERA design can then be formally approved by the sponsors and review board in accordance with organisation policies around delegated authority. The partners can then move forward into making the alliance happen, confident they are going to be organised for success. Phase 4, alliance launch, is where all the components of the ERA get implemented and the first fruits of the collaboration come about.

PITFALLS TO AVOID

The ERA Map provides a summary test with questionnaires on how the partners might need to build their effective relationship architecture. It can be tempting to rush ahead and plot the partner without having completed the prior work first. By all means do so as a quick checkpoint, and share it with the partner too, but failure to do the groundwork beforehand might lead into the wrong architecture being constructed which will either lead to performance failure or relationship failure.

Other pitfalls to avoid at this stage include:

■ Trying to execute and build the alliance, solving all due diligence issues in advance of the launch phase. Be careful about rushing ahead without a formal contract or ERA principles agreed.

■ Not being prepared to pull out. While significant investment is likely to have been made thus far, consider the opportunity costs of a wrong decision over the longer term. If this phase has not proceeded as planned, and issues are of the partner's making, consider the contingency list of partners identified in Phase 2. It is likely that much of the work conducted in this phase so far will still be relevant.

■ Underestimating the importance of due diligence despite good relationships. Consider the large organisation that failed to complete due diligence effectively. It found that after the outsourcing alliance commenced it had overestimated the value of assets in one area and failed to manage the launch and transition in the manner envisaged. Despite its close relationship with its customer partner, over a six-month period it lost an additional £5 m which significantly affected profitability over the alliance life.

■ Overengineering the ERA approach. What is shown above is considered for high value and important alliances which will almost certainly need individual relationship architectures. For lower tier alliances it is likely that a more standardised approach using the components noted above will suffice.

■ Partners needing to make significant changes to their business as usual operations in order to execute the alliance tasks. Even if they say they are prepared to do so, making fundamental changes, for example by building new delivery capability, integrating new risk management systems, or learning a new solutions sales method and reporting process, will take time. It is likely that unless investment is made in training and change management initiatives for affected staff, the change will fail, compromising alliance success.

■ Failing to ensure that the alliance team can make a difference. Roles without responsibility, for example P&L accountability or ability to influence key decisions, will lead to suboptimal performance or alliance failure.

■ ERA is called ERA for a reason. Without the relationship, the alliance will fail and governance alone will be worthless. So if investment is needed in the relationship then make it happen, and measure the change by monitoring relationship health as a key metric.

SUMMARY OF TOOLS NEEDED FOR PHASE 3

■ Tools from Phase 2 plus
■ Alliance timeline exercises
■ Due diligence report
■ ALLIANTIST ERA Map and questionnaires
■ ALLIANTIST ERA components

PHASE 4: ALLIANCE LAUNCH

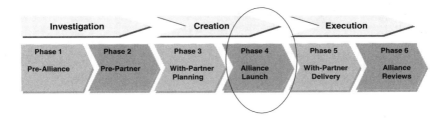

CONTEXT

Phase 4 is the end of the beginning. The hard work really starts now. There is only one opportunity for a successful launch and key stakeholders will be watching closely. Despite popular belief a successful launch includes far more than a press release and in itself can deliver favourable returns if well received by customers, share-holders and interested commentators. As was reported in Part I, organisations with a positive reputation and capability for partnering saw share price gains even on announcing alliances.

Having played a key supporting role during the alliance investigation and early creation activities the baton of alliance leadership formally gets passed onto the alliance manager. Assuming the alliance manager has been involved early on the need for knowledge transfer and potential for delay is mitigated. The resources that were instrumental in leading the creation of the alliance (commercial negotiators, lawyers and so on) will now step back, although should remain available for clarification of any issues as the launch progresses.

PHASE 4 AIMS

Having done all the preparatory work in Phases 2 and 3 this phase is about implementation and delivering early successes to create positive momentum. There are two key outputs for this phase as outlined in Table 17.1, each of which in practice is executed in parallel.

Table 17.1   Phase 4 output checklist.

No.	Phase 4 output	Tick when completed	Comments
A	Project and change management activities undertaken and ERA implemented to each partner's satisfaction.		
B	Formal announcement and launch to the wider external stakeholder groups and interested parties.		

OUTPUT A: PROJECT AND CHANGE MANAGEMENT

Alliance launch projects of any value require effective project and change management; however, depending on the value and type of alliance some activities will be more formal than others. Project launch activities like administration, planning, workstream delivery monitoring, stakeholder and risk management are coordinated from the project office which reports into the alliance manager. 'Change management' per se should not stick out like a sore thumb, it is merely an umbrella phrase that incorporates the tools, processes and mindset necessary to help people work through and implement the desired change successfully. Many of the principles for successful project and change management have already been discussed in earlier phases, including work breakdown planning, stakeholder communication and risk management. There are also many explicit change management philosophies but one which is common sense and works well in practice is that developed by John Kotter, the author of *Leading Change*[104]. Deloitte Consulting People & Change Practice advocates use of this methodology in particular for large change projects and points to many successes with it. It has eight principles, many of which have been implicitly used so far in Phases 1–3:

1. Create a sense of urgency
2. Build the guiding team
3. Get the vision right
4. Communicate for buy-in
5. Empower action
6. Create short-term wins
7. Don't let up
8. Make change stick

Building on those principles the leaders need to demonstrate the right behaviours and create urgency for the successful launch and implementation, for example by demonstrating why things cannot stay the same and why the alliance vision is so attractive. Communication strategies derived from the earlier stakeholder plans need to be targeted based on the stakeholder power and interest as expressed earlier. The contents are important but the vehicle for communication is also crucial, especially where the alliance disrupts individuals' lives, for example in staff transfer, major role change or redundancy. Past experience suggests the harder the impact of change is on someone, the more personal the communication needs to be. 'Town hall' announcements and large-scale communication can set the scene but each person will want to understand how it affects them. Communication is nothing without action following it and the alliance manager and sponsor need to ensure that any obstacles identified earlier are removed, and investments needed for success made swiftly. This could include the need for new equipment, training, work redesign, reward changes and other aspects noted in the chapter on collaboration. Creating short-term wins is essential for maintaining momentum so the principle of 30–60–90 day plans with clear deliverables can aid focus and results orientation.

Some of the Phase 1–3 Investigation and Creation team will no doubt still be involved in this phase but the ERA design will have shown additional delivery and governance-based resources required for success. Early delivery champions and advocates should now be identified, if not before in Phase 2, to help demonstrate the right behaviours to others that follow, and to help implement the early designs for real life activity. For example, in a joint go-to-market sales alliance it is worth getting an account team from each partner working closely together to hone the sales related tasks from the task lists created in Phase 2 and demonstrate how they work in practice (e.g. with a beach head client) so that during formal launch, the broader delivery resources can see their colleagues supporting it in practice through a live case study. This will make wider ramp-up of service somewhat easier and enable fine-tuning along the way. Similarly the other alliance touchpoints such as marketing, operations and service should also work together as required in their relevant workstreams on bringing their relevant ERA components to life. The operational governance bodies should be implemented such that at the end of the first 30 days the governance body members get informed of progress and can either reward progress or invoke consequences and keep up the urgency and pressure for success. The earlier investments in crafting relationship building plans also need to be integrated into the workstream tasks so that individuals build trust and relations in their partners as well. A simple plan overview would therefore look something like the example shown in Figure 17.1.

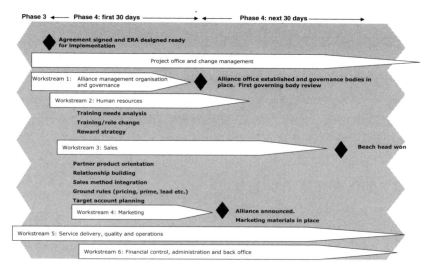

Figure 17.1 High-level example of a joint go-to-market alliance project plan.

OUTPUT B: ANNOUNCING THE ALLIANCE

In parallel with output A the partners will need to agree when the alliance should be unveiled to the wider stakeholder groups of customers, suppliers, other partners, competitors and shareholders. Timing is essential to avoid losing any first mover advantage (assuming the alliance aims to achieve that) but also not too early that the interested parties feel the alliance is more about smoke and mirrors and logo sharing than substantial value add. Communications strategies will be derived from the value proposition work and exercises undertaken in Phase 2. Both partners should have pre-agreed the 30–60 day marketing plan and any public communication activity. Having successfully completed the early tasks in output A the organisation can now execute that much desired press release, safe in the knowledge that behind its marketing activity there is operational excellence and no threat of customer rejection.

PROGRESS TO PHASE 5

Having implemented the ERA and successfully launched the alliance, the temporary project office and supporting resources can be closed down or phased out. The partners should now be well into the delivery phase and executing on their commitments.

PITFALLS TO AVOID

As with earlier phases consideration needs to be given to the level of engineering required, for example in project management and change management. Prince II project management methods may be completely over the top for most alliances, but for long-term, high value, complex and important collaborations, for example building a ship, they could be highly relevant. Other examples include:

■ Don't underestimate the importance of relationship building and early involvement of workstream champions, ideally introducing them in Phase 2 if the opportunity merits it.

■ Losing momentum early on will kill the alliance in no time at all. Maintaining strong and consistent communications with desired behaviours, led from the sponsor down, is essential for success.

■ Deal with disputes quickly, using the agreed dispute resolution mechanism if appropriate.

■ Do not tolerate mistakes or disengagement; use them as positive lessons to learn from and penalise noncollaborative behaviours for all to see.

SUMMARY OF TOOLS NEEDED FOR PHASE 4

■ Those from previous phases plus
■ Alliance launch and project management
■ Change management

## CHAPTER 18

PHASE 5: WITH-PARTNER DELIVERY

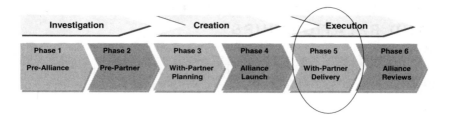

CONTEXT

Having successfully launched and stabilised the alliance, the alliance moves into delivery phase. In order to understand what happens during 'delivery' this chapter looks through the lens of the alliance manager. There is no typical 'day in the life' or 'week in the life' of an alliance manager as the profile of time spent changes from week to week although there are some common themes.

PHASE 5 AIMS

During this phase there are two key outputs: delivery of the results and management of the stakeholders to ensure results are achieved in an efficient and effective manner. Table 18.1 summarises the outputs.

Table 18.1 Phase 5 output checklist.

No.	Phase 5 output	Tick when completed	Comments
A	Deliver the alliance results in accordance with the relationship business plan.		
B	Develop and manage relationships with the stakeholders internally and externally.		

OUTPUTS A AND B: RESULTS AND RELATIONSHIPS

Outputs A and B are inextricably linked so it is worthwhile considering the two together. To achieve the desired results and keep relationships healthy, the focus of an alliance manager's time changes over the duration of the delivery phase and will differ depending on the type of alliance. However, there are some common activities as shown in Figure 18.1 which implicitly also touch on other phases offering a constant 'check and balance' that the alliance continues to deliver the desired value.

The work breakdown is underpinned with relationship management, targeted at the various internal and external stakeholders. The general/senior management profile of work reinforces the SACKED characteristics of alliance managers which were first highlighted in Chapter 13. Examples of an alliance manager's

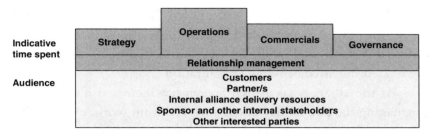

Figure 18.1 Alliance manager task profile.

challenges and activities needed to achieve results are scattered throughout the book, but a few examples of successful alliance managers delivering in practice will help bring this phase to life.

Steven Sharpe is the alliance manager at Reuters for its key outsourcing relationship with Fujitsu which delivers IT field services, distribution and logistics to important clients in the UK. This alliance helps Reuters' clients access relevant information and data via complementary applications and systems to trade in the equities, fixed income, foreign exchange, money, commodities and energy markets around the world. The financial markets trade billions of pounds each day and consequently there is a huge risk if service suffers. Steven has strong background knowledge of Reuters' operations and client environment, coupled with a good understanding of the future business opportunities and threats facing Reuters and its clients. He has managed and developed the relationship since 2001 and has a team supporting him. He also has other responsibilities outside of the alliance although it remains his primary focus.

Steven is responsible for the strategic direction of the alliance which makes a significant contribution to Reuters' UKI business. As such he works closely with his team, sponsor and other senior management to ensure the direction of the alliance remains aligned with Reuters' broader strategic goals. He also spends his energies on maintaining strategic fit and positive relationships by working closely with Fujitsu. Steven recently led the strategic review and planning of where to grow and develop the relationship for ongoing mutual benefit and with his specialist support team recently extended the alliance scope and duration.

As the alliance has grown Steven has increased his resources managing the day-to-day operations. His team works closely with Fujitsu's alliance team and the 100 plus Fujitsu delivery resources who execute the-day-to day business tasks on time and to clients' satisfaction. During the early days of the relationship it was not all plain sailing and much work, including some tough decisions, was required to convert the intentions of the alliance into reality. This task was made much tougher due to the general resistance to change of those impacted, many of whom were transferred to Fujitsu from Reuters under TUPE. Steven cites a 'dogged determination' and positive outlook as reasons for his success along with the ability to bring people along by offering a clear vision of the future and maintaining focus. He has made changes happen, for example by co-locating the Reuters and Fujitsu operations teams together to aid the relationship and ultimately improve service. He also introduced incentives and encourages Fujitsu's participation in Reuters' events to drive better collaboration and to help ingrain Reuters' culture and objectives into its staff. His key phrases are about openness and inclusion, where clients and other Reuters colleagues would struggle to tell whether a member of the alliance team was a Reuters or Fujitsu employee. Relationship management underpins all the tasks within the role. Activities for ongoing relationship building are undertaken regularly, either as standalone events, or tacked neatly onto the back of formal sessions such as review meetings.

Bi-weekly operations meetings focus purely on service delivery, reviewing client surveys and performance reports and act as two-way open forums to discuss how to maintain or improve service to clients and gain mutual benefit. Steven has designated financial and commercial resources focused on the alliance and they spend time assessing the costs of the alliance and its returns on investment. Monthly commercial meetings with Fujitsu establish actual performance versus forecasts and both parties work together to reconcile accounts and 'close out' the prior month performance, then align targets for the next period. This is made much easier by both parties sharing the same IT systems for service delivery, and working with the same information. There are significant risks for the UKI business, so time is dedicated to effective governance of the alliance. This implicitly includes some of the tasks above but explicitly addresses formal risk management and control for Reuters. The contract between the partners for the most part stays in the filing cabinet. However, there are underlying safeguards, for example service level agreements, joint policies around client engagement and how to deal with problems. These are regularly reviewed at governance meetings to ensure they facilitate alliance success, not stifle it, while protecting the parties from unnecessary risk or surprise. Steven complements the regular governance and reviews by undertaking a formal partner and alliance review annually adopting principles similar to that expressed in the next chapter – Alliance reviews.

To offer a contrasting alliance example, this time a short-term joint go-to-market alliance, Phil Mehrtens was alliance manager for Thus. Phil led its recent pilot alliance with O2 to test the market attractiveness of a new service. It was the first fully integrated communications proposition for small growing businesses. The short pilot provided valuable market feedback on the proposition, sales channels and fulfilment process for both Thus and O2 and built a solid relationship for future development. The common themes of strategy, operations, commercials and governance were all evident again, although this was a small team so the alliance manager role was much more hands on in each area of delivery. Having helped architect the alliance Phil knew the pilot was groundbreaking for Thus so stakeholder management internally was a large part of his role. Effective communication on the strategy and both 'soft' and 'hard' benefits needed to be shared with internal managers who naturally felt investments could be better directed elsewhere. Similarly as the partners had not worked together before, effort was put into joint communications and internal roadshows in parallel with the strategic and commercial activity. Phil was the first point of contact within Thus for partner related queries, also acting as the initial ambassador for the alliance and leading regular governance reviews. From a commercial viewpoint Phil took responsibility for negotiating the initial trial terms and finessing them as the alliance progressed through its pilot period. Operationally, he programme managed and governed the technical delivery resources and worked directly on both marketing and sales engagement overseeing the joint value proposition turn from effective marketing collateral into sales. At the end of the pilot, recommendations were made on where and how to take the alliance further, based on the trial learnings.

In a final example, Robert Hayward, Head of Strategic Partnerships for BT Mobility & Convergence, works with the relevant executive sponsors to set direction and strategy and lead the relationship with BT's Mobility & Convergence Strategic Partners. He works closely with organisations like Intel and Vodafone to drive achievements of commercial targets set around revenue, costs, innovation, customer satisfaction and quality. For example, BT and Intel entered into a strategic marketing alliance in January 2004 that includes joint R&D and marketing initiatives around the next generation of mobile broadband and Wi-Fi solutions. By undertaking this alliance BT and Intel are together helping create a new digital society where convenience, speed, innovation and flexibility are set to become the norm. From a strategic perspective Robert oversees the overall alliance direction for BT Mobility & Convergence and informs the strategic choice (make, buy, ally). Once it is determined that an alliance is needed he develops strategies and plans with his team and the partners to ensure delivery. Robert takes overall responsibility for the entire relationship with his partners, looking across the multiple touchpoints at the sell-with, buy-from and sell-to delivery activity. From a governance perspective Robert leads partner summits at least twice annually that include the relevant CEOs and has broader stakeholder board meetings four times a year alongside more regular delivery and relationship management activities that his team drives on a day-to-day basis.

The three examples above could not be more different in terms of delivery focus, duration, scope, scale and complexity. Yet there are many parallels with these alliances and those mentioned earlier, including the HP BT complex relationship led for HP by Hugh Barton. The role of an alliance manager in every phase, but in particular delivery, has its frustrations but can be one of the most exciting roles in an organisation. Outside of the CEO, there are few other roles where one can work across the whole organisation and drive activity that can have such a significant impact on performance. The importance of relationship management cannot be underestimated. Effective, continual communication is at the heart of it because many alliance managers have no real decision-making power or P&L responsibility, and rely on virtual resources to deliver the alliance goals. The virtual resources and independent P&L owners may also be less interested in the broader alliance goals and care more about short-term wins for their profit centre rather than the longer-term relationship benefits set out in an alliance plan.

Another of the biggest parallels is the continued need to push against the cultural tide, attempting to apply collaborative alliance behaviours and practices in organisations that are not easily organised for extended enterprise operation. Yet these alliance managers have done it well, although it is clear from the statistics that most do not and they along with their organisations unfortunately make up the 70% of alliances that fail. Consistent feedback from alliance managers that succeed in delivery are about the traits discussed in

Part I being evident: alliance spirit, inclusion, trust and an unswerving tenacity to drive through organisation and partner 'treacle' in the pursuit of success. These comments reinforce the importance of attaining CSF 1 and having prepared well in the earlier phases of this ICE Map. Imagine how much more successful these and other alliance managers could be with dedicated resources driving the alliance, along with their organisations achieving CSF 1, and having an ability to partner that leading alliance brands exhibit?

Even being provided with the right tools and systems can help them succeed, as again there were parallels in feedback that for many alliance managers success is achieved despite ineffective tools. Whether it was forcing ineffective CRM systems into alliance use, lacking useful stakeholder and change management tools or formal relationship building budgets, everyone can see room for improvement in this field and felt that increased returns would materialise from further investment in building alliance capability.

PROGRESS TO PHASE 6

In reality, Phase 6 alliance reviews, is conducted during alliance delivery but presented as a separate phase for ease of presentation and to take into account that point in time when the alliance ends, as discussed in the next chapter.

PITFALLS TO AVOID

Avoid part-time alliance resources and tacking on alliance activity to areas that are not effectively aligned with the alliance goals. Investments and benefits should be considered for dedicated resources and separate P&L accounts for material alliances and complex relationships. Another pitfall to avoid during delivery is to focus purely on results without considering the relationship health along the way. Many alliances go on for years and the strength of individual relationships will also determine the strength of the organisation's relationship too. Challenges arise in long-term alliances, for example in pharmaceutical or ship building where alliance team members and sponsors, as well as organisation strategy, can change over the course of many years. Being able to provide continuity of alliance focused resources is good but always ensure a professional handover, ideally having the resource swap underpinned with a wealth of pertinent and consistent information held in an alliance repository.

Other pitfalls are covered in more depth during alliance review and take into account the need to maintain alignment on the inputs to alliance success, rather than just focus on the results and relationship per se.

SUMMARY OF TOOLS NEEDED FOR PHASE 5

■ Components from earlier phases, for example business plans, risk and stakeholder management tools, performance reporting scorecards and so on
■ Alliance and partner repository that offers an alliance portfolio and partner centric view of operations, integrated back into organisation-wide systems where appropriate. This includes:
  (a) Repository for alliance and partner documents (internal and external)
  (b) Alliance relationship management functionality including project management capabilities

## CHAPTER 19

PHASE 6: ALLIANCE REVIEWS

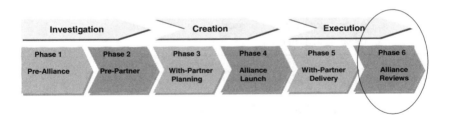

CONTEXT

During Phase 3 the partners should have agreed ground rules towards partner and alliance relationship reviews. This phase therefore addresses what aspects to include in formal alliance reviews while in delivery (Phase 5). It complements anticipated informal reviews that are undertaken on an ongoing as needed basis during the alliance.

PHASE 6 AIMS

The aims of the alliance review are to ensure that the alliance continues to produce the desired results for the partners, exploit new opportunities as they arise and where appropriate make course corrections as needed along the way, including alliance exit, when appropriate. Table 19.1 highlights the two key outputs of this phase.

Table 19.1   Phase 6 output checklist.

No.	Phase 6 output	Tick when completed	Comments
A	Objective assessment of the partner and alliance relationship performance.		
B	Actions and next steps necessary to exploit new opportunities, undertake course corrections or seek alliance exit.		

OUTPUT A: OBJECTIVE ASSESSMENT

As demonstrated in Part I, some 70% of alliances fail to meet their objectives, and given the increasing financial and reputational risks from alliance activity, regular alliance assessment is essential. Partner and alliance assessment should be undertaken on a regular basis and many partners would argue they probably do so, especially where new mutually beneficial opportunities arise. In addition, the regular governance meetings would seek to address ongoing performance of the alliance towards its targets and consider course corrections if needed.

However, past experience suggests that these types of alliance review are not as well structured as they could be, and rarely get to the underlying causes of problems or threats and focus more on one partner than the other. Most effort is expended on looking at alliance results and external factors affecting results such as market or customer activity. Therefore an annual assessment, or six month review for large complex alliances, should be considered which offers a complete review across both partners and the alliance itself. If conducted in a systematic consistent fashion, the assessment can become the baseline for ongoing partner learning and alliance improvement, adding real value to long-term collaborations. Assessment should also be considered where the alliance is failing or not delivering in the fashion originally anticipated by the partners.

ALLIANTIST PARA (Partner and Alliance Relationship Assessment) Map offers a more comprehensive assessment of both partners and the alliance itself. The map can be used by alliance managers although for formal reviews it may best be assessed by an independent party to the alliance. The PARA Map not only addresses the alliance effects, it also looks at the causes of success or failure as well. Figure 19.1 highlights the nine dimensions that should be assessed.

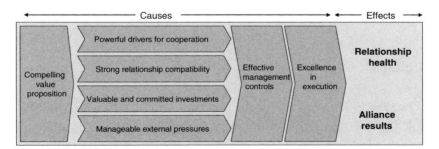

Figure 19.1   ALLIANTIST PARA Map.

Effects

Most organisations that do measure the effects will focus on tangible alliance results. Performance metrics should relate back to the original alliance goals and will ideally include leading as well as lagging indicators in a scorecard. For example, in a simple co-selling alliance leading indicators will include metrics such as pipeline strength, marketing activity and joint initiatives such as new products launched. Lagging indicators will address value creating areas such as products sold, revenues gained, markets entered and specific wins/losses. As touched on earlier, if the alliance has co-opetition or is a nonexclusive alliance, metrics around value destruction should also be considered. These could include partner activity with competitors and business risks in the alliance itself. The assessment should review progress towards the targets and also provide a sanity check that the metrics remain appropriate.

An area that is addressed less often in alliances is around relationship health yet this is where alliance results can be seriously affected in the future. Measuring relationship health can provide good insight into the future success and is an indicator of how close the organisations and individuals are during the alliance. Assessment should take into account partner satisfaction measured across the key stakeholders. Other relationship health metrics to consider include assessing the alliance spirit, degree of trust between the parties as well as the amount and frequency of activities that contribute to relationship building.

Causes

The PARA Map highlights the inputs or 'causes' of alliance success. Each of these inputs should have been considered and architected effectively at Phases 2 and 3, making the assessment straightforward. Few organisations look in this fashion at the inputs during an assessment yet it makes so much sense to do so. There are seven 'causes' which are inextricably linked and together they produce the effects noted above:

- **Compelling value proposition:** the assessment should ensure that the value proposition remains compelling to the participants; customers and both partners as well as other key stakeholders such as investors. Often the value proposition falls out of step with the evolving market offerings or the forecasted costs and benefits for one or both parties turn out wrong and subsequently mean an impact to one of the other causes.

- **Powerful drivers for cooperation:** the assessment should look to determine whether the partners remain aligned in their motivation for the alliance. Looking at factors such as mutual need, strategic fit and other factors originally highlighted under the TOPSCORER Map 'S' strategic fit dimension the review should assess whether the partners have good reason to remain aligned. It may be, for example, that one partner has decided that the partner rewards are so attractive and it has learnt enough from the partner that it decides to enter the market itself. As a result the mutual need diminishes and the partners become fierce competitors with each other.

- **Strong relationship compatibility:** reviews should seek to reinforce that there are strong relationships at the various touchpoints across the alliance and the factors affecting relationship fit under the TOPSCORER 'R' Relationship continue to grow positively. These include assessing the factors that affect collaboration as expressed in Part II such as leadership styles, structures and control, values and beliefs as well as systems and technology alongside teamworking and individuals where reward strategy and personal drivers need assessing.

- **Valuable and committed investments:** having made the commitments during the earlier phases it is not uncommon for organisations to step back from those commitments and refocus their resources elsewhere, especially if the alliance is not delivering the desired results. This then compounds the problems. Similarly it is not unusual for one party to invest more resources than anticipated in order to achieve success. Assessment should therefore look at original promises of the assets and investments proposed versus those in play at the time of review, as well as the assets or other investments that may be required for success, if different. For example, commitments to provide an alliance manager full time may have turned into a part-time focus with the individual not displaying the right SACKED characteristics.

- **Manageable external pressures:** the TOPSCORER Map highlighted 'O' as being about outside pressures. This aspect of the assessment derives from that and seeks to understand what other pressures exist that might be affecting alliance success. This could be resource conflicts where the alliance manager from one partner has other alliances to manage, through to higher order pressures such as potential organisation change of control that may affect productivity and morale, or external pressures such as regulatory factors.

- **Effective management controls:** this part of the assessment seeks to establish whether the partners have introduced the controls highlighted in Phase 3 around the ERA Map components. Factors to consider include business plans, governance bodies, ground rules, safeguards, reporting and measurement systems as well as clear policies, for example around sharing information, training, decision-making, investments and regular alliance reviews outside this formal assessment.

- **Excellence in execution:** this part of the assessment should seek to establish whether the previous six inputs join up and work well in practice, not just on paper, and to what extent the partners collaborate during alliance operation itself and overcome issues on a day-to-day basis.

Having conducted the assessment around the nine dimensions noted above, the review team should have prepared a report for discussion with the alliance managers and onward submission to the strategic governance board. The report should highlight strengths and weaknesses across each dimension and where appropriate make recommendations for change as discussed in output B.

OUTPUT B: ACTIONS AND NEXT STEPS

Having received the formal review, the alliance sponsor, alliance manager and other members of the alliance team should consider their organisation's interests prior to a combined alliance governance body meeting. In some circumstances the findings and actions may be entirely positive, meaning decisions are relatively easy for each organisation, and the governance body session becomes quite straightforward. Examples outside of 'business as usual' include the organisation that saw its share of the rewards growing faster than its partners, despite its own investments being somewhat lower. After considering its negotiation options it agreed to a redistribution of some of the rewards to the other partner in order to maintain positive relationships, with the agreement that once the partner's forecasted benefits materialised, the earlier model would be reintroduced. In another case, the review suggested that there were problems emerging in one partner and the relationship health metrics indicated lower than expected partner satisfaction on the ground, alongside reducing returns for both parties. The underlying causes established some changes in rewards and resourcing constraints which had affected alliance delivery resources motivation. As a result of looking at the underlying inputs, the problem was identified and works undertaken to address the issue.

There are occasions, however, when differences cannot be resolved and it is time for the alliance to be closed down or substantially redefined. For example, one partner was continually being let down by the other, despite regular sponsor assurances to address the problems. Sadly, as a result of an organisation restructure since the alliance commenced many problems were out of her control and the alliance became less important for the organisation, despite her own views. Both partners were suffering although the opportunity costs for the 'innocent' party were significant. As a result of a well-crafted exit strategy based on targets and milestone deliverables agreed in Phase 3, the innocent party terminated the alliance, taking sole rights of the newly created IPR (by way of agreed compensation) and worked alone until it could find another partner.

In any alliance exit, positive or negative, the wind-down or change process should be managed professionally between the parties in particular where external customers are concerned. In addition, consideration should be given to each organisation's overall alliance reputation and identity as alliance failure and poor performance on exit will affect any aspirations towards developing an alliance brand.

PROGRESS

At this stage of the lifecycle the alliance will do one of three things:

1. Continue to mature and deliver well until it reaches its end of life when the parties depart
2. Succeed and possibly lead to change in relations, such as new alliances, or a merger or takeover
3. Fail and despite turnaround efforts, termination is the sensible solution

By adopting the three critical success factors as an overarching philosophy and following the VIP, ICE and ERA Maps, organisations and their partners will have the choice of (1) and (2), rather than just (3)!

PITFALLS TO AVOID

Many organisations are apprehensive about closing down alliances even when they know they are not delivering desired results. They also fear seeking turnaround solutions in case their partner chooses to exit or catches them underperforming. However, if positioned well, the formal alliance review should be seen as an opportunity to encourage both partners to improve and drive the alliance to new, mutually beneficial heights. Other pitfalls to avoid include:

- Failing to address obvious problems and issues when they arise. Informal reviews and alliance governance meetings should address performance on an ongoing basis as well, although in a less structured fashion to the PARA Map review.
- Sycophantic reviews between alliance managers suppressing operating problems may aid their personal relations but will do little for results if underlying problem causes remain untreated. Objective and independent reviews should be considered at least annually for large alliances.

SUMMARY OF TOOLS NEEDED FOR PHASE 6

- ALLIANTIST PARA Map and technology system to hold reviews and scorecards for future baselining.

## CHAPTER 20

THE JOURNEY TO ALLIANCE BRAND AND WINNING ALLIANCES

*B*eing the owner of a leading alliance brand means great rewards and a super reputation for partnering. But it is not easy to achieve; indeed even reaching alliance brand status is tough in itself and not for the uncommitted. To make an omelette one needs to break a few eggs in the process. Sustainable competitive advantage is often said to be myth but having gained an alliance brand that might no longer be the case. With a positive reputation and results from alliances and an extended enterprise that can adapt and evolve as opportunities and threats arise it will enable organisations to effect their strategic goals more quickly and effectively than their competitors.

The book has sought to help in terms of understanding why having an alliance brand is necessary for future business success. In addition, it has demonstrated how to get great business results and a positive reputation for alliances by following the three

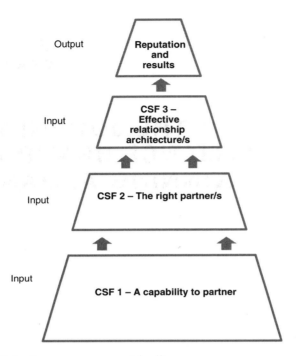

Output

Input

Input

Input

Figure 20.1   Steps to success with alliances.

critical success factors shown in Figure 20.1 and using ALLIAN-
TIST Maps and tools to aid the journey.

As the book draws to a conclusion here are some final points
to share which intend to help you launch new initiatives in this
field and achieve positive successes quickly.

GETTING STARTED

Each organisation is at a different level of maturity with respect
to their alliance activity so prescribing a one size fits all approach
to getting started is not ideal. As with the maps in the book, they
are not the territory, and activity on the ground will differ from

organisation to organisation, although there are some common issues to consider. For example, it is tempting to jump right in and get cracking on selecting new alliance partners, or review the performance of existing partners by using the maps and tools from Part III. Having been under pressure to do the same in the past without first aligning the internal environment (CSF 1), experience suggests the efforts will fail or not succeed in the manner envisaged. For example, one organisation recently expressed a desire to get inside their existing partner base, shake it up and put in place more effective relationship architectures to drive up performance. Within five minutes of the first clinic it became clear that they were not yet ready to put their partners under such positive pressure because they themselves hadn't achieved much around CSF 1. As such some internal initiatives were first undertaken based around ALLIANTIST VIP Map that helped address obvious issues and positioned the organisation more effectively for growth with its partners.

Consider this approach as one way to go forward if your organisation is at an early stage of maturity with its alliance activity:

1. Undertake the alliance brand quick test at www. ALLIANTIST.com or in Appendix 1. Identify obvious areas of strength and weakness, opportunity and threat, noting thoughts about what improvements are necessary and their likely costs and benefits.

2. Prioritise the areas of benefit less investment in a brief proposal and outline a high-level roadmap, looking for quick successes along the way to ensure ongoing senior stakeholder buy-in. Paul Davies, Director of Procurement Excellence in the Police Service (PEPS), has a neat (and ironic) phrase which is 'don't just rob the bank, do the petrol stations on the way'. Given the pace of change in organisations today, few people will wait patiently for their first return.

3. Look for a senior sponsor who can drive and support the
    changes, not least to help assemble the team and budgets
    needed for success. Having secured sponsorship consider the
    benefits of validating your alliance brand quicktest findings
    with an independent alliance brand audit before making
    wholesale changes.

If a relevant sponsor is not forthcoming then think carefully about
how much support the actual initiative will have in practice.
Perhaps a broad alliance brand building programme will not work
at that time. It may not be a priority in the organisation. Other
potential routes for progression include starting with a business
unit, geography, function or product set that can stand alone and
be a pilot on behalf of the organisation.

More mature organisations that are aligned internally and have
much of the VIP Map addressed and attained CSF 1 may wish to
look more closely at their alliance infrastructure to ensure it is
optimised in terms of people, processes, tools and systems. Reviewing existing partner and alliance activity with ALLIANTIST
PARA Map is also a positive step to portfolio optimisation and
enhanced returns on investments. The PARA Map can also
be adapted for addressing alliances with differing values and
importance.

Alliance brand is clearly symbiotic so all the partners in the
portfolio can benefit. In some instances working closely with a
strategic partner as a pilot to effect mutually beneficial improvements around CSF 1, 2 and 3 in parallel can also help, but care is
needed to avoid distractions and undue partner pressure.

Organisations that are less interested in building an alliance
brand itself will still enjoy many opportunities for a positive return
on investment from the book. The exercises, tools and commentary throughout the book can make a difference to how an organisation not only manages its alliance activity but also its overall
business. Even using the maps simply as checklists, or keeping the

book on the desk and referring to it from time to time, will help improve your probability of alliance success and mitigate hitherto unforeseen risks.

STANDING OUT FROM THE CROWD

Alliance brand index

Organisations with leading alliance brands will stand out from the crowd but there are not many and partnering opportunities to work with them are limited. However, organisations without any form of alliance brand are not going to actively promote their weaknesses so sorting the good partners from the bad can take precious time yet is essential for success. Growing forces such as the increasing transparency required for reporting and compliance on alliance activity will also aid partner identification and selection in the future. However, that still means trawling far and wide in the first instance.

The principles expressed within this book will help the organisation and its partners raise the bar on performance but in the future a new transparent model of alliance performers will also emerge; alliance brand index. Alliance brand index is similar in approach to other well-recognised league tables and indices such as BusinessWeek/Interbrand's Global Brand Scorecard, and the Harris-Fombrun Reputation Quotient[TM]. It will help alliance brands improve their value and marketability even further and enhance their reputation to an even wider audience of potentially interested parties. At the time of writing alliance brand index remains an embryonic initiative and will take time to reach a level of maturity where it can add real value for a wide range of participants. Take a look at www.alliancebrandindex.com to see how you can participate.

BS 11000

The British Standards Institution (BSI) is collaborating with PSL on developing the world's first relationship management standard; BS 11000. Intended for launch late in 2006 the aim is to offer a code of practice and framework for businesses to manage their internal and external relationships more effectively.

If initiatives like alliance brand index and BS 11000 can do for alliances what the Global Brand Scorecard and BSEN ISO 9000 have done for their respective audiences then the success rate of alliances is sure to improve in the coming years. Keep tuned to www.ALLIANTIST.com for more information.

ALLIANTIST SERVICES

Despite being an alliance solution specialist with an advisory arm, ALLIANTIST believes that organisations need to develop a core competence in this field and should hold their alliance management skills and infrastructure internally. Alliance management is not an area to outsource or delegate to others on an ongoing basis. Help may be required from time to time on building the initial alliance capability using the VIP Map, or supporting alliance ICE Map investigation and creation, alliance turnarounds and PARA Map reviews. ALLIANTIST offers expert advisory services, coaching for aspiring alliance practitioners and can offer internal alliance training programmes for organisations and their partners too. The maps, tools and methods outlined in the book are also available both as licensed methodologies for manual use or to embed in existing technology systems. High value, low cost ALLIANTIST software that incorporates the maps, tools and methods is also available. For more information, contact mark.darby@ALLIANTIST.com

CONCLUDING REMARKS

Everyone needs a little luck along the way. With this book by your side your probability of success has increased significantly. As Arnold Palmer once said 'the more I practice, the luckier I get'. Practice using the methods and maps in this book and you might get real lucky with the prize being a leading alliance brand, standing out from the crowd with a great reputation and results from your alliance activity!

ALLIANCE BRAND
QUICK TEST

*T*his self-administered quick test should take around 10 minutes and is focused on the inputs for success and reflects the elements highlighted in Part II around ALLIANTIST VIP Map. At this level of inquiry there is no real consideration of the outputs in terms of alliance results or reputation. The online and updated version of the quick test is available at www.ALLIANTIST.com along with more information on how to undertake deeper reviews and assess the alliance outputs as well as inputs.

Allocate a score between 1 (poor) and 5 (excellent) to each question in Figure A1.1. Sum each of the individual elements (e.g. clarity on strategy and direction) and calculate your percentage results in Figure A1.2. Scores under 60% in any element or overall should be deemed RED, i.e. high risk with no evidence of alliance brand characteristics. Scores over 60% but under 80% should be deemed AMBER, indicating some risk, but portraying signs of some alliance brand characteristics. More detailed output-based

	ALLIANTIST	Alliance Brand – Quick Test Diagnostic©		

Assign a score into the relevant cell below

Poor 1 2 3 4 5 Excellent

Strategy and direction

#	Poor	1	2	3	4	5	Excellent
1	There is confusion over our business strategy and direction and no or few stakeholders understand it						There is absolute clarity on our business strategy and direction and all stakeholders understand it
2	Our 3rd party alliances and partner relationships compromise our strategy						Our 3rd party alliances and partner relationships complement our strategy
3	We 'spray and pray' in our alliance relationships – quantity over quality						We are very focused with our alliance relationships – quality over quantity
4	We have no idea of our dependency on third parties for delivery of our strategic goals and objectives						We have a clear idea of our dependency on third parties for delivery of our strategic goals and objectives

Core competences

#	Poor	1	2	3	4	5	Excellent
5	There is no understanding of our core competences						There is a clear understanding of our core competences
6	We have no focus and pretty much attempt to do everything ourselves without working with others						We only focus on what we do well and where appropriate work with others for everything else
7	Core competences held by our partners determine the success or failure of our company						Core competences held internally determine the success or failure of our company

Strategic choice

#	Poor	1	2	3	4	5	Excellent
8	We have no idea whether to make, buy or ally when considering execution of strategy						We have complete clarity and understanding on when to undertake make, buy or ally decisions
9	Teams responsible for make, buy and ally activity do not work closely together nor operate to an agreed policy						Teams responsible for make, buy, ally activity work closely together and operate to an agreed policy

Asset attractiveness

#	Poor	1	2	3	4	5	Excellent
10	We have no idea what assets the organisation has nor their value to us or others						We have clarity on the organisations assets and their value to us and others
11	Our assets are ineffectively used in alliance and partnering activity						Our assets are effectively used in alliance and partnering activity
12	There are no policies or processes regarding the use of our assets in alliance activity						There are clear policies and processes regarding the use of our assets in alliance activity

Collaboration

#	Poor	1	2	3	4	5	Excellent
13	There is no correlation between strategy and dept/personal objectives						Strategic objectives are translated into dept and personal objectives
14	There are no effective mechanisms in place to encourage collaboration between depts and individuals both internally and externally						There are effective mechanisms in place to encourage collaboration between depts and individuals both internally and externally
15	The organisation culture and working environment stifles collaboration both internally and externally						The organisation culture and working environment enables collaboration both internally and externally

Governance

#	Poor	1	2	3	4	5	Excellent
16	There are no effective reporting and controls in place to align overall alliance activity and performance into the broader organisation internal controls						There are very effective reporting and controls in place to align overall alliance activity and performance into the broader organisation internal controls
17	There are no coordinating mechanisms in place to address multiple relationships with a party which might include customer, supplier and competitor activity						There are very effective co-ordinating mechanisms in place to address multiple relationships with a party which might include customer, supplier and competitor activity

Alliance Infrastructure

#	Poor	1	2	3	4	5	Excellent
18	There is no understanding of the performance of each alliance versus its original goals nor the overall alliance portfolio return on investment						There is a good understanding of the performance of each alliance versus its original goals and the overall alliance portfolio return on investment
19	There is no explicit method or consistency in the way that resources and investments are allocated to alliances or partners						Resources and investments are allocated to alliances and partners based on a clear and consistent method
20	The alliance organisation is informal, peripheral to the core of the business and has no senior management leadership						The alliance organisation is embedded into the heart of the business and has a high profile senior leader
21	There are no or few trained qualified or experienced staff in place to execute the alliance programme activities in the optimal fashion						There are enough trained, qualified and experienced alliance staff in place to execute the alliance programme activities in the optimal fashion
22	Customers and partners would say that the alliance organisation adds no value to the firm and is a nightmare to work with						Customers and partners would say that the alliance organisation adds real value to the firm and is easy to work with
23	Alliance propositions are not well thought out or subject to any form of due diligence or stakeholder cost/benefit analysis						Alliance propositions are subject to effective stakeholder cost/benefit analysis and appropriate due diligence undertaken in a consistent fashion
24	There are no explicit or effective policies, tools or processes in place to aid selection of the right partners						Effective and explicit policies, tools and processes exist to aid selection of the right partners
25	There are no tools, processes or policies in place to ensure or monitor execution of alliance commitments, tasks and other obligations during the lifecycle						Effective tools, processes and policies exist to ensure execution and monitoring of alliance commitments, tasks and other obligations during the lifecycle
26	No technology solution is in place to aid collaboration and to enhance decision-making as well as the development, protection and sharing of knowledge and information internally and externally with partners						Suitable technology solutions are in place to aid collaboration and to enhance decision-making as well as the development, protection and sharing of knowledge and information internally and externally with partners

Figure A1.1 Alliance brand quick test.

Element	Total score	Max available	%	RAG status
Strategy and direction		20		
Core competences		15		
Strategic choice		10		
Asset attractiveness		15		
Collaboration		15		
Governance		10		
Alliance Infrastructure		45		
		130		

Figure A1.2   Quick test results.

analysis on results and reputation will help determine whether these are emerging alliance brand characteristics (i.e. good results but no reputation) or laggard alliance brand characteristics (i.e. poor results but a good reputation). Organisations scoring over 80% in each element, and overall, are likely to be displaying leading alliance brand characteristics.

This is a high-level self-diagnostic designed to give you an overview of the typical areas that may create or destroy value from an alliance perspective in your organisation. It will help you to determine whether you need to undertake further investigation into the underlying causes surrounding alliance performance. ALLIANTIST offers no warranties from this free diagnostic exercise.

REFERENCES

1. Michael Treacy and Fred Wiersema (1996) *The Discipline of Market Leaders*. HarperCollins
2. Alfred Rappaport (1998) *Creating Shareholder Value*. Free Press
3. For example, Michael Porter (1980) *Competitive Strategy*. Free Press; Michael Porter (1985) *Competitive Advantage*. Free Press
4. Michael Porter (1985) *Competitive Advantage*. Free Press
5. Michael Porter (1980) *Competitive Strategy*. Free Press
6. Most strategy books give a critique of Porter's strategies but for a good example see Boyett and Boyett (1998) *The Guru Guide*. John Wiley & Sons
7. http://www.btplc.com/Thegroup/Companyprofile/Ourstrategy/Ourstrategicpriorities.htm
8. Michael Treacy and Fred Wiersema (1996) *The Discipline of Market Leaders*. HarperCollins
9. Michael Porter (1980) *Competitive Strategy*. Free Press
10. Michael Porter (1996) What is strategy. *Harvard Business Review*, Nov–Dec
11. Kenneth R. Andrews (1980) *The Concept of Corporate Strategy*. Richard D. Irwin Inc.

12. William F. Glueck (1980) *Business Policy and Strategic Management,* 3rd edition. McGraw Hill
13. George Stalk, Philip Evans and Lawrence E. Shulman (1992) Competing on capabilities: the new rules of corporate strategy. *Harvard Business Review,* Mar–April
14. Henry Mintzberg and James Brian Quinn (1992) *The Strategy Process Concepts and Contexts.* Prentice Hall
15. Anthony Robbins various tapes and books
16. Barry Nalebuff and Adam Brandenburger (1996) *Co-opetition.* HarperCollins
17. Mark Darby and Richard Punt (2004) Survival of the fittest. Extended Enterprise white paper. Deloitte MCS Limited
18. CEO challenges 2004 perspective and analysis. Conference Board
19. Michael Porter (1996) What is strategy. *Harvard Business Review,* Nov–Dec
20. Combined Code, section 41 Turnbull guidance, July 2003
21. Cnnfn.com 1999
22. Tom Copeland, Tim Koller and Jack Murrin (1995) *Valuation, Measuring and Managing the Value of Companies,* 2nd edition. John Wiley & Sons Inc.
23. *Harvard Business Review,* June 2000
24. www.SEEDA.co.uk
25. Robert Spekman, Lynn Isabella and Thomas MacAvoy (2000) *Alliance Competence. Maximising the Value of Your Partnerships.* John Wiley & Sons Inc.
26. Jordan Lewis (1999) *Trusted Partners. How Companies Build Mutual Trust and Win Together.* The Free Press
27. Jordan Lewis (1999) *Trusted Partners. How Companies Build Mutual Trust and Win Together.* The Free Press
28. Jordan Lewis (1999) *Trusted Partners. How Companies Build Mutual Trust and Win Together.* The Free Press
29. Various sources including IBM and Siebel websites, white papers, Association of Strategic Alliance Professionals (ASAP) and personal experience
30. Warnock Davies (2001) *Partner Risk Managing the Downside of Strategic Alliances.* Ichor Business Books/Purdue University Press
31. www.news.bbc.co.uk, 16 January 2001

32. Jeffrey H. Dyer, Prashant Kale and Harbir Singh (2001) How to make strategic alliances work. *MIT Sloan Management Review*, Summer

33. William Gordon, Bud Moeller and Dominic Palmer (2000) Becoming an alliance partner of choice. Accenture Outlook point of view

34. Mark Darby and Richard Punt (2004) Survival of the fittest. Extended Enterprise white paper. Deloitte MCS Limited

35. The State of Alliance Management (2002) A special ASAP research report into alliance capability

36. Mark Darby MBA (2001) Achieving competitive advantage in the age of the virtual enterprise. University of Reading

37. Elena Berton (2005) More biotech, pharma alliances ending in tears. Dow Jones Newswires

38. www.news.bbc.co.uk, 4 November 2005

39. http://www.theregister.co.uk/2004/11/18/csa_nukes_eds

40. www.news.bbc.co.uk, Tax credit fiasco costs EDS £71m, 22 November 2005

41. Parliamentary Office of Science and Technology, July 2003, No. 200, Report Summary

42. A. Cox and C. Lonsdale (1998) *Outsourcing a Business Guide.* Earlsgate Press, p. 26

43. Yves Doz and Gary Hamel (2000) *Alliance Advantage.* Harvard Business School Press

44. http://www.weforum.org/securitysurvey, Corporate brand reputation outranks financial performance as most important measure of success. World Economic Forum, January 2004

45. Ronald Alsop (2004) A good corporate reputation draws consumers and investors. *Wall Street Journal*

46. Ronald Alsop (2004) A good corporate reputation draws consumers and investors. *Wall Street Journal*

47. David Taylor (2003) *The Brandgym: A Practical Workout for Boosting Brand and Business.* John Wiley & Sons

48. David Taylor (2003) *The Brandgym: A Practical Workout for Boosting Brand and Business.* John Wiley & Sons

49. William F. Glueck (1980) *Business Policy and Strategic Management,* 3rd edition. McGraw Hill

50. Tom Blackett (1989) Brand valuation. Establishing a true and fair view. In John Murphy (ed.) *The Nature of Brands.* Hutchinson Business Books

51. William Gordon, Bud Moeller and Dominic Palmer (2000) Becoming an alliance partner of choice. Accenture Outlook point of view

52. David Taylor (2003) *The Brandgym: A Practical Workout for Boosting Brand and Business.* John Wiley & Sons, p. 7

53. Brad Van Auken (2003) *Brand Aid.* AMACOM

54. David Taylor (2003) *The Brandgym: A Practical Workout for Boosting Brand and Business.* John Wiley & Sons

55. J. Rockart (1979) Chief executives define their own information needs. *Harvard Business Review,* Mar–Apr

56. Ben Gomes-Casseres (1998) Strategy before structure. *The Alliance Analyst,* August

57. Michael Porter (1996) What is strategy. *Harvard Business Review,* Nov–Dec

58. Michael Porter (Rowan Gibson, ed.) (1998) Rethinking the future. Nicholas Brearley

59. www.about.reuters.com

60. Geoffrey A. Moore (1999) *Crossing the Chasm,* 2nd edition. Capstone

61. Craig S. Fleisher and Babette E. Bensoussan (2003) *Strategic and Competitive Analysis.* Prentice Hall

62. Barry Nalebuff and Adam Brandenburger (1996) *Co-opetition.* HarperCollins

63. Jay B. Barney (1996) *Gaining and Sustaining Competitive Advantage.* Addison Wesley

64. Gary Hamel and C.K. Prahalad (1990) The core competence of the corporation. *Harvard Business Review,* June

65. Gary Hamel and C.K. Prahalad (1994) *Competing for the Future.* Harvard Business School Press

66. P. Selznick (1957) *Leadership in Administration.* Harper & Row

67. E.T. Penrose (1959) *The Theory of Growth of the Firm.* Blackwell

68. Gary Hamel and C.K. Prahalad (1994) *Competing for the Future.* Harvard Business School Press

69. Michael Treacy and Fred Wiersema (1996) *The Discipline of Market Leaders.* HarperCollins

70. John Micklethwait and Adrian Wooldridge (1997) *The Witch Doctors.* Mandarin

71. Kevin P. Coyne, Stephen J.D. Hall and Patricia G. Clifford (1997) Is your core competence a mirage? *McKinsey Quarterly,* No. 1

72. Heene and Sanchez (eds) (1997) *Competence Based Strategic Management*. John Wiley & Sons
73. Heene and Sanchez (eds) (1997) *Competence Based Strategic Management*. John Wiley & Sons
74. Heene and Sanchez (eds) (1997) *Competence Based Strategic Management*. John Wiley & Sons
75. Thomas Durand (1997) Strategising for innovation: competence analysis in assessing strategic change. In Heene and Sanchez (eds) *Competence Based Strategic Management*. John Wiley & Sons
76. Michael Porter (1980) *Competitive Strategy*. Macmillan Free Press
77. J.B. Barney (1991) Firm resources and sustained competitive advantage. *Journal of Management*, Vol. 17
78. Jay B. Barney (1996) *Gaining and Sustaining Competitive Advantage*. Addison Wesley
79. Jay B. Barney (1996) *Gaining and Sustaining Competitive Advantage*. Addison Wesley
80. J.A. Klein and P.G. Hiscocks (1994) Competence based competition: a practical toolkit. In G. Hamel and A Heene (eds) *Competence Based Competition*. John Wiley & Sons
81. J.A. Klein and P.G. Hiscocks (1994) Competence based competition: a practical toolkit. In G. Hamel and A Heene (eds) *Competence Based Competition*. John Wiley & Sons
82. Mark Sirower (1997) *The Synergy Trap: How Companies Lose the Acquisition* Game. Free Press
83. Geoffrey Moore (2000) *Inside the Tornado*. Capstone publishing
84. www.brandfinance.com, The increasing importance of intellectual property, Brand Finance (2000)
85. John A. Byrne (1993) The virtual corporation. *Business Week*, 8 February
86. Edgar Schein (1992) *Organisational Culture and Leadership*, 2nd edition. Jossey Bass
87. Warren Bennis and Robert Townsend (1995) *Reinventing Leadership*. Piatkus
88. T. Deal and A. Kennedy (1982) *Corporate Cultures: The Rites and Rituals of Corporate Life*. Penguin
89. www.BP.com values page
90. See www.in-alto.com for a good insight into KAI
91. www.wholebeing.co.uk

92. Michael Armstrong and Helen Murlis (2001) *Reward Management*, 4th edition. Kogan Page

93. www.COSO.org

94. Applying COSO Enterprise Risk Management Framework: The Institute of Internal Auditors presentation, 29 September 2004

95. Cisco and Microsoft's tricky partnership, Marguerite Reardon CNET Networks, http://news.com.com/Cisco+and+Microsofts +tricky+partnership/2100-1033_3-5768872.html

96. www.about.reuters.com

97. www.cisco.com

98. TUPE – Transfer of Undertaking Protection of Employment legislation

99. John Moore (2004) Unisys unwraps services strategy. *The Channel Insider*, 4 November

100. Mark Darby and Richard Punt (2004) Survival of the fittest. Extended Enterprise white paper. Deloitte MCS Limited

101. Philip Kotler (1991) *Marketing Management Analysis Planning and Control*. Prentice Hall

102. For the background to BATNA see Roger Fisher and William Ury (1991) *Getting to Yes*, 2nd edition. Penguin

103. http://www.citrix.com/English/aboutCitrix/caseStudies/ caseStudy.asp?storyID=22884

104. John Kotter (1996) *Leading Change*. Harvard Business School Press

INDEX

Compiled by Indexing Specialists (UK) Ltd